COLORADO

A Liquid History & Tavern Guide to the Highest State

Thomas J. Noel

Fulcrum Publishing
Golden, Colorado

For Vi,
who is always there in the morning
with coffee

Copyright © 1999 Thomas J. Noel

All photographs copyright © 1999 Thomas J. Noel, unless otherwise noted.

Library of Congress Cataloging-in-Publication Data
Noel, Thomas J. (Thomas Jacob)
    Colorado : a liquid history & tavern guide to the highest state /
Thomas J. Noel.
       p.   cm.
    Includes bibliographical references and index.
    ISBN 1-55591-260-5 (pbk.)
    1. Bars (Drinking establishments)—Colorado—Guidebooks.
2. Colorado—Social life and customs. 3. Colorado—History.   I. Title.
TX950.57.C6N64   1999
647.95788—dc21   98-49390
                                        CIP

Cover photo of a Creede, Colorado, "tent" saloon,
courtesy of the Colorado Historical Society.
Back cover photo of Paul's Place in Denver, currently known as My Brother's Bar,
Tom Noel Collection.

Book design by Patty Maher

Printed in the United States of America
0 9 8 7 6 5 4 3 2 1

Fulcrum Publishing
350 Indiana Street, Suite 350
Golden, Colorado 80401-5093
(800) 992-2908 • (303) 277-1623
www.fulcrum-books.com

Contents

Acknowledgments

Thanks to:

Chubby Aiello, Chuck Albi, Gene Amole, Sam and Carrie Arnold, Louisa Ward Arps, Sandra Dallas Atchison, Bob Baron, Paul and Janet Barrett, Ed and Nancy Bathke, Bart Berger, Bill Bessesen, Hugh Bingham, Larry Bohning, Robert Brown, Smiling Jack Brown, Jack Brozna, Cec Burkhardt, Lew Cady, Patty Calhoun, Nels Carman, Kirsten Christensen, Norm Clark, Dave Cole, Susan Collins, Dick Conn, Bill Convery, Bill Coors, Alan and Marcy Culpin, Janet Cunningham, Joan Day, Joan Deegan, Joanne and Edwin Dodds, Jim and Lorena Donahue, Lyle W. Dorsett, Becky Dorward, Connie Douglas, Mike Ducey, Bill Dutton, Don Ebner, Richard and Emogene Edwards, Peg Ekstrand, Jay Fell, Rosemary Fetter, Ellen Fisher, Peggy Ford, Daniel Forrest-Bank, Mark S. Foster, Joe Fuentes, Dennis Gallagher, Richard Gardner, Eleanor Gehres, Barbara Gibson, Marcia and Jeff Goldstein, Breck and Mary Lynn Grover, Andy Gulliford, Dave Halaas, Eric Hammersmark, Steve Hart, Jim Hartmann, Phil Hernandez, John Hickenlooper, Benny Hooper, Bill Husted, Margaret Jacob, Jim and Angelo Karagas, Kate Kienast, Jack Kisling, Dick Kreck, Steve Leonard, Liston and Barbara Leyendecker, Patty Limerick, Rebecca Lintz, Gary Long and Kathy Hoeft, Patty Maher, Terry Mangan, Augie Mastroguiseppi, Laura McCall, Jay Mead and Carol Svensen, Pat Mendoza, Ree Mobley, Chocolate Dan Monroe, Charlie Moore, Marcie Morin, Judy Morley, Jack Murphy, Gary Nafa, John Nallen, Ron Neeley, Janet Noel, Jim and Chris Noel, Vi Noel, Barbara Norgren, Cathleen Norman, Allen Nossaman, Angie Ortiz, Eric Paddock, Phil Panum, Ed and Martha Quillen, Dale Reed, Neil V. Reynolds, Martha Ripley, Kevin Rucker, Bill Russell, Sam Scinta, Clark Secrest, Karle Seydel, Virginia Simmons, J. Sebastian Sinisi, Duane Smith, Jack Smith, Bill Spahr, Jimmy Spinelli, Eileen Sullivan, Wayne Sundberg, Lori Swingle, Gennifer Thom, Gerry Thomas, Marne Tutt, Thayer Tutt, Jan and Phyllis Updike, Dave Waltrip, Tom Ward, Rebecca Waugh, Tom and Jan Weaver, Elliott West, Luther and Judy Wilson.

And thanks to many others I've forgotten, alas, in the course of the past thirty-four years of barstool research. I'll treat if I see you in heaven.

Publisher's Preface

The subjects of taverns, drinking, and camaraderie predate Dr. Thomas Noel and his book *Colorado: A Liquid History*. Many authors have researched and written on these subjects, from Aristophanes to Isak Dinesen. They are quoted throughout the text.

The gathering of people together to share a beverage is an ancient custom. Dionysus, the Greek god of grape growing, and Bacchus, the Roman god, were special gods who celebrated the fermentation of grape juice into a more interesting beverage.

The Greeks have their taverna, the French their café, the Germans their rathskeller, the English their pub (public house) and Colorado natives their neighborhood watering hole. Samuel Johnson in 1776 was quoted by Boswell as saying: "There is nothing which has yet been contrived by man by which so much happiness is produced as by a good tavern or inn." From its first settlements, many Colorado residents have shared that belief.

Whether they call it a bar, a saloon, a tavern, a cocktail lounge, or for the years between 1919 and 1933 a speakeasy, people have sought and found a social gathering place where drink was available, laughter flowed, and the affairs of the world could be discussed.

This book does not deal with the alcoholic, boozer, drunk, or lush. Some people cannot handle alcohol. People should not drink and drive. In many cases, they should not drink and walk. We believe very strongly in the social drinker—the person who goes to a tavern for companionship, laughter, and a quiet drink. The issue for such a soul is one of where to drink, what to drink, and with whom.

On the subject of choice of beverages, opinions differ widely. Some prefer beer, ale, lager, or porter. Some prefer wine in its infinite labels. And some prefer liquor straight or in cocktails. Some even prefer bottled water, specifying the make, amount of bubbles, and perhaps even year that the water fell from the sky and was gathered. A good bar serves all. And a good bartender can serve them up with a smile and also be a listener, arbiter, and confessor. For the services of a good saloon keeper move beyond the mere dispensing of beverages.

The ability to provide a drink, mix a good martini, pour a Guinness properly, select

---

I will make it a felony to drink small beer.
—**William Shakespeare**

Alonso of Aragon was wont to say in commendation of age, that age appears to be best in four things—old wood best to burn, old wine to drink, old friends to trust, and old authors to read.

—*Francis Bacon*

wine, and even, without smiling, serve a Scotch and ginger ale, Virgin Mary, or absinthe (absinthe makes the heart grow fonder) is a particular talent. To combine service with the ability to remember how many home runs Babe Ruth hit, what year Michael Jordan started in the NBA, who were Nixon's vice presidents, and what to do when your lover has dumped you, puts the men and women behind the bar in an honored place. No wonder some people select their watering hole with more care than they select their cars, apartments, or dates.

Since the earliest Colonial days in New England, some Americans have insisted on establishing behavioral controls on others. As Mark Twain wrote: "Nothing so needs reforming as other people's habits." For nineteen years after World War I, Prohibition made social drinking the government's business. But Americans balk when someone tries to legislate their private personal habits and morality. No sooner was Prohibition the law of the land than bootlegging sprang up to quench the public thirst. The law was unenforceable, especially in the cities. Prohibition was repealed and, gradually through the century, liquor laws have been liberalized throughout the country.

Liquor there is ... but how I miss the Bar!
I miss a certain attitude of mind,
Congenial, which I seek but never find
Except beneath the golden triple star
Which from the brandy bottle shines afar.
I miss a type of jest that was designed
For roaring barrooms warmed with booze,
*   and kind—*
Good gawd! how low and coarse my real tastes are.
I miss an ambling, splay-foot waiter's beak,
Which like some rare peninsula of hell
Glowed through the humming barroom's
*   smoky reek—*
I miss the lies I used to hear men tell
Over the telephone to waiting wives—
What sweet aromas had these joyous lives!

—*Don Marquis*

Finally there are the results of drinking—great discussions, new friends, strained relationships, hangovers, and morning-after resolutions. Two writers who once worked for *The New Yorker* had comments appropriate to this subject. Robert Benchley wrote: "The only cure for a real hangover is death." And Dorothy Parker said: "One more drink and I'll be under the host." So moderation, my friends.

And now a few words about our author. Born in Cambridge, Massachusetts, Tom Noel moved west at an early age. Tom has led walking tours of Colorado and its buildings, including saloons, for a number of years. As a writer he has erased the line between nonfiction and fiction. He has followed in the footsteps of the early western editors who often reported on things that had not yet had the decency to occur.

For some years, Tom has been doing research on the liquid history of Colorado with many of Colorado's leading citizens. Peter De Vries once wrote: "I love being a writer. What I can't stand is the paperwork." Tom follows this pattern, preferring the sociable work of research to the sober work of writing.

Although many have commented on taverns and drinking, Dr. Thomas Noel brings to this subject the enthusiasm of the student and the professionalism of the historian. I am pleased to have assisted Dr. Noel in his voyage of discovery.

—Robert C. Baron

Let us have wine and women, mirth and laughter,
Sermons and soda water the day after.
—Lord Byron

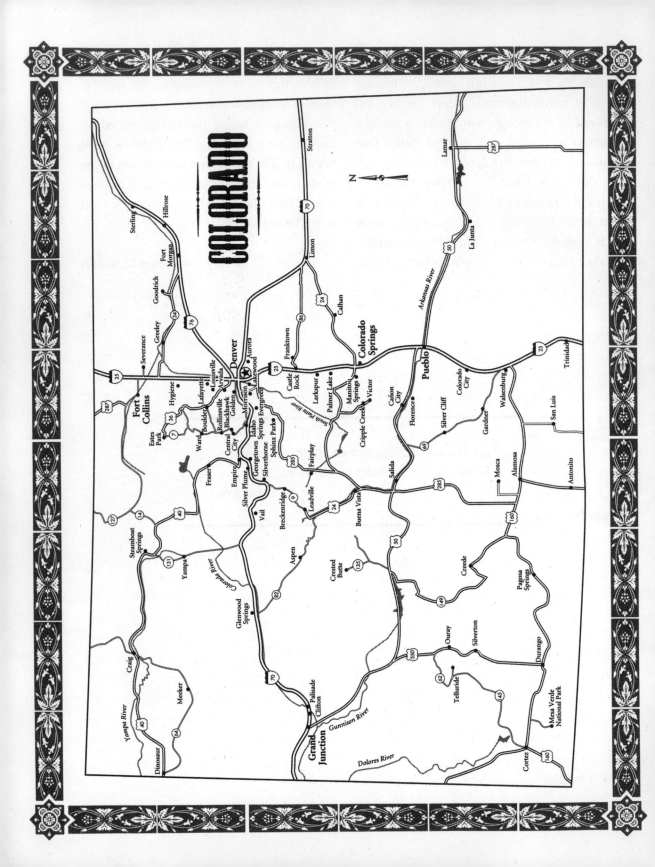

Introduction

I f you leveled the highest state, you would stand at 6,800 feet above sea level. The sky would probably be sunny and the air a little nippy. High, thin air and the absence of a large, moderating body of water allow temperatures to rise and fall quickly. A 30-degree difference in temperature often separates night from day. Thermometers can drop from balmy to frigid in a matter of hours. In other words, Colorado is frequently too hot or too cold. This helps explain why some of us patronize saloons for temperature, as well as altitude and attitude, adjustment.

Taverns are also a terrific source of local history. Colorado is a state whose territorial government was conceived and born in a tavern—Uncle Dick Wootton's saloon on Cherry Creek. Much subsequent political action has been tavern-related, as saloons are a favorite place to wheel and deal.

Bars overflow with folklore as well as history. For instance, you hardly ever see jackalopes in the wild anymore, but they can still be found in a few old taverns, usually on a wall with other stuffed critters. In search of jackalopes and other things, I began surveying bars early. As a nineteen-year-old college student, I found work-study employment making student identification cards.

This enabled me and some friends to get a head start on the bar survey of Colorado. Of course we already had visited many 3.2 bars, where patrons ages eighteen or older were welcome until the state outlawed these joints in the early 1990s. Underage drinking is a long tradition, a rite of passage. In some bars in Colorado, young babies only had to coo—"Coo … Coo …"—and the bartender would produce a Coors beer. Youngsters have also been raised on red beer or tomato beer, a health food combining a bit of tomato juice.

Pursuing higher education as long as I could, I completed a dissertation in history at the University of Colorado at Boulder. For that research, *The City & the Saloon: Denver: 1858–1916,* I systematically visited every licensed and unlicensed after-hours club, bar, lounge, nightclub, and tavern in Denver—some six hundred establishments.

In each bar, I, and any companions I could enlist, compiled 3-by-5 note cards. We recorded the bar name, address, date, and hours of our attendance. Then we attempted to describe the building exterior and interior, the quantity and nature of the clientele, transactions, the type of music, graffiti, prices, and any other information of possible interest.

Sometimes the bar survey led to trouble. Folks in some of the shadier joints suspected that we were federal narcotics agents or the local vice squad. A few times, I carelessly left the bar survey note cards in the tavern and had to go back for them the next morning. This proved embarrassing in one of Denver's more Neanderthal bars, Joe's Cave, which supposedly started out long ago as a dugout on Federal Boulevard. I had noted a brawl, the aroma of urine, graffiti galore, and rather barbaric behavior in general. When I returned the next day, Joe glared at me from behind the bar. He handed over my note cards, which he had edited heavily. Sure enough, he had cleaned up his place, at least on my cards, to meet health department rules and other standards of civility.

In a few bars I got into fights, such as the old Store, a stucco Spanish Colonial Revival–style fortress nightclub on East Colfax Avenue. There I learned a hard lesson. Do not fight for a woman, even if she came in with you. I wound up in University Hospital, and I never heard from her again.

Wounded or not, visiting every bar in the city and county of Denver is not as simple a job as you might think. Bars are constantly opening, closing, burning down, or changing names. So I took to checking every address where there ever was a bar. Sometimes the bar was gone, closed, or converted to something else.

America needs a greater sense of community, a sense of place, of local allegiances, and neighborhood bars help promote that.

Watching *Cheers* reruns on television isn't the same. A neighborhood bar is generally not new and trendy, but old and funky. It is not a place to see and be seen. Local taverns are a place to hear musicians and politicians, poets and cranks; to see local art and hear neighborhood news; a place for memorable parties, singing, dancing, tears, and good times.

Since completing the Denver bar survey of 1965 to 1978, I have not been idle. I have expanded the study, hoping to visit every bar in Colorado. So far, about seven shoe boxes are crammed with 3-by-5 cards on Colorado bars, arranged by county, town, and street address. In this book I focus on the most interesting taverns in terms of history, clientele, decor, and location. Antique, storied bars shed light on a community, its characters, and its past.

Some of these legendary watering holes are gone. Colorado is a boom-and-bust state with twice as many dead towns as live ones. The mountains are littered with old mining towns, the plains stained with failed farming communities. Saloons have a much shorter life expectancy—often only a year or two or three. So there are at least fifty dead bars for every live one you find. Prohibition alone wiped out a thousand Colorado saloons.

A few of the taverns herein will be ghosts by the time this book gets into your hands. For these defunct bars, the entries are not guides but obituaries. Most of these taverns, however, are still flowing and worth a visit for their flavor and history, if not their libations and food.

Breweries, too, have disappeared at an alarming rate. Back in the 1880s, even small communities tended to have their own suds maker. Denver alone had more than twenty-five breweries between 1859 and 1916, when statewide Prohibition burst the bubble. Prohibition broke most of the breweries, although a few survived on a diet of "near beer." Four remained until the 1950s: Walter's in Pueblo, Schneider's in Trinidad, the Tivoli in Denver, and Coors in Golden. In 1969 the Tivoli closed, leaving only Coors.

Then a miracle happened—small brewpubs and microbreweries began to make an incredible comeback. Since the Wynkoop Brewing Company opened in Denver in 1988, more than a hundred other brewpubs have opened around the state. Budweiser opened a huge branch of its St. Louis brewery in Fort Collins, and microbreweries (where beer is made but not sold for on-premises consumption) began springing up all over Colorado. Although this book hardly does justice to the current renaissance in local brewing, it does include a sampling of some of the better brewpubs.

Colorado's first saloons were adobe cantinas in the San Luis Valley (see Alamosa, Antonito, and San Luis). During and after the 1858–1859 gold rush, many more taverns sprang up, often made of canvas, dirt, and logs. Only a few of these evolved into more distinctive brick or stone edifices (see Aspen, Breckenridge, Denver, and Telluride).

The oldest masonry saloons have round arched windows and doors and decorative brick cornices. Some even aspire to be stylish, be it Italianate, Romanesque, or neoclassical.

Inside, many saloons feature Neoclassical backbars with columns, arches, cornices, and Greek and Roman trim such as garlands, swags, and egg-and-dart or dentiled molding. Ideally, the decor is also graced by semi-classical paintings of nude maidens and bare-chested male athletes.

Many of the fanciest backbars have a bronze plaque identifying them as the creation of the Brunswick Company. John M. Brunswick founded the firm in Cincinnati in 1845, originally to make pool tables. After his brother, Joseph, joined the firm, they also began making backbars, bowling equipment, bank fixtures, saloon tokens, and other wood furnishings. In 1874, Brunswick merged with a Cincinnati rival, the firm of Julius Balke, and in 1884 with H. W. Collender, a New York pool table maker. The firm soon had offices in St. Louis, Chicago, and other large cities. Under the names Brunswick, Brunswick-Balke, Brunswick-Balke-Collender, and since 1960 the Brunswick Corporation, it made many of the fine wooden furnishings showcased in bars. Today

Brunswick still makes pool tables and pool and bowling equipment. They no longer manufacture backbars, although independent woodworkers make handsome replicas.

Traditional altars of King Alcohol are classically inspired, just as the exteriors of elegant nineteenth-century saloons architecturally tended to reflect classical Greece and Rome. Even false-fronted frame saloons generally had bracketed cornices and pedimented windows derived from Greek Revival architecture. No matter how primitive or dilapidated, even the lowest dive, country roadhouse, or stagecoach inn generally has at least a few feeble pretenses at neoclassicism.

Taverns tend to be conservative institutions in traditional style, usually old, buildings. Only in rare cases do bars venture into a modern style, be it Art Deco, Streamline Moderne, Modern, or Postmodern. The Cruise Room of Denver's Oxford Hotel has been restored as a prizewinning example of an Art Deco interior. Another unusual departure is Silver Cliff's geodesic dome bar, complete with a silvery exterior skin.

Much more commonly, the "good old days" is the standard barroom theme. New bars are often built to look old. Old bars may be renovated to look even older. Bars are bastions of history and traditionalism drowning in nostalgia. They are retreats to a mythical golden past and an escape from present troubles.

Despite historical structures and traditional decor and behaviors, bars are not usually considered edifying institutions to be dignified with local or national register landmark designations. No matter how striking their "barchitecture," saloons are often regarded as signs of decay and degeneracy and banned from stylish neighborhoods. Bars frequently seem to be the last step in a building's decline, inviting urban renewal. Taverns gravitate to old, worn outbuildings that have exhausted other uses. Turnover in such places is a blessing as new owners usually at least add a new coat of paint.

The tavern as an institution, as well as a building type, is underappreciated. This book gives a voice to people—and an institution—that usually escape dry history books. Bars have made and shaped history. They themselves have revealing histories and are great places to collect tall, short, and winding tales.

Readers and critics, please note, this is not footnoted history. Names have sometimes been changed to protect the guilty. I have tried to stay close to the truth, or at least to the spirit of the truth.

Is one of your purposes on earth to find the perfect old-time saloon? To settle into some cheery, beery, historic tavern founded by thoughtful ancestors? To find a comfortable seat and be waited on promptly? To find someplace where all are equal and friendly? This book hopes to take you there.

Alamosa
Elevation: 7,574 feet

A riverside cottonwood grove gave its Spanish name to this town, laid out in 1880 by the Denver & Rio Grande Railroad. The railroad bought a 1,608-acre townsite on the west bank of the Rio Grande for its San Luis Valley headquarters. Town founder Alexander C. Hunt, a former territorial governor of Colorado and president of the D&RG Construction Company, brought in many of Alamosa's early frame and log buildings on flatbed railcars from Fort Garland, the previous end-of-track town, and plunked them down on newly platted lots. A few of these structures survive south of the tracks, at 312 and 411 8th Street and 621 9th Street. Governor Hunt's old mansion still sits on the western edge of Cole Park, where a replica of the original depot serves as the Chamber of Commerce and visitor center.

In the semiarid desert of the San Luis Valley, the most conspicuous landmarks are water tanks: Alamosa's old rocket-shaped tank (1920s), fed by six deep artesian wells, is now rivaled on the skyline by a 1980s onion-shaped tank. This new bright blue and white tank is an indication of Alamosa's steady, if slow, growth to a 1990 population of 7,579. Though the water tanks are easy to find, the town's notable taverns are harder to discover.

Alamosa is bigger than it looks. For local color, try the 500 block of State Street, once anchored by the now-gone Victoria Hotel, next to the once-bustling D&RG Depot and vast, now forlorn, railyards. In Mack's Bar and Pool Hall, 506 State Street, started by Mack Borotti, you can mingle with spinach cutters, potato planters, and lettuce pickers. At the Purple Pig on Main Street, the bartender controls bikers, college students, and

1

migrant workers with a sawed-off cue stick. If that doesn't work, he also has an electric cattle prod and a shotgun. All of this induced me to honor the homemade signs: "There will be no tabs given. This is a bar, not a bank," and, above the pickle jar, "Tip Your Tender."

Ace Inn Restaurant & Lounge
326 Main St. (se corner of Denver St.), (719) 589-9801

Forty-two-ounce margaritas, enchilada tortes, chiles rellenos, and guacamole flautas make this a cool hot spot. It began as a modest house that George and Viola Nestor converted to the Ace Inn in about 1939. Ed and Paul Quintana enlarged the premises, the menu, and the reputation after taking over in the 1980s. Peg and Monte Collins, proprietors since 1994, have maintained the place as an old favorite. Don't miss the back room, a veritable museum featuring twenty-eight rifles, including flintlocks. Homey black vinyl booths and barstools, paneled walls, a tile ceiling with fluorescent lighting, and a padded horseshoe-shaped bar adorn this inexpensive, friendly place located a block east of the junction of U.S. 160 and Main Street.

Jameel's Lounge
520 State Ave., (719) 589-0566

"Daddy" Jameel, a Palestinian, welcomes anyone here, including migrant laborers. "I've had this place since 1964," he reported. "Then it was the Indian Grill and before that a Chinese restaurant." This is said to be the most dangerous bar in town. If you are arrested there, however, remember that the owner also operates Jameel's Bail Bonds. Signs on the walls suggest behavioral problems: "First fight. Last Drink." "NO profanity. Men or women." "No stacking drinks during Happy Hour."

I made the mistake of arriving in a sports coat and the whole bar bristled. One swarthy, scared-looking fellow whimpered, "Jesus, he looks like my lawyer!"

"I didn't dare come in here sometimes," Jameel confessed, "except that I own it. Sometimes the lettuce pickers bring their lettuce knives. Don't let 'em cut you. Those knives are so dirty you'd die of infection, even if the cut didn't kill you."

Jameel seemed to have eyes in the back of his head during our discussion. He could spot and stop trouble quickly. When migrant workers eat and drink here, Jameel treats them well. "I don't ask 'em what they want. I just serve 'em good steaks. And whiskey. Not just beer. I'm a little guy and some call me a damned A-rab," he added, "but I have straightened out the toughest bar in the valley."

Antonito

Elevation: 7,888 feet

Antonito (yawn-toe-knee-toe), a Spanish-accented village in the San Luis Valley, lies 5 miles north of the New Mexico border. Like many valley villages, it has been largely bypassed by the twentieth century. Even the Cumbres & Toltec Scenic Railroad, which supposedly starts in Antonito, actually begins a mile south of town. The C&TSR snubbed Antonito's handsome old stone D&RG depot to build a fake new framed one.

Few tourists stop in town on their way to Taos and Santa Fe. Even fewer visit the El Ortiz Tavern, where I first met Angie in the summer of 1966. I was working as a roustabout west of Antonito at a dude ranch, The Rainbow Trout Lodge, headquartered in a two-story, peeled-log cabin on a celebrated trout stream called Conejos ("rabbit"), which runs as fast as a jackrabbit from the silvery San Juans into the Rio Grande.

"Antonito was the toughest town in the state when I first struck it in the late 1870s," according to engineer William Walk, who spent forty years with the Denver & Rio Grande. In memoirs published in *The Colorado Magazine* (November 1947), Walk remembered the early years of the town, which was founded in 1880: "It was a railroad town with lots of Mexicans and Indians." Its only street paralleled the track and was lined with wood shacks consisting of dancehalls, gambling dens, restaurants, a laundry, and saloons.

Originally an Anglo railroad town with a Presbyterian church, an opera house, and the Palace Hotel, Antonito is now predominantly Hispanic. In 1940 the population peaked at some 1,300. Since then, Antonito has dwindled to about 900 citizens.

El Ortiz Tavern
513 Main St. (U.S. Hwy. 285), CLOSED

After days rousting about the dude ranch, I joined Julio Archuleta, Ernie Marquez, and other employees for visits to the El Ortiz on Antonito's faded Main Street. Even back then, the El Ortiz usually looked deserted. A "For Sale" sign shared the front window with tubs of geraniums whose riotous red blossoms meant that Angie was still running the place.

Antonito's ancient adobe tavern, the faded El Ortiz, stands on the main street of the small Hispanic town in the San Luis Valley.

Angie Ortiz has auburn hair and a sunny smile. She struck me as the brightest and fastest talker in town. And she ended her dances with a cartwheel. "I married Ricardo Casias," Angie explained once, "because he was the best dancer in Antonito."

Angie and Ricardo had turned the tavern into a dance club and, on occasion, a dinner club, with Angie cooking on the huge, old cast-iron range. The ancient building had been Ira Green's dry goods store until Angie's father, Gaspar Ortiz, bought it. He helped Angie and Ricardo switch to wet goods. Angie decorated the 18-inch-thick adobe walls with her high school butterfly collection, properly mounted on balsa wood with pins and neatly printed labels in Latin. Other walls displayed Angie and Ricardo's wedding photo, choice *Playboy* centerfolds, framed prints of John F. Kennedy and Jackie Kennedy, and a large colorful painting of Nuestra Señora de Guadalupe.

Angie and Ricardo acquired a pool table and installed a spiffy, easy-to-clean linoleum floor over the dirty, splintered, and stained floorboards. Angie also had a mini-library in the bar. The last time I looked, that shelf had well-worn copies of *Webster's Collegiate Dictionary, Family Health Guide Medical Encyclopedia, You and the Law, Pie Cook Book,* and *How to Increase Your Word Power.*

Angie put a sign over the doorway, "Peace to All Who Enter Here," and called everyone "honey." Yet she could throw out troublemakers in seconds, usually outshouting them in the process. She kicked them out in either

English or Spanish, allowing the customer to pick the language of eviction.

Rarely did Angie turn gloomy. But late one night, I recall hearing her sigh, "Tomas, the El Ortiz will always be in limbo. I will never be able to escape it. No one's ever offered me even one peso for this place. Antonito is doomed."

It all started, she explained, back in the 1850s, when the first New Mexican settlers came up the Rio Grande into Colorado. They hoped for a more promising place than the high, dry desert of the San Luis Valley. But the lead mule stopped and would not budge. The New Mexicans pulled and pushed. They kicked and swore and prayed. But it just stood there, stubborn as a jackass. Finally, someone noticed that the statue of Nuestra Señora de Guadalupe had fallen off the creature's back and landed on the banks of the Rio Conejos.

So the pioneers built the little town of Guadalupe with a chapel where the statue had landed. But the statue made a mistake: she had the people build the town on the north bank of the Conejos, where a flood washed most of it away. The people rebuilt the town on the higher, south bank and re-named it Conejos, but named the new chapel for Guadalupe. It is now the oldest operating church in Colorado.

When the railroad came in 1880, D&RG officials tried to get the people of Conejos to give them land and bribes to bring in the railway. Otherwise, General William J. Palmer threatened, Conejos would become a railroadless backwater. The people only laughed. So the D&RG bypassed Conejos to build the railroad town of Antonito a mile away. Antonito quickly became the largest town in Conejos County, a major sheep and cattle center with a big perlite mill. Of course the Guadalupe Church and the courthouse stayed in Conejos. No one told the D&RG about the Guadalupe statue.

The ultimate fate of a town founded by railroad and real estate developers instead

A tub of geraniums brightens the storefront of the El Ortiz Tavern, posted with the prayer "Peace to All Who Enter Here."

of by heavenly guidance troubled Gaspar Ortiz, founding father of the El Ortiz Tavern. A wiry man with a wispy moustache, he leaned against the high-backed booth. His dim eyes grew sharper as he looked into the past. "My great-grandfather came from Spain. My father, Gaspar Florentino Ortiz, was here when the railroad came down from Alamosa. The Spanish people didn't want the railroad. They thought it would bring in bad people. They were right. Once the railroad came, we lost this land."

The old man, whom people called Jasper, looked at Angie. She is a beautiful woman. You would never guess she was a grandmother, but she was changing her granddaughter's diaper on the bar. Gaspar's eyes left his oldest daughter and focused again on the past. "My great-grandfather from Spain was a *rico*. Gaspar Avenue in Santa Fe is named for him. My other grandfather, Jim Archuleta, my mother's father, ran 100,000 head of sheep west of here in the county they named for his family.

"My father was postmaster here and he named the little town south of us for our family, Ortiz. Once Antonito was rich with sheep. I was born in 1886 and can remember driving thousands of sheep down Main Street to the railroad cars headed for Denver. Sheep were to us what buffalo were to the Indians.

The people of the San Luis Valley ate lamb, wore wool, slept in wool blankets, and even made the windows of their homes out of sheepskin. Those were the happy days. Millions were made in the sheep business. But little of that money stayed in Antonito, except for the Warshaurer Mansion a block away, where the old sheep tycoon Fred Warshaurer killed himself one night."

The last time I visited Antonito I found the El Ortiz closed down. So were most of the other bars I used to visit there: the Dutch Mill, the El Rio Bar, the Cumbres Cafe, the Gold Nugget, and the Sweetwater Saloon. The Rainbow Night Club, with its huge curvilinear parapet crowning a white stucco facade on the outskirts of town, has been closed since at least the 1950s. Even longer gone was the Hoffman Saloon, which used to face the D&RG depot. A turkey vulture circled overhead.

I found Angie in the back rooms of her closed bar. She was living there alone. Gaspar and Ricardo were dead. She looked old and tired and was covered with debris from the firewood she was stockpiling for the winter. "Ricardo and I had California retirement dreams ...," she began softly. She could not finish. Slowly, the cloud passed from her face and the old sunny smile rose again. "Hey, honey. Here's a quarter for the jukebox."

Arvada

Elevation: 5,337 feet

With its large arts complex, museums, and a rejuvenated downtown, Arvada is one of Denver's most progressive and history-conscious suburbs. Long an agricultural hamlet of several hundred citizens, it became one of Jefferson County's fastest-growing towns after World War II. With a population of more than 95,000, Arvada is now Colorado's sixth-largest city.

The Arvada Flour Mill Museum at 5580 Wadsworth Boulevard is a relic of the agrarian past, a 30-foot-tall wooden structure that produced Arva-Pride flour. Arvada agrarians incorporated in 1904 as a dry town, but a few notable watering holes have sprung up since.

Arvada Tavern
5705 Olde Wadsworth Blvd.,
(303) 424-9905

Located in the Olde Towne Arvada Historic District, this 1910 blacksmith shop evolved into an auto repair garage during the 1920s. After it became a tavern in the 1930s, the outdoor stairs were moved indoors and the chimney was removed. This small, nondescript, two-story gray brick building is a favorite of old-timers who fancy the antique popcorn machine and one of Colorado's oldest shuffleboard tables.

Fred Gaglia, owner of the bar for decades, tried to rename it "Fred's Arvada Tavern," but regulars saw no need for the change. The forty barstools are occupied mostly by blue-collar males. If women show up, they may be asked to the little dance floor next to the jukebox. Legendary regulars include Bubble Up, who drinks out of an upraised Coors bottle, sending up giant bubbles.

Some of the bar veterans still remember the night a guy with a double-barreled shotgun came in to rob bartender Eddie

Krantz. When the robber ordered him to lie on the floor, Krantz stared down the barrel and told him, "Everybody I know dies lying down. If you're going to kill me, you do it while I'm standing up." The guy left. They caught him outside; his gun was loaded and he had a dozen shells in his pocket. Nowadays it's a more peaceful place, although not yet heavenly. A home-made sign over the pool table warns, "In case of argument or foul language, table will be closed."

The Beer Lover's Prayer

Our Lager,
Who art in barrels,
Hallowed be thy drink.
Thou will be drunk, I will be drunk,
At home as thou art in the pub.
Give us this day our foamy head,
And forgive us our spillages
As we forgive those who spill against us.
And lead us not to incarceration,
But deliver us from hangovers,
For this is the beer, the bitter, and the lager forever.
Ahhh-men.

—Anonymous

Aspen

Elevation: 7,908 feet

Prospectors from Leadville discovered silver along the Roaring Fork River near its junction with Castle, Maroon, and Hunter Creeks. There they founded Ute City in 1879, appropriately honoring the natives. Shortly thereafter, the Utes slaughtered Indian agent Nathan Meeker by ramming a stake down his throat. Ute City was quickly renamed "Aspen" in 1880.

Aspen's pay dirt did not pay off until the Denver & Rio Grande Railroad steamed into town in 1887, followed by the Colorado Midland Railroad in 1888. Jerome B. Wheeler of Colorado Midland put Aspen on the map by building a large smelter, a fine hotel, an opera house, and a fabulous mansion that now houses the Aspen Historical Society.

During the flush times, Aspen sported some twenty-three saloons and the town drank sixty barrels of beer a day in winter and ninety barrels a day in summer. Heavy beer consumption inspired the construction of the Aspen Brewing Company at the north end of Mill Street at the base of Red Mountain. Alarmed at Aspen's alcoholic intake, the Woman's Christian Temperance Union (WCTU) opened an Aspen office in 1887 and began to wage war on the saloons and brothels of Durant Street.

The WCTU fought a losing battle in what was briefly Colorado's premier silver city: in 1891, Aspen and Pitkin County outproduced even Leadville and Lake County. During the early 1890s, Aspen, complete with streetcars and a population of some 5,000, was the third largest city in Colorado, preceded only by Denver and Leadville. The silver crash of 1893 and repeal of the Sherman Silver Purchase Act changed all that. The price of silver sank from about $1.32 to only 59 cents an ounce. Aspen silver

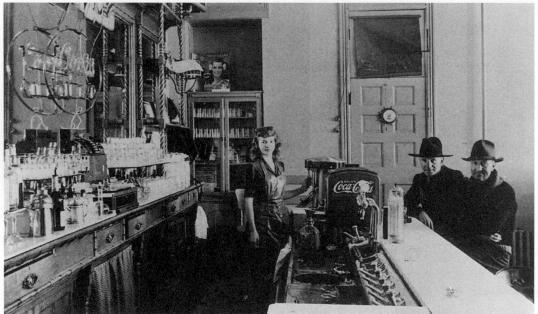

Aspen's Hotel Jerome Bar evolved from a silver mining–era saloon (top) to a soda fountain (bottom) with statewide Prohibition in 1916. Like many hard drink places transformed into "soft drink parlors," the Jerome sometimes offered stronger concoctions than Cherry Cokes. Old-timers still remember "Aspen Crud"—milk shakes laced with whiskey. Photos courtesy of the Aspen Historical Society.

production dipped to about $3.7 million in 1894, half of what it had been in 1893. Silver and lead mining continued to be Aspen's major industries, but the town's population had tumbled to a low of 705 by 1930. Not until the 1980s would Aspen's population equal that of the 1890s.

The silver crash hit Aspen hard. One old miner, Jacques Bionis, supposedly blew himself to heaven by placing three sticks of dynamite under his hat and lighting the fuse—a fuse long enough to allow him to finish his last pint of beer. At the Hotel Jerome Bar, one of two old-time saloons to survive Aspen's long decline, a visitor asked one of the old codgers, "Hey, Pop, have you lived here all your life?"

The old geezer peered at the questioner and mumbled, "Nope, not yet."

"What makes this town so slow?"

"Well, sonny, I'll tell you. The people in Aspen are all mineralized. They've got silver in their hair and lead in their pants."

Aspen's many slick new saloons range from Planet Hollywood, where they charge even for souvenir menus, to its first striptease joint, Club 81611. Oops, scratch them both. Planet Hollywood, despite its glitzy 1994 opening with megastars Don Johnson, Sylvester Stallone, and Arnold Schwarzenegger, went out of orbit in 1998. The strip club was undone in 1996 when an ordinance was pushed through city council banning nude dancing and the depositing of tips in dancers' clothing. At the following landmark taverns, you will find people very well clothed in this most fashionable town, a Glitter Gulch whose extravagant homes and lifestyles would astonish its silver-grubbing founders.

The Cantina
Main and Mill Sts.
(on the se corner of Mill St.),
(970) 925-3663

This is a fine Mexican restaurant where even during the high season you can usually find a chair or a barstool, as they have 230 seats indoors and out. The combination of lots of glass, sun, and plants makes a bright spot out of this corner building, which once housed the old YMCA.

Flying Dog Brew Pub
424 E. Galena St., (970) 925-7464

In a subterranean hole with naked brick walls, Aspen's first brewpub was opened by George Stranahan in 1991. The building has housed many pubs in the past—Pinocchio's, Loretta's, Pablo's, The Blue Moose, and Johnnie's Rendezvous, among others. The Flying Dog boasts the cheapest hotdogs and best amber ale in Aspen. Even dogs are welcome in this casual, laid-back bar. The mint tray is filled with complimentary dog biscuits to help wash down the pub's legendary Doggie Style Amber Ale.

Hotel Jerome Bar
330 E. Main St., (970) 925-5518

A picture of Jerome B. Wheeler, who wore a beard that mice could hide in, hangs behind the front desk. He built this three-story brick hotel for $160,000. The old hotel had eighty tiny rooms. I can remember staying here for $16 a night in the 1960s. The rooms were so small you had to go outside in the hall to put on your boots. Those little rooms have been converted to twenty-seven luxury suites with marble bathrooms bigger than the old bedrooms, and Jacuzzis and gold water faucets.

The hotel and its saloon have been the town gathering place since they first opened in 1889. Originally the bar occupied the corner storefront, which is now a clothing shop, and a barber shop occupied what is now the bar. This legendary saloon has huge mahogany doors, silver chandeliers, and ceiling fans hanging from a high tin ceiling. The unusual golden oak backbar has delicate filigree that looks Japanese.

During Aspen's drowsy decades from 1893 to the 1950s, the hotel became more of a boardinghouse. Few businessmen or travelers came to the dying silver city, and indigent miners found cheap room and board at the hotel, which was struggling to stay open and hungry for any customers.

During Prohibition the saloon survived, disguised as a soda fountain that served "Aspen Crud," a vanilla milk shake laced with booze.

The hotel's 1985 restoration/expansion included new I-beam supports and footings, along with a sixty-six-room addition. One of the new spaces is a second watering hole, the Antlers Bar, featuring elk antler chandeliers and antler-legged tables. Neither saloon serves Aspen Crud or Aspen ditch water. The latter flowed freely until the 1950s, when the city removed its ubiquitous water ditches, used for irrigation, fighting fires, and diluting firewater.

The Red Onion
420 E. Cooper Ave., (970) 925-9043

I first visited the Red Onion in the summer of 1965 while hanging out at the Aspen Writers Workshop. Writers often got into at least verbal fights with local ranchers, cowboys, construction workers, and hay stackers. I usually went with a grizzly old poet who was working on a long epic poem, an ode to President Lyndon B. Johnson. It was in the Onion that he finally decided on a title to his masterpiece, "F**k You with Flowers."

I think he may have been the same poet who left these words above the men's room urinal:

> *Rowdy, howdy*
> *By gum golly*
> *You're welcome*
> *to Aspen, Colorady*

This old-time, long, narrow barroom lies behind a Victorian storefront on the Aspen mall. Tom Latta, an early-day city councilman, built the saloon in 1892, as the pediment atop the cornice and the inlaid entry-floor tile proclaim. An *Aspen Times* reporter, probably influenced by free libations, pronounced Latta's saloon "the handsomest in the West." During Prohibition Tim Kellaher kept the place open as a restaurant and lived upstairs with his family. Johnny Litchfield, a veteran of the 10th Mountain Division and Camp Hale, bought the place and gave it its present name. The two-story, red brick building retains its tile floor, pressed metal ceiling, and big corner booths. The antique front bar is golden oak with Gothic arches framing inlaid, white wooden flowers. On top of the Second Empire–style backbar sits a porcelain couple—somehow they have avoided destruction despite all the commotion that still makes this one of Aspen's liveliest nightspots.

A 1948 photograph on the wall shows the Red Onion surrounded by only a few log shacks and weedy vacant lots. Today the lots are built or overbuilt around the Onion, a small old-timer with a Victorian red brick façade and pressed metal cornice. Although the rear gambling hall is now a dining room, the upstairs brothel an office space, and the jazz cellar closed, the Red Onion remains a pungent reminder of Aspen's naughty past.

Ask the bartender for "The Red Onion Alumni Association Reflections & Names for Past Visitors." This thick black notebook is rich in memories, including an account of the night Jack Kennedy danced here and the days "when Aspen was a ghost town and people were moving abandoned homes down to Glenwood Springs." Of skiing in the 1950s, one customer wrote: "You had to climb uphill—or ride the boat tow, which had nice warm blankets. Then we skied down Aspen Mountain straight into the Red Onion."

Aspen's pungent Red Onion, one of the few saloons open in 1952, when Mary Hayes took this photo, is no longer alone amid dogs and vacant lots. The Aspen Mall, in-fill buildings, and many newer watering holes now surround this boisterous liquid landmark. Tom Noel Collection.

Ute City Banque Restaurant & Bar
501 E. Hyman (on the corner of Galena St.), (970) 924-4373

Ute City, the initial name of Aspen, is commemorated by this elegant inn. Inside, a grand backbar frames an old safe dating from the days when Wells Fargo officed here, followed by the Aspen State Bank and the Pitkin County Bank. When the bankers moved out in the 1970s, this became the Ute City Banque, one of the town's more elegant restaurants and long-lived saloons. Henry Cowenhoven, an Aspen patriarch, erected this landmark in 1890. He used the distinctive orange-red sandstone from the nearby Peachblow Quarry. Local stonemasons carved the gorgeous arches, columns, and decorative trim to give this hospitable landmark Aspen's finest façade.

*Myself, I can endure the drouth
With stoic calm, and prayer.
But my feet still seek a railing
When a railing isn't there.*
                    —**Don Marquis,**
          The Old Brass Railing

Woody Creek Tavern
2 Woody Creek Plaza, (970) 923-4585

Located 7 miles northeast of Aspen on Colorado 82, the Woody Creek Tavern was immortalized by Hunter S. Thompson when he smoke-bombed it on April 29, 1989. The gonzo journalist subsequently apologized in writing and promised never to do it again. Even he appreciated the good, inexpensive food in this crowded joint with nine tables and a small bar. Tile floors and the low acoustic tile ceiling overhead, as well as walls jammed with stuffed animals, photos, and memorabilia, make this an intimate tavern. Raucous and unpretentious, catering to blue-collar locals, it is an antidote to the chic upvalley lounges in Glitter Gulch.

Aurora

Elevation: 5,342 feet

Aurora started out in 1891 as Fletcher, the darling of Denver developer Donald K. Fletcher. He subsequently absconded with city funds and citizens renamed their town for the Roman goddess of the dawn. She awoke slowly, not shining until the 1920s, when the new Fitzsimons Army Hospital and Denver Municipal Airport helped boost the population to 2,295. Greater growth came with the establishment of Lowry Army Air Field, Buckley Army Air Field, and Rocky Mountain Arsenal.

When Lowry Field opened in 1938, its eastern edge, Havana Street, began to develop as a commercial strip, drawing business south from Aurora's original main street, East Colfax Avenue. After 1945 many ex-servicemen returned to raise their families under the spacious, sunny skies where they had trained. By the 1990s the ambitious city of some 250,000 had annexed more than 100 square miles in Adams, Arapahoe, and Douglas Counties, becoming Colorado's second largest city in terms of area.

Aurora Seed & Feed on East Colfax Avenue, a longtime landmark of the hamlet's early days as a farm and ranch town, became Sgt. Pepper's Night Club in the 1980s, epitomizing Aurora's transformation. Aurora has grown away from its original main street, but Colfax remains the place for barhopping—and trouble. Aurora cops still heavily patrol the bar-lined avenue where pioneer marshal Alfred G. "Pop" Stiff used to lie in wait with his deputy, a pet parrot. Pop, who had a long white beard, stopped troublemakers by shooting out their tires with his shotgun and then had the parrot scold them. Pop's home base was the now-defunct Bus Tavern at East Colfax and Dallas Street, then the east end of the Number 15 Colfax streetcar line.

Blue Lady Lounge
9700 E. Colfax Ave. (at Emporia St.), CLOSED

A life-size reclining nude with a blue Bette Davis face made this neighborhood tavern famous. "Crippled Eddie," a polio victim, painted her in 1951 with a 4-inch brush to commemorate the building's 1924 origins. It started out as Aurora's first movie theater, the Hollywood, until the Fox Theater (now the Aurora Fox Arts Center) opened in 1946 at 9900 East Colfax. Marie Copenhaven operated the Blue Lady as Cope and Marie's until 1986, when it was shut down for overenthusiastic liquor service regardless of the hour or the age of the customer. After losing its liquor license, the Blue Lady became a pawn shop.

Cozy Inn Bar
11310 E. Colfax Ave., (303) 366-9418

Started around 1910 as a false-fronted frame saloon, this place is not only cozy but cheap. For decades "Mom" Fernette Pope offered 7-ounce beers for a dime and hamburgers for 15 cents. She also made the Cozy cozy for soldiers from Buckley and Fitzsimons and airmen from Lowry. In turn, they made her a 6-foot Christmas tree and a model of the bridge from the war movie *Bridge over the River Kwai,* using swizzle sticks welded together with cigarette lighters.

Mom has mothered her customers since the 1950s. She is usually the first to know who is sleeping with whom, who is pregnant, who is engaged, and who is getting divorced.

"People confide in a bartender before anybody else," she said, "because a good bartender knows how to keep a secret. I also follow the bartender's code: The three things you don't talk about are politics, religion, and wives."

Mom can be tough, though. She packs a baseball bat behind the bar. "That," she explained, "is my persuasion stick at two in the morning when they don't want to go home. I don't really hit anybody, but whomp 'em on the butt where they keep their wallets. I run this place; the customers don't."

Emil-lene's Sirloin House
16000 E. Smith Rd., (303) 366-6674

To reach this steak house, turn south off Smith Road at the vintage cocktail sign and head down a corduroy dirt lane until you see a circle of covered wagons. These wagons and a large grove of cottonwoods along Sand Creek hide the low-slung, ramshackle cinderblock-and-frame building. Emil-lene's claims to be Aurora's second-oldest tavern—and a far more colorful steak house than any of those chains in downtown Denver.

The tiny bar jammed into one corner is decorated with the international "No" symbol superimposed on a pooping bull. On the opposite wall, a large bull head has red eyes that light up whenever someone in the three small dining rooms pushes a cocktail service button. The wood-paneled rooms have low tile ceilings with fancy chandeliers. One room surrounds a huge cottonwood tree that has been decapitated at the roofline on orders of the Tri-County Health Department to keep bugs, birds, and rodents from getting into the bar. And in this remote rural area there are critters galore—bugs and rodents eager to escape the raccoons, deer, foxes, and magpies.

The alligators are gone, according to Emil Kuchar, who founded this place with his wife, Charlene (the other half of Emil-lene's). Kuchar, the son of a Walsenburg coal miner, said, "My father always told me don't coal mine for a living if you want to live. That was the only advice he gave, and I followed it. I started working in the restaurant business at age twelve. I worked for Frank Emmerling, who opened this sirloin house in 1958 as Frankie's. Before that is when the alligators were here. This used to be the Mystery House, a fun house filled with optical illusions, creaky floors, and an arena where you could watch local cow and farm boys wrestle the gators. It all came to an end when an alligator de-armed one local youth." Or so Frank swore at the bar underneath the "No Bull" sign.

Frankie's was also notorious for the craps and poker games. Hidden away out in the countryside, it was a gamblers' mecca, so long as they treated the Adams County sheriff and all eight of his kids to free dinners. But a new sheriff raided the place, making the front page of both *The Denver Post* and the *Rocky Mountain News*. For a remote steak house that has never advertised and is probably unknown to 95 percent of all Denverites, the gaming raids were

Why don't you slip out of those wet clothes and into a dry martini.

—Robert Benchley

terrific publicity. Emil-lene's has been legendary—and well patronized—ever since.

Emil bought the bar from Frank in 1972 for $100,000 and has since sold it to his daughter, Karen L'Anglais, and son, Jay Lombardi. The menu is unwritten but easy to remember: T-bones, sirloin, filet, fresh baked salmon, crab legs, lobster, lamb chops, and roast chicken. Each meal comes with a generous iced vegetable tray, soup or salad, spaghetti and beef marinara sauce, French bread, and baked or fried potatoes.

Emil-lene's is a folksy, friendly country place, complete with two "lonely hearts" tables at the entrance for viewing all entering patrons for possible romantic encounters. Extraordinarily fine, fast, and friendly service; good bountiful meals; and, best of all, the funky rural setting make Emil-lene's a must. After dinner, explore the adjacent cottonwood grove along Sand Creek. It used to be Pop Stark's ranch. He wasn't much of a rancher, but he made a fortune selling sand, leaving the area with sinkholes, bogs, and wetlands. The city of Aurora recently purchased 60 acres next to Emil-lene's 4-acre site (complete with horseshoe throwing pits) to preserve as a wetlands. Emil hopes they will reintroduce alligators, which he claims he'll add to Emil-lene's menu.

Gully Homestead
200 S. Chambers Rd.
(ne corner of E. Alameda Ave.),
(303) 360-8545

At the east end of the Colfax streetcar line, passengers could see a ranch miles off to the southeast. That homestead has been there since the early 1890s, when it was started by the Gully family from Tipperary, Ireland. Out on Tollgate Creek, the Gullys were by themselves—and liked it that way.

Once in a while John, the youngest son of Thomas and Temperance Gully, drove steers and dairy cows into Denver's Wazee Street corrals. He sold them, hit a few Larimer Street saloons, bought supplies with the remaining cash, and headed back out to the High Plains. Another Irish son of the sod, John Delaney, moved in next to the Gullys and married their daughter, Bridget.

Aurorans wanted little to do with the Gullys and Delaneys. In venerable East Colfax bars, old-timers still talk about the Gully boys, the three sons of John and Bridget who never married and mostly raised hell. After John died in 1915, his sons took to making moonshine and staging rodeos. The ranching business suffered, but revelers enjoyed getting smashed at these Sunday afternoon celebrations. The last of the Gully boys, Edward, died in 1962, just as suburbia was about to swallow the homestead his grandfather had established a century earlier.

As subdivisions and shopping centers closed in, the city of Aurora salvaged the venerable Gully Homestead House and the Delaney Homestead House and Round Barn. They became the centerpiece of what is now a 160-acre Aurora City Park site at the junction of two waterways, Tollgate Creek and the Highline Canal. The round frame barn (ca. 1900) is the only one left in Colorado. A variety of outbuildings, including a railroad boxcar and a cinderblock silo, document farm and ranch activities over the past century. In addition to John Delaney's clapboard farmhouse (1892), the park contains the ranch house, where the Thomas Gully family lived in the original single-room clapboard house with a later two-room addition. The full-width front porch is a good vantage point for watching the local prairie dog colony and trying to imagine the wild, boozy rodeos at Aurora's first unofficial saloon.

The Plainsman
652 Peoria St., (303) 366-6478

Since 1953, Aurorans have gravitated to this well-named watering hole supervised by a giant buffalo head behind the bar. The buffalo has guarded a rambunctious saloon with country-and-western music, pool tables in the back, and free bowls of popcorn and tacos. The Plainsman also offers homemade soups, a Mexican-American menu, and down-home fun. Because The Plainsman is so popular with Aurora flatlanders, the owners opened The Plainsman II at 3124-D South Parker Road (303-696-7225) and the Plainsman III at 15400 Smith Road (303-361-6184).

The Store
8975 E. Colfax Ave., CLOSED

Before it was burned down in the spring of 1972 and subsequently leveled, The Store resembled a fort whose concrete walls were painted and textured to look like an adobe outpost. It had bars and dance floors upstairs and down, a cover charge, and live music. In 1971 I was slugged in the mouth for defending my date from a fellow who was trying to shake his cigarette ashes into her hat.

The Zanza Bar
10601 E. Colfax Ave., CLOSED

Among Aurora's most memorable liquid landmarks was this country-and-western bar. Behind two green metal saguaro cacti, it jumped with excitement for fifty years before dancing off into history in 1994. The Zanza Bar entertained airmen from Lowry Air Force Base during World War II. Many of them fell in love with Denver and the local gals they met. Inside you could usually find live bands and couples dancing in snappy cowboy outfits, hats, and boots. The cinderblock walls had Technicolor murals of western scenes, including some particularly memorable moments in The Zanza Bar. The Zanza Bar Motel was available next door if couples grew amorous. This pioneer country-and-western bar closed in 1994 and has been obliterated. Its real cowboys and cow-

girls, as well as wannabes, would be flabbergasted at today's new country-and-western joints with electronic bulls to ride and $10 shots and beers.

Zephyr Lounge
11940 E. Colfax Ave., (303) 364-8981

Barry Melnick has owned the Zephyr Lounge since 1947 and still opens it six days a week for the 7 A.M. happy hour. Although the bar no longer looks like a streamlined railroad diner or serves its famous Z-burger, not much else has changed. "This is an old-time bar," admitted Melnick. "People sit in the same chairs and tell each other the same stories one hundred times. It's quiet; it's peaceful. I had the grandfathers, the fathers, and now the sons in here. As long as I'm healthy, I'll stay open. I couldn't stay home and watch TV. And I'm a health guy; I don't smoke or drink."

Black Hawk

Elevation: 8,042 feet

Black Hawk, the "City of Mills," was named for its first gold mill—a quartz mill built by the Black Hawk Company of Rock Island, Illinois. Strategically located at the confluence of Gregory Gulch and North Clear Creek, this 1860 gold camp became Colorado's first ore-processing hub.

Colorado's first great smelter, Nathaniel P. Hill's Boston and Colorado Smelter, opened in 1868. It salvaged the sputtering gold rush by applying a process imported from Swansea, Wales, to cook recalcitrant gold ores. By the 1870s, fifteen stamp mills were crushing ores for twenty-five smelters that darkened Black Hawk with sulfurous smoke. To feed the smelters, much of Gilpin County was deforested for charcoal. Twenty-four hours a day, the town throbbed to the beat of the stamp mills, where huge steel- or iron-tipped lead weights pulverized the ore.

Miners and smelter workers cooled off in Black Hawk's numerous saloons. By 1865 the six-year-old town had thirteen watering holes. In the early days, the town also had three breweries: the Chicago Brewery (1873–1885), the John Edwards Brewery (1862–1865) in Chase Gulch, and the Kirby & Barnes Brewery (1877–1878).

Prohibition did not dry up this mining town. A relic of the speakeasy days is the Bootleggers' Cabin at 3873 Colorado 46 in Golden Gate Canyon State Park. This 16-by-24-foot log cabin, the only moonshiner's resort on the Colorado Register of Historic Places, is hidden on a forested, secluded hillside above Ralston Creek. Along the creek, a large pit contains remains of wooden barrels, many rusty metal hoops, and even the skeleton of the 1920s Dodge truck in which the "squirrel whiskey" was delivered.

Like other mining towns, Black Hawk squeaked through thin times with the help of moonshine. Old mines made great places for secret distilleries. After the railroad abandoned service there in 1941, Black Hawk survived the drowsy decades because it had the only gas station in the county. People stopped for gas and sometimes wandered into the saloons, which sustained the town after mining and milling profits shriveled to a pittance. The Golden Gilpin Gold Mill is the sole survivor of the many mills that rimmed the town and consumed the surrounding forests for charcoal fuel.

In 1900, 1,200 people lived in Black Hawk; by 1990 the population had dwindled to 227. Although people disappeared, many of the buildings remained, since Black Hawk had never suffered a major fire. Gambling began to change the scene in 1991, and old retail shops and mill sites were replaced by casinos that a modern-day William Blake might also characterize as "dark Satanic mills."

Churches grabbed the high ground in mining towns such as Black Hawk, but a far greater number of saloons flourished in the town's lower regions. 1864 photo by George Wakely, Tom Noel Collection.

Gambling has always been popular in Black Hawk, but not cheating—as this public hanging suggests. Tom Noel Collection.

Besides the town's casinos and taverns, don't miss the Lace House at 161 Main Street, a house museum since 1974. Lavish decorative wood detail makes this a postcard model of how Carpenter's Gothic trim could enhance a miner's shack.

Black Forest Inn, Casino & Hotel
260 Gregory St., (303) 642-0415

Wilhelm "Bill" Lorenz, a German-born innkeeper, converted two old miner's cabins into this Teutonic lodge in 1958. A favorite town character and former mayor, Lorenz is one of the few old-timers to transform a sleepy, small-town business into a big-time casino operation. He added the casino in 1992 and moved the mountain behind his inn to make room for a hotel.

Cuckoo clocks, red-and-white-checkered tablecloths, rustic decor from the German Alps, and the Rathskeller make this a memorable stop. Lorenz is usually around with tempting suggestions such as hot apple strudel or one more Teutonic elixir. Three generations of the Lorenz family have maintained this hospitable haven, complete with a children's arcade and German food, beer, and wine that make it one of the finest feasts in the Little Kingdom of Gilpin County.

Bull Durham Casino
110 Main St. (ne corner of Gregory St.), (303) 582-0810

William Fick, a Prussian immigrant, built heavy-duty "Black Hawk Wagons" with large double wheels for mountain use. His thriving wagon-building, repair, and blacksmith shop moved into this two-story gran-ite building with a fancy brick front. To make a few extra dollars and get some free Bull Durham chewing tobacco, Fick allowed the large Bull Durham sign to be painted across the façade. It is one of the few remaining signs out of thousands painted nationwide by traveling crews of the American Tobacco Company. After a women's organization complained about the bull's conspicuous private parts, the company sent an employee around the country to paint a fence over the offending member. The sign and the building were restored and recycled in 1991 for a casino.

Bullwhacker's Casino
101 Gregory St., (303) 271-2500

J. E. Scobey's Billiard Saloon occupied this 1864 brick commercial structure before the Knights of Pythias purchased it in 1885. The second-story round-arched windows were matched by arched windows on the first floor before conversion to solid plate-glass storefronts. The frequent floods sweeping down Gregory Gulch to bathe Black Hawk have filled in the original first floor, which is now the basement. The building, also known as the Knights of Pythias Hall, is completely surrounded by the giant, four-story Bullwhacker's Casino (1992), which has preserved only the façade of the old hall. Here and in many other casinos, cheap contemporary rooftop screens hide mechanical systems and destroy any neo-Victorian illusions suggested by the rest of the building.

Crook's Palace
200 Gregory St., (303) 582-5094

In claiming to be Colorado's oldest tavern, the Palace traces its ancestry to a demolished 1860s saloon on the same site. Tom Crook opened the current establishment around 1900. A classic storefront with chandeliers in the twin front windows adorns this tiny, old-time saloon. Two reclining nudes

Crook's Palace is one of the few small, historic saloons to survive the transformation that gambling brought to Black Hawk. Since gaming became legal in three mining communities in 1991, Black Hawk has become Colorado's most popular casino town.

embellish one wall, while other walls display frilly, mock-Victorian murals with trompe l'oeil couplings showcased between the staghorns.

Corinthian columns dignify the matching cherrywood front and backbars, as does the egg-and-dart trim with which classical Rome celebrated fertility. The backbar frieze is an orgy of bas-relief ribbons, garlands, and bells; the front bar is free of video poker screens. According to the late Dowell Blake, the front and backbar came from an old saloon in Russell Gulch. Dowell was the only regular ever honored by Crook's Palace with a free lifetime supply of Budweiser. He is gone now, but the brass sign is still on the bar in front of his stool: "Dowell Blake Drinks for Free." His portrait lingers on the backbar. Dowell, who was born in Black Hawk where his family owned a mill and opened the Texaco station, told me that even Prohibition did not dehydrate Crook's Palace. "It became a card club, pool hall, and soft drink parlor. Down in the basement, where the beer cooler is today, was a speakeasy."

The pine plank floor is worn white, the brass foot rail is shiny and splitting from heavy use, and the barstool seats have been contoured by regulars. From the barstools oldtimers once squinted at the daily changes in gold and silver prices scribbled on a chalkboard. Nowadays gamblers, also struck with gold fever, peer into slot machines.

Sammy, a former teacher at Denver's East High School, manages this place with authority and flair. "We try to keep the slot machine noise down and the conversations up," she confessed in a late-night 1996 interview. She joined us in one of the preferred pastimes of Crook's regulars: tossing quarters onto the top of the backbar. This sport keeps the bartender lively, as barstool aim is not always on target. Tossed quarters more often than not plink off bottles and the backbar mirror. When the firing of quarters becomes too hot and heavy, the barmaids have been known to disarm customers by dragging them to the back room to dance.

Gilpin Hotel Casino
111 Main St., (303) 582-1133

This three-story, sand brick hotel incorporates an older wooden building that is said to have housed the first town newspaper and school. The stone cellar is the Mine Shaft Bar. In 1991 and 1992 the Gilpin Hotel was rehabilitated for a casino career. On either side, neo-Victorian casinos (1992–1993) of brick and stone draw some design inspiration from this venerable hotel.

The casino complex sports five bars and three restaurants, including Lucille Malone's on the second floor. From this second floor, Lucille, a schoolteacher, jumped to her death; a passionate love affair had earned her condemnation as a "loose woman" and dismissal from the Black Hawk School. In the evening Lucille is sometimes still spot-

Before gaming brought monstrous, multistory casinos to Black Hawk during the 1990s, the Gilpin Hotel, with its basement Mine Shaft Bar, was the biggest deal in town.

ted on the second floor, a fragile, dark-haired figure in a pale nightgown. Embrace her, for she will bring you good luck.

Rohling Block Inn & Casino
160 Gregory St., (303) 582-3063

J. H. Phillip Rohling, a Prussian immigrant who became a merchant and mayor of Black Hawk, operated "the largest dry goods store in the county" in this 1886 two-story, red brick landmark, now reshuffled for the Rohling Block Inn & Casino.

Boulder

Elevation: 5,363 feet

B oulder has insulated itself from the rest of Colorado with miles of open space and some peculiar laws. These have ranged from a ban on alcohol to a pacifist foreign policy that bans nuclear weapons within the city limits. Boulder has strict noise ordinances and height ordinances limiting downtown buildings to 33 feet, the height of the local cottonwoods along boulder-strewn Boulder Creek, where gold discoveries gave birth to the town in 1859.

Among Boulder's quirks was a Prohibition ordinance not repealed until 1967. Initially this was a wet town. "I have never seen a city of this size," marveled a reporter for the *Boulder County News* in 1880, "with so many saloons and so few drunks." Saloons initially clustered along Pearl (Main) Street and in the red light district around the railroad depot at 9th and Canyon. Editor Lucius C. Paddock of the *Boulder Daily Camera* complained that passengers alighting from railroad cars were welcomed by "prostitutes, pimps and gamblers."

Paddock and other reformers persuaded townsfolk to vote for local Prohibition in 1907. Even after national and statewide repeal of Prohibition in 1935, the town of Boulder clung to its high, dry principles. However, by the 1950s booze could be bought at unincorporated "islands," which contained the Harvest House, The Sink, and a notorious North Boulder strip joint, The Bus Stop. Another favorite dive, The Drum Tavern at 1534 Pearl Street, was founded in 1952 by Carl Drum. A later owner renamed it The Broken Drum. Rather than being fixed, it was razed in 1982 for a parking lot. Yet another famed old saloon, the Timber Tavern at the southwest corner of Arapahoe and Folsom, now peddles health foods. Canyon Park Dance Hall stood where the County Justice Center now sits.

Celebrated restaurants in the foothills, such as the Flagstaff House, maintain well-stocked wine cellars. So does the Greenbriar Inn at U.S. 36 and Left Hand Canyon Road, which Reudei Zwicker of Nuremberg, Germany, opened in 1967 as the Little Gas Station. He converted the old gas station to a bar and added a dining room to what became Boulder's first four-star restaurant.

Although better known for consumption of tofu and Celestial Seasonings teas, the city boasts several microbreweries, including the large Boulder Brewery at 2880 Wilderness Place, which has a barroom. Consider starting your pub tour at the Boulder Historical Society in the fabulous old Arnett House at 646 Pearl Street. They have brochures, maps, books, and walking tour guides that will lead you to the following liquid landmarks.

Although Boulder is now blessed with a half-dozen breweries, only one supplied the nineteenth-century town. Founded in 1889 as the Boulder Brewery, it became the Boulder City Brewing Company and then the Crystal Springs Brewing & Ice Company. This suds maker at 954 Arapuhoe Street went out of business in 1911. Photo courtesy of the Colorado Historical Society.

Hotel Boulderado
2115 13th St. (nw corner of Spruce St.), (303) 442-4344

When no private parties stepped forward to build a downtown hotel, a spirited public subscription drive bankrolled this one, which was built in 1908 and city-owned until 1940. Inside, a large stained-glass dome covers the spacious lobby and ornate staircase. Note the lobby's original desk, safe, and Otis elevator, and sample some water at the Arapaho Glacier fountain.

After Boulder finally repealed its local Prohibition ordinance in 1967, the city's first bar, the Catacombs, opened in the hotel basement. It remains a great place for live music, pool, and late-night cavorting by subterraneans. The corner storefront with its bright plate-glass windows is now the Corner Bar, handsomely appointed with a bull moose head on the backbar celebrating Theodore Roosevelt, the Bull Moose presidential candidate in 1912. T. R. never visited there but F.D.R. did, which perhaps helps to explain why Boulder votes Democratic.

Old Chicago Saloon
1102 Pearl St. (se corner of 11th St.), (303) 443-5031

Louis Garbarino's 1880s false-fronted saloon sold two schooners for a nickel and threw in a free lunch, attracting a low-end clientele who gave his joint a reputation as Boulder's most disreputable groggery. During Prohibition, it was rehabilitated as Garbarino's Garage. After happy days returned in the 1930s, Walt and Hank opened a 3.2 beer dive here.

In 1977 it became Old Chicago, serving deep-dish pizza and more than 110 different beers. Posters from the Chicago Art Institute and maps of the Chicago Transit System adorn this place, notable for its old backbar with four marble columns framing a classic mirror with colored-glass grape clusters. Note the bronze plaque commemorating those who have drunk all 110 brews on Old Chicago's World Beer Tour. This hot spot at Garbarino's old saloon thrived and has been cloned in what became a nationwide franchise of some forty-five Old Chicagos during the 1990s. Sip your suds in the open-air patio on the mall or in back on the sunny side.

Red Lion Inn
38470 Boulder Canyon Rd., (303) 442-9368

This Old World stone-walled and -floored bratskeller is warmed by a venerable Great Western coal burner. On sunny days you can wander out to the beer garden bordering Boulder Creek. The inn attached to the bar is the creaky-floored, hewn log and stone headquarters of what started out in the 1870s as Blanchard's Ranch. In 1963, Chris and Heidi Mueller opened it as the Red Lion Inn, now a legendary resort of many small, private dining rooms. The Muellers have installed a mountain lion to guard the entry. Their rustic inn on Boulder Creek is a liquid landmark, notable for fine wines as well as good prime rib, sauerbraten, and Wiener schnitzel. If there's a wait for dinner, try the mini-bar, which has only four stools.

Tom's Tavern, according to founding proprietor Tom Eldridge, is an island of reality—complete with old-fashioned hamburgers and pitchers of beer—in the land of tofu popularly known as the People's Republic of Boulder.

The Sink

1165 13th St., (303) 444-SINK

During the 1960s and 1970s when I was at CU, students sat around here in puddles of beer, smoked pot, and watched *Batman* and *Star Trek*. My Mumsie was at CU during the 1930s, and remembered this as a fancy place, Summer's Sunken Gardens, with an elegant fountain in the center of the dining room. Patrons nicknamed it "The Sink."

The Sink sank lower and lower over the years. To hide the grime, the lights were lowered, the walls were painted black, and bright red paint was slapped on the low overhead pipes. Mobs of students consumed oceans of beer sold by the quart. After a 1995 restoration, the reincarnated Sink still lives in this two-story house with a tacked-on storefront. Among gobs of graffiti, the place's crowning achievement is a re-creation of Michelangelo's *The Creation of Man,* with God handing down a Sinkburger to Sink Rats in the "Sink-stine Chapel." Lloyd Kavich, a beatnik artist from San Francisco, and his sidekick, Streamline the Rat Dog, painted many other vivid cartoonlike sequences, often featuring the Sink Rats. The eternally sophomoric clientele are still primarily university students gravitating to beauteous Boulder, the Athens of the Rockies.

Tom's Tavern
1047 Pearl St. (nw corner of 11th St.), (303) 442-9363

In 1962 young Thomas Eldridge bought the two-story, red brick Trieze Mortuary. In the basement where they kept the corpses, Tom stored his liquor. The bartender who took me down there had to unlock a panel of floorboards behind the bar. We descended the ancient plank steps to the subterranean tombs. The basement has a dirt floor and rubble stone walls. I saw no skeletons, caskets, or embalming fluids, but rather a reassuring stockpile of wet goods.

Upstairs, the modernized interior features old photographs of a morbid Mr. Trieze standing in his undertaker's top hat and Prince Albert tails at the corner entry, looking for customers. Customers are no problem for Tom's Tavern, which annually sells some 80,000 of its famous cheeseburgers and hamburgers. It's a basic burger with fresh lettuce, a healthy slice of tomato, and a thick slice of crunchy white onion on a sesame-seed bun.

"I started in the bar business in 1959 when I was twenty-one," Eldridge reminisced in 1995. "It's a wonder Tom's has lasted this long. And you know, I like it even better now than I did then! Wonderful customers. Wonderful employees."

Amid all the flighty, fantastic happenings in Boulder and its ever slicker Pearl Street Mall, this no-nonsense tavern is a reality check on the People's Republic of Boulder. When the clean-living citizens outlawed smoking even in bars, Tom successfully ran for city council in 1997 to protect his and other taverns from Boulder's neo-Puritans.

Walnut Brewery
1123 Walnut St., (303) 447-1345

Of a half-dozen Boulder County brewpubs, this was the first; it opened in 1980. A huge buffalo head graces the walls of this popular restaurant and brewpub, which boasts, among other notable beers, Buffalo "In Gold We Trust" Gold. The landmark building has a live music stage perched over the front entry, offering musicians some protection from adoring fans and bottle-tossing critics. This is a hot spot, but the antique fire extinguishers have been converted to lanterns.

The West End Tavern
926 Pearl St., (303) 444-3535

Part of a retail complex in the old Boulder Armory, this groggery has a rooftop bar where troopers once kept an eye on potential troublemakers. A subterranean beer cellar features improvisational comedy and live music. At the antique bar, complete with brass rail and tile floor, they serve premium brews and swell sandwiches. The beer garden on the roof is a popular observatory for watching Pearl Street Mall shenanigans and clandestine smoking. Remember that in Boulder the fine for smoking pot is only $100, but tobacco gets you ninety days and a $1,000 fine.

Breckenridge
Elevation: 9,603 feet

Gold panners first prowled the upper Blue River in 1859. Fearing the Utes and the weather, they built a stockade supposedly called Fort Mary B, for Mary Bigelow, the only woman in the party. Fort Mary B evolved into Breckenridge.

Gold in the 1860s, silver in the 1880s, and turn-of-the-century gold dredging bankrolled the rosy times. In between, Breckenridge weathered hard times that doomed thirty-seven other mining towns in Summit County. Breckenridge's golden age began in 1882 when the narrow-gauge Denver, South Park & Pacific Railroad snorted into town to haul out gold and silver and haul in supplies and people.

By 1880 the town had eighteen saloons and three dancehalls on Main Street. Growing at railroad speed, Breckenridge soon boasted three smelters, an opera house, and even a convent, hospital, and finishing school, all run by Benedictines. The monks and nuns soon despaired of saving the town, however. Father Rhabanus Gutmann complained that "all the roustabouts, rascals, loose women, adulterers … find their way to Breckenridge" and that his parish was "a disgrace to the name of St. Mary."

The number of saloons and mines began to taper off by 1910 when Breckenridge went into virtual hibernation. The town shrank to less than 300. The drowsy decades ended with an avalanche of development triggered by the opening of the Breckenridge Ski Area, completion of Dillon Reservoir, and the opening of I-70 and the Eisenhower Tunnel in the early 1960s. By 1990 the town had grown to 1,285, nearly its mid-1880s peak population. A dozen new saloons opened, but none outshone the old Gold Pan, which has quenched Breckenridge's thirst since 1879.

The Angel's Rest
110 S. Ridge St., (970) 453-8585

Paul Mahoney opened this far-from-angelic spot in 1973 as Breckenridge's first 3.2 bar catering to eighteen- to twenty-year-olds. The name came from the original Angel's Rest, an 1880s tavern in Indiana Gulch, a quarter mile east of Dyersville on the Boreas Pass road. The resurrected Angel's Rest opened in a metal-roofed 1880s log cabin that once housed L. L. Hillyers's Assay Office, where Colorado's largest gold nugget was weighed and returned to finder Tom Groves in 1887. Tom took his prize around town swaddled in a blanket, showing it off to one and all. "Tom's Baby," as the 13-pound, 7-ounce prize was christened, wound up on display—to this day—in the Denver Museum of Natural History.

The Brown Hotel
208 N. Ridge St., (970) 453-0084

An 1880s house became the Brown Hotel in 1898 when Tom and Maude Brown expanded this primitive hewn log structure and facetiously gave it the name of Denver's finest hotel. Captain Brown, an Englishman, installed Summit County's first bathtub at his palace. The Brown never closed, surviving even the slowest years. Today it is a terrific restaurant and swell mini-bar, but only ghosts occupy the upstairs rooms.

Gold Pan Saloon
103–105 N. Main St., (970) 453-5499

The Gold Pan Saloon has stoutly resisted the transformation of a ramshackle mining town into a cute ski and summer resort. Behind the swinging doors of Breckenridge's oldest saloon, raucous regulars fight off the invading tourist armies. Its dinginess also shields it from stray tourists. This bar is actually two tipsy clapboard buildings leaning on each other atop wobbly log foundations. The north half is a linoleum-floored restaurant; the south half is the barroom, with rough plank walls, a faded hardwood floor, and a potbellied stove. Several antique frame additions are tacked on to the rear where wooden stairs stumble up to a second-story apartment.

Rubberneckers poking into the Gold Pan may be discouraged by behavior designed to send greenhorns skedaddling. Regulars can even outsnarl the mountain lion atop the mahogany backbar. The Brunswick-Balke-Collender Company of St. Louis made this classic altar of Bacchus with egg-and-dart trim and Ionic columns framing a huge mirror whose centerpiece is a rusty gold pan with broken clock hands. Barstools are more or less reserved for regulars, who also fancy the ore-car track substitute for the traditional brass foot rail.

Long ago the Gold Pan was a respectable place called The Palace. It served trout; customers could pick one out from a huge aquarium in the front window. A bar has been on the spot paying taxes ever since 1865, although the first part of the current buildings was apparently erected in 1879. Over the years, under various names, the building has housed bars, a bowling alley, and a funeral parlor. It may have taken its current name from the Gold Pan Mining Company, a giant placer mine opened in 1899. The huge Gold Pan complex was demolished in the 1960s and redeveloped as the Breckenridge Resort where the slick Belltower Mall is today. The Gold Pan Saloon, however, never closed, even during Prohibition. Like Breckenridge's crusty miners, the Gold Pan lingered in the nineteenth century, even after the town's first streetlight was installed just outside its swinging doors at the corner of Main and Lincoln in the 1980s.

The television is usually off; it cannot compete with the show put on by Gold Pan regulars. In the 1970s, when I first jumped into the Pan with some friends, we were eighty-sixed in less than two minutes. Before I knew it, the shaggy, huge bartender was yelling at one of our party: "You calling me a liar? I didn't shortchange you, you

Then fill a fair and honest cup, and bear it straight to me;
The goblet hallows all it holds, whate'er the liquid be;
And may the cherubs on its face protect me from the sin,
That dooms me to those dreadful words,
"My dear, where have you been?"

—Oliver Wendell Holmes

bitch! Here's all of your money back, all of you." With a ferocity that struck me as feigned, he picked up our drinks and kicked us out. There is a horseshoe over the front door of the Gold Pan. You may need to rub it for luck to get in.

I only gained comfortable admission after befriending a shaggy employee. Like a lot of mountain men, Travis never used a last name. He was a blond, blue-eyed talker whose wild stories could be bought with beer. Both his and my details may be fuzzy. Travis had been among the squatters who lived in the tiny mining town of Tiger on the Swan River about 7 miles northeast of Breckenridge. Although he never stooped to mining, like other leisured indigents he sometimes used the Gold Pan as a labor market. As late as the 1980s, one could go to the Gold Pan early in the morning to be picked up for day labor, carpentry, and construction work. The Gold Pan provided not only breakfast but also take-out sack lunches for day laborers.

"Once," Travis beamed, taking a swig that drained his longneck bottle, "the Gold Pan hired me to clean the place up. Anyway, thirteen whores once lived up there. The town used to bust those gals regularly and fine 'em whenever the town treasury was low. The gals got even by taking late-night potshots at the town bell. You can see the bell tower of the courthouse from the top of the Gold Pan. Even with a pistol it's pretty easy to ring that bell.

"Sure, we have fights in here, but what the hell. We listen when customers tell us, 'Hell, we're having a hell of a good time. What the hell, we'll pay for everything we break.'" The diamond dust mirror on the backbar was shattered after the Colonel got drunk one night.

"The meanest S.O.B. in here was a little guy who was part Injun. One night I saw two rednecks hassling him. He keep telling 'em to bug off, but they wouldn't. They were big guys. Finally he had enough. He jumped on one of the guy's lap, grabbed his ears, and bit the tip of his nose off. He spit it out and yelled, 'You're lucky I'm not hungry!'"

Travis spoke expansively about the preachers' bench along the south wall of the saloon. He cleaned up not only the Gold Pan but also the drunks, taking a social worker's interest in scientifically sorting out troubled people. "We have a regular order of positions at the Gold Pan. Position number 1 is watching the ant races—head down on the bar. Position number 2 is falling backwards off the bar stool. Tequila Tom once did that holding a bottle of Jose Cuervo and never spilled a drop. Position number 3 is passed out but still standing. They only rock when you push 'em—they don't fall. That position has been achieved by only one person—Louis. Position number 4 is passed out here on the preachers' bench. May the sweet baby Jesus piss on me if I'm lying—I've laid out more people in this pew than you can imagine."

Reginald Grey bought the Gold Pan in 1988 and began rehabilitating it, transforming the north half into a good restaurant with soft classical music. The barroom proved tougher to clean up. Hoping to further civilize the place, Reggie inaugurated a "skirt night," when anyone wearing a skirt is given free drinks. This, however, has created other unforeseen problems of cross-dressing, reminiscent of earlier days when Helen Rich and Belle Turnbull visited the Gold Pan in their blue jeans and flannel shirts.

Helen Rich, a Lost Generation novelist, traveled from her native Minnesota to Paris, California, and Colorado Springs, where she worked as the society columnist for the *Colorado Springs Gazette Telegraph* before retiring to the Blue River backwater of Breckenridge.

There she shared the still-standing, one-story cabin at 317 North French Street with an old friend, Vassar-trained poet Belle Turnbull, who had retired from teaching English at Colorado Springs High School in 1940. They lived modestly without indoor plumbing, electricity, or a telephone—devices they considered unnecessary—from 1940 until their deaths in the 1970s.

In their prose and poetry, these two writers captured the essence of Breckenridge during its drowsy decades before the 1960s ski boom. They knew the place at rock bottom during the 1940s and 1950s when the population sank to under 300 and the Gold Pan was about the only saloon still open. Both wrote of the town's climate, its old miners, and the dredge boats that almost consumed it.

"There is no great hurry about anything here," Helen said of Breckenridge. Belle "felt stifled below timberline." Helen once wrote to her editor in New York, "I love these mountains almost extravagantly and nearly die of homesickness when I have to be away from them."

Turnbull's best-known works are a novel in verse, *Gold Boat* (Houghton Mifflin, 1940); a poetry anthology, *The Tenmile Range* (The Prairie Press, 1957); and a novel, *The Far Side of the Hill* (Crown, 1953). Rich's *The Willow Bender* (Simon & Schuster, 1950) and *The Spring Begins* (Simon & Schuster, 1947), are among the first environmental novels. They deal with the effects of mining on the earth and on human beings.

You can no more keep a martini in the refrigerator than you can keep a kiss there. The proper union of gin and vermouth is a great and sudden glory; it is one of the happiest marriages on earth and one of the shortest-lived.

—Bernard DeVoto

Of the Gold Pan, Helen wrote in *The Willow Bender* about "the juke box going boo-boo-boo-be-boop-boo" and the day the dredge boat man came in to announce that the gold gobblers were going to devour Breckenridge.

Along the bar the talk was drowsy and the men slouched comfortably over their drinks, taking the last dram of rest before another Monday broke over the ranges. In the back room the cards were falling softly and without excitement, the chips clinking their special music and a syllable said now and then. The dawdling talk stopped momentarily when the door opened, and each head turned to see who had come in. Some of the men were underground miners [speaking] in voices rasped a little by mine dust, friendly with liquor.

[The bartender] with a slight inclination of his head suggested a space down at the end of the bar ... put out the glasses and poured the whiskey to the farthest arc where the liquor rounded the top of the glass and one more drop would have spilled over on the bar.

The Hob Nob Pub
200 S. Ridge St., (970) 453-8099

A once-ramshackle 1882 miner's cottage is now a cozy, elegant public house serving afternoon tea. Settle into one of the large easy chairs by the fire for tea, beer, cocktails, scones, fish and chips, or other pub grub. This new, old-fashioned place boasts a player piano, darts, and terrific bay window views of Breckenridge and the Ten-Mile Range.

Shamus O'Toole's Roadhouse Saloon
115 S. Ridge St., (970) 453-2004

"This place is such a shambles," Shamus once confessed, "it would be hard to mess it up. So we'll let anyone in, even bikers, hippies, tourists, and dogs." Shamus and some sidekicks built this ramshackle tavern in 1976 "so we'd have a place to drink free." Inside, the brick floor and ore-car foot rail provide heavy-duty footing for tipsy customers. The walls are smothered with slogans ("Unattended Children Will Be Sold Off"), stag heads, Irish memorabilia ("Parking for Irish Only"), and four-leaf clovers. A dance floor and stage host memorable live music and rituals in which people have been flung—or have jumped—out the window.

Shamus is the bar's central attraction with his storied past as a political advance man, bartender, ski instructor, businessman, and biker. "All four of my grandparents came from Ireland," he told me. "When I discovered that Breckenridge did nothing for St. Patrick, I initiated the St. Patrick's Day Pub Crawl. It's a race to drink a beer in all seventeen local bars, then come back to Shamus. The prize is a case of beer."

Buena Vista

Elevation: 7,954 feet

Buena Vista, with its splendid view of the Collegiate Range to the west, lives up to its name. Pioneer prospectors, the story goes, named the peaks for their girlfriends: Mount Flossie, Mount Fannie, Mount Daisy Mae, Mount Lulu, and so forth. After Buena Vista developed aspirations to respectability, the peaks were renamed Oxford, Harvard, Yale, Princeton, and Columbia in 1896 by I. D. Whitney, a professor at the Harvard University Mining School. Cottonwood Creek and the Arkansas River converge here, as did three railroads. Buena Vista became a raucous center for railroaders, teamsters, cowboys, and miners. The town later lost ore-processing, smelting, and railroad business, as well as population and the county seat, to faster-growing Salida.

Buena Vista, however, retains two of Colorado's wildest old-time saloons, not to mention a notable former brothel. "Cockeyed Liz" Marshall's bordello, The Palace, is now an apartment house. It is two doors west of the grand old Chaffee County courthouse, which has been converted to the Buena Vista Heritage Museum. The latter celebrates in nifty exhibits Buena Vista's grimy, rowdy origins as a railroad town, its mining days, and the local cattle industry. The Climax Mine and other local holes are now closed, and in 1997 the Union Pacific abandoned the Arkansas River line from Cañon City to Minturn, leaving Buena Vista a much quieter town from which to contemplate the fabulous snowcapped Collegiate Peaks. If those peaks are ever returned to their original monikers, one should be named Zelda.

If you spend too much time in Buena Vista's legendary twin taverns, The Green Parrot and the Lariat, consider the Webb Hotel (1885) at 414

East Main, now elegantly restored as a bed-and-breakfast, the Meister House. Other notable possibilities are the Adobe Inn, the Blue Sky Inn, the Buena Vista Bed and Breakfast, the Mountain Shack, and Potter's House Bed & Breakfast. Rustic inns also make the Cottonwood and Mount Princeton Hot Springs west of town a terrific place to stew the morning after.

The Green Parrot Bar
304 E. Main St., (719) 395-8985

The Parrot and the Lariat, competitors since the 1930s, have inspired locals to quip, "No matter which joint you go to, you'll wish you were in the other." Zelda Upchurch, the Wagnerian blonde bartender at the Parrot, told customers sternly as they entered, "Give me your hat and coat." She stored them behind the bar. If you went across the street to the Lariat, you went coatless and hatless.

Many abandoned hats line the Parrot's walls to this day.

"Zelda was the biggest, strongest woman I ever saw," reported June Shaputis, Buena Vista town clerk and historian. "She could literally lift an offensive customer off his barstool and throw him out the door. If two guys got to fighting, she put one under each arm and butted their heads together. You should have seen her the night John Whitlock jumped up on the bar and pissed up into the

Buena Vista's Main Street bristles with salty saloons in fancy Italianate buildings such as The Green Parrot.

ceiling heater to make it sizzle. She spun him around over her head to shake the trouble out of him, then threw him out that door."

Thanks to Zelda's love of law and order, the Green Parrot, long the toughest bar in town, became tame. A river rock propped open the door of this 1880s red brick saloon the last time I visited. Superstrong, custom-made barstools had stout, round log legs and backs. Zelda's ghost seemed to preside over what is now a genteel café. Before its 1930s conversion to this legendary saloon, pool hall, and dancehall, the tough old Green Parrot was Harvey Mear's Confectionery Shop, filled with sugar and spice and everything nice.

Lariat Saloon
206 E. Main St., (719) 395-9494

The troublemakers whom Zelda tossed out of the Green Parrot moved across the street to the Lariat, known to locals as "The Rope," as in "at the end of your rope." Tables and seats lost in action have been replaced by wooden benches and picnic tables. The replacement bar foot rail is a huge, sturdy hewn log. The battle-scarred old backbar and high ceiling have been patched up with loads of memorabilia, including the observation "If a**holes could fly, this place would be an airport."

At one time the post office, this handsome 1885 brick building now has a sign out front: "We Sell & Service Hangovers!" Inside, elegant chandeliers attempt to dignify often raucous behavior at the bar, pool table, shuffleboard court, and dance floor.

Just across from The Green Parrot on Main Street, the rival Lariat Saloon boasts of selling and servicing hangovers.

Connie Cameron bought the place in 1985 and cracked down on some of the horseplay. She eighty-sixed "Stinky Dave" Jardine and his dogs and Tim Roby and his horse.

In this far-famed cowboy bar, the knotty pine walls are seared with the brands and barbed-wire specimens of local cattlemen who have long drunk here with their cowboys, horses, and dogs. Nowadays most of the wild stuff happens in bar stories and in the westerns you can check out of this saloon's little lending library.

Calhan

Elevation: 6,507 feet

Calhan is an agricultural hamlet founded in 1888 and named for an official of the Chicago, Rock Island & Pacific Railroad. His name was Callahan, but the post office shortened it. This tiny town east of Colorado Springs had a big-hearted barkeeper memorialized in a locally venerated tavern. The town's other great marvels are the two Russian Orthodox churches. Soaring over the prairie, these lovely frame landmarks, crowned by onion domes and Slavic crosses, shelter tiny cemeteries with lonely tombstones, including Curly's.

And always, if he had a little money, a man could get drunk. … Then there was no loneliness, for a man could people his brain with friends, and he could find his enemies and destroy them.

—John Steinbeck
The Grapes of Wrath

Curly's Place
**425 Colorado Ave. (sw corner of 4th St.),
(719) 347-2517**

Although in disrepair, this solid parapeted brick building looks like it can stand a good deal of neglect. Bert Skaggs converted this Ford sales and showroom to a John Deere tractor outlet and painted his name on the side. The Skaggs family leased it during the 1980s to Abraham Lincoln Tressler. "He was the most beloved man in Calhan," his widow told us. "Everyone called Abe 'Curly' for his beautiful black hair. When he died in 1991, the town gave him a five-day wake. And his spirit still visits us here, asking for another V.O. and Coke and playing his jukebox favorite, 'Whiskey River.' "

Cirrhosis killed Curly at the age of fifty-one. But his name lingers on one of the tattered old, vinyl-backed barstools, next to other labeled thrones of great patrons, living and dead. A huddle of regulars gathered at the bar. The talk turned to Curly and they wouldn't let us pay for a drink. He was discussed with the reverence usually reserved for saints.

This huge, shrinelike bar is still decorated the way Curly liked it, with musty, mangy animal heads, a bra, a jockstrap, a primitive life-size reclining nude, and a homemade sign: "Nobody Is Ugly After 2 A.M." Even a three-legged, scruffy-looking dog is welcome here. In this casual saloon, there is no bar foot rail, but there is a tornado cellar, an electric dart game, two pool tables, a parquet dance floor, and a stage for the weekend bands.

The waitress gave us another beer and got the country-and-western jukebox to sing, "If I said you had a beautiful body, would you hold it against me?" "We know everybody in here," she told us. "Or get to know them. Nobody was a stranger to Curly. People come out from Colorado Springs, just because they're lonely. At Curly's Place you can always find somebody down-home to talk to."

Cañon City
Elevation: 5,332 feet

Cañon City sprang up in 1859 near the point where the Arkansas River disappears into the Royal Gorge. City founders hoped it would become the gateway to rich gold and silver mines on the upper Arkansas, but the Civil War cut off traffic along the southern route west. Although immigration dried up, Cañonites could at least cry in their own beer. Inspired by the "pure water and abundance of wild hops," Bateman and Litsell opened a brewery in 1860, and libations have been available happily ever after.

Cañon City hoped to capture the title of state capital but lost that plum to Denver. Cañon was offered a consolation prize, a choice of the state university or the state penitentiary. Cañon picked the prison, figuring inmates would be better behaved than faculty and students, notorious for carousing and troublemaking in local bars. That tale is not true, one scholar tells me, but it's too good to erase. City government incorporated, met, and held court in the upstairs hall of Murray's Saloon at 305 Main Street in what is now an antique shop.

Brother's Bar
625 Main St., no phone available

The Rex Theater marquee, ticket window, and double doors survive in a building that became a notorious biker bar, now reborn as a boater's bar. After getting off the river, kayakers, rafters, and other water rats retreat to this long and narrow, dim and funky old dive. Boaters toast the rapids they've run, tourists they've soaked, and proclaim the Arkansas is now "America's Most Rafted River."

Although boaters now outnumber bikers, Harley Davidson posters and paraphernalia adorn the walls. The high ceiling displays a 1939 Western Flyer tricycle, bicycles, and a 1949 Simplex motorcycle, but nary a raft, kayak, or canoe. Two pool tables, $4 pitchers of beer, and free happy-hour hotdogs and chili make this a popular joint, whether you're wet or dry.

The Cañon City Opera House
**nw corner of 5th & Main Sts.,
no phone available**

Behind a two-story conventional brick façade lies a spectacular opera hall–turned–nightclub. Beneath the high pressed-tin ceiling with skylights, the upstairs hall retains the old Cañon City Opera House stage, seating, original stained-glass signage, and a semicircular balcony with ornate cast-iron railing. Bas-relief garlands garnish the proscenium arch and chandeliers illuminate the side aisles. The original hardwood floor squeaks during the live music dances here. And after the bar closes, you can recover downstairs in the Dragon Gate Chinese Restaurant.

Hotel St. Cloud
& Silver Lining Saloon
**627–631 Main St. (corner of 7th St.),
(719) 276-2000**

As the silver-mining era faded in Silver Cliff, the original site of this three-story brick hotel, the building was dismantled and hauled into Cañon City. It reopened as the

Cañon City's Hotel St. Cloud has a heavenly Silver Lining Saloon that attracts angels and Hell's Angels alike.

Hotel St. Cloud for notable guests such as Buffalo Bill Cody, Calamity Jane, and western movie idol Tom Mix, who briefly made Cañon City a mini-Hollywood. The Second-Empire mansard-roofed hotel boasted the town's first elevator and elegant interior details, such as the high pressed-metal ceiling in the Silver Lining Saloon. The saloon sports a grand old backbar with handcarved garlands and swags. Also garlanded and swagged are the waitresses, who look, as one jaded woman put it, "like hussies in old dancehall red, yellow, green, and blue dresses with ostrich feathers."

Kate's Old Strathmore Lounge
331 Main St. (nw corner of 4th St.), (719) 275-1141

To celebrate Cañon City's first grand hotel, town founder Anson S. Rudd wrote a poem, which included the following lines:

I came in on a special train …
And as I cut a swell,
I put up at McClure's Hotel
Where all great minds do gravitate
To regulate affairs of state …

William H. McClure built this three-story palace of the public as the McClure House. Twenty years later, an Englishman, allegedly the Earl of Strathmore, bought the hotel and gave it his name. The Fremont County Bank's 12-foot-high corner storefront became a saloon after the bank moved across the street. Five pool tables, foosball, pinball, darts, and two bars keep this place

lively, while the original woodwork and fireplace keep it warm. Kate, a city councilperson as well as a tavernkeeper, has made the corner saloon a place where locals still "gravitate to regulate affairs of state." Less ambitious tipplers head around back to McClure's Saloon on the hotel's rear alley.

Le Petit Chablis
512 Royal Gorge Blvd., (719) 269-3333

In this funky 1888 house with a small but spirited garden, Daniel and Leigh Petit uncorked in 1989 an exquisite French restaurant with a wine list that defers to Daniel's native land, Burgundy.

Merlino's Belvedere
1330 Elm Ave., (719) 275-5558

In 1946, Joe and Tony Merlino opened a tavern in what is now the bar of this large and celebrated Italian *ristorante*. The fine food, drink, and hospitality attracted crowds and led to numerous expansions. Merlino's now boasts a subterranean Mediterranean Room, a Roman Room, a Grotta Sotteranea, and a mini-bar. The lavish decor includes arches framing painted scenes of old Italy, plastic Ionic columns, and classical statuary and grape-leaf upholstery celebrating the grandeur that was Rome.

Owl Cigar Store
626 Main St., (719) 275-9946

This is without question the best old-time pool, snooker, cigar, soda fountain, beer, and hamburger joint in Colorado. The front door is guarded by a stuffed barn owl perched on a giant cigar. Inside is a long narrow hall with linoleum over the old plank floor and acoustic tile hiding the old pressed-metal ceiling. Boxcar wainscoting adorns the walls that showcase trophy-size trout. The marble-topped front bar also has marble trim, while the barstools are shiny red vinyl and chrome. The oak backbar has zigzag Art Deco framed mirrors. The Seeburg Wall-o-Matic jukebox features oldies but goodies such as the Beach Boys, James Brown, the Beatles, and Tammy Wynette, usually accompanied by the clickety-clack of busy billiard balls. Above the pool tables and dollar-an-hour snooker table, note the big "NO PROFANITY" sign. It is enforced. Discreet bets on pool and other athletic endeavors are still okay, and pinup girls adorn the collection of antique calendars from local businesses that help to make this a crackerjack museum.

Along with full bar service, the house specialty is the long-famed Owl Burger, a greasy gut-buster. If one patty is not enough, try the "double-double" or "triple-triple," which come off the grill faster than any franchised burger. Red plastic ketchup squirters, old-fashioned salt shakers, and Coors red ash trays are at each barstool and table. Other options are fries, eggburgers, ham and cheese sandwiches, not to mention rich old-fashioned shakes and malts.

This has always been the Owl Cigar Store, according to the old-timers who mingle with all ages here, including young

The Owl Cigar Store in Cañon City is Colorado's finest surviving specimen of an antique institution—the pool hall–saloon–café–smoke shop.

mothers teaching their children to play pool. At one time a pool hall that parents warned their children about, the Owl is now a family place where all sorts of folks feel at home. The third generation of Santillis—brothers Pete and Roxy—still run this family business.

Oh yeah, you can still buy cigars here. Not the big-city stogies that cost $10 to $50 each, just cheap old King Edwards, Dutch Masters, and Swisher Sweets—but no Owl Cigars, the extinct brand memorialized by this diamond in the rough.

Santa Fe Depot Restaurant & Bar
410 Water St. (corner of S. 4th St.),
(719) 269-7076

This gracious 1913 Atchison, Topeka and Santa Fe depot of red brick under a red tile roof was restored as a restaurant and bar in 1997. Local brews and a good wine list complement the pizza, calzones, soups, and salads. Outside tables overlook a riverside park and a take-out station for Arkansas River boaters.

Castle Rock

Elevation: 6,202 feet

Some urbane curmudgeons say the suburbs lack soul. I'm not so sure after a recent tour of America's fastest-growing patch of suburbia: Douglas County. In the county seat, Castle Rock, where the monumental butte prominent from I-25 suggests cosmic favoritism, are three spiritual centers of note.

Castle Cafe
219–223 4th St.
(nw corner of Wilcox St.),
(303) 814-CAFE

Prominently sited opposite Courthouse Square, this 1901 two-story hotel has street-level storefronts that over the years have housed saloons, a shoe store, a dancehall, apartments, Hi's Western Store, and, most memorably, the Castle Cafe. Builders Jim and Frank Fetherolf originally ran the hotel with the Tivoli Saloon in the corner storefront. Quarry workers, railroad men, and cowboys gathered in this lively, if not rowdy, town social center.

When Prohibition came in 1916, the saloon became a restaurant famed for its chicken dinners. When drinking days returned, it became the Castle Cafe with a wall mural showing the foothills and the Castle Rock formation. When I visited in the 1970s, they drank a lot of tequila and listened to juke-box country-and-western artists such as the Sons of the Pioneers, whose big hit was "Tumbling Tumbleweeds." The waitress told me the upstairs hotel had been converted to apartments and "the hotel never had a name or needed one. It was the only hotel in town."

Restored in 1996 as a splendid old-time restaurant and bar, it once again offers superb chicken dinners pan-fried to order and a lively bar. Hardwood floors, high ceilings, and big bright transom windows shine on the folksy, clichéd cowboy paintings on the wall and a slick New West oil by Denver artist David Parker.

The Old Stone Church
210 3rd St., (303) 688-9000

This heavenly bar and restaurant has reasonably priced, tasty food and drink, but no pound cake, which is the name hungry early explorers gave Castle Rock. Too bad it is not Pound Cake today—the Rocky Mountain empire is crawling with Castle Rocks, but has no place named Pound Cake.

In 1888, Catholics opened St. Francis of Assisi, a country Gothic chapel of locally quarried lava stone from some of the surrounding "pound cakes." After the parish moved to a larger church in 1966, the old church was reborn as a culinary experience. It retains the choir loft, confessional, and stained-glass windows of the Blessed Virgin, the Sacred Heart, and St. Teresa of Avila, although St. Francis was moved to the new church at the top of 5th Street. The stained glass now illuminates a different sort of altar: a backbar. The churchy decor includes a church register, where you can sign in and get credit for fulfilling your Sunday obligation. The bathrooms are labeled "Brothers" and "Sisters." An outdoor café occupies the old church cemetery, from which all bodies have supposedly been exhumed. Specialties of the chaplain (bartender) include a tart ale brewed in Faversham, Kent, by Shepherd Neams ("Britain's Oldest Brewers"), with a memorable taste and a memorable name: "Bishop's Finger."

I feel sorry for people who don't drink. When they get up in the morning, that is as good as they are going to feel.

—Anonymous

Pino's Place
3 Wilcox St., (303) 688-8159

An 1889 brick house, now stuccoed, had become a liquor store when Italian immigrants Pino and Pina Arini bought it in 1993. They converted it to an Italian *trattoria* with fine Italian food and vino. Pino's children help run this haven of old-country delights.

Central City
Elevation: 8,496 feet

Born in the 1859 gold rush, Central City sparkled as Colorado's first major mining town. Outgrowing even Denver, it was Colorado Territory's most populous city during the 1860s. Other mining towns subsequently eclipsed it, but Colorado's first golden city proved remarkably resilient as a mining town.

During the town's golden era, 1895–1914, the population, mine output, and number of pubs peaked. During the flush times, twenty saloons flowered in Central. Another fifteen watered nearby Black Hawk, Nevadaville, and Russell Gulch. Louis J. Carter, who was born in Central City in 1891, recalled that these taverns had "curtained front windows, swinging doors set back six to eight feet from the front entrance, a bar running lengthway of the main room, one or two wine rooms adjacent to the rear entrance, from two to six card tables.

"Under the table top and at the right corner, next to the leg, a small boxlike shelf was set in. The shelf was large enough to hold a beer mug. With this set up, card playing never interfered with the player's drinking nor his drinking with his card playing. There was no charge for the use of the table. All that was required was that a round of drinks be purchased after each game. Beer was served in six to eight ounce mugs for five cents a glass. Whiskey was served in a two ounce glass and the customer served himself from a bar bottle … fifteen cents a drink or two for a quarter."

The ornate front and backbars had "two rails at most bars—one on the outer edge of the front bar and one at the foot of the bar. There were no stools at the bar. I know of no more relaxing and comfortable position than that of having one foot on the foot rail and one elbow on the bar-rail.

"No keeper of a bar would want his drinks to be classified as 'slop.' He therefore prepared and served drinks of authority in special cups and mugs, properly marked and highly adorned. The guests, and that they were, set out to prove the old saying, 'You can't fly on one wing.'

"Every saloon had from one to three very ornate slot machines in the usual five, ten, and twenty-five cent sizes. On every saloon bar ... there was a leather cup about the size of a tea cup with five dice. The customer could call for the dice and shake with the house to see if they paid double or nothing."

Gaming returned in 1991 when Colorado voters approved it for Central City, Black Hawk, and Cripple Creek. Since then, a dozen casinos have sprung up, as well as a gay gaming joint, The Coyote. Most have authentic façades and faux-Victorian innards, but the façade is brand-new on the instant "Victorians" such as Harvey's Wagon Wheel, a $61-million subsidiary of Harvey's Casino Resorts of Lake Tahoe, which dwarfed even the Glory Hole. Opened in 1994, this casino/hotel has 228,000 square feet, 938 slot machines, and 24 gaming tables. Harvey's centerpiece is an exploding mine shaft made of synthetic rock, despite all the real rock around Central City. Harvey's boasts a two-story waterfall, Colorado's largest family electronic-games arcade, a four-story parking lot blasted out of Mammoth Hill, and two bars.

On a much more modest scale, an old-time casino/saloon has been

There is something they put in a highball
Which you'll notice one day, if you watch;
And it may be the soda
But judged by the odor,
I rather believe it's the scotch.

—Ogden Nash

reconstructed in the Gilpin County Historical Museum. Exhibits range from a beautiful roulette wheel from the Gold Coin to a spiffy little backbar from Crook's Palace in Black Hawk to a grandiose slot machine, "The Judge," from the Toll Gate. The museum has material on many of Central City's saloons and the town's two breweries, the Central City Brewery (1866–1895) on Dory Hill and the Rocky Mountain Brewery (1862–1890) of the Mack Brothers, whose stone ruins linger a mile west of the Opera House on upper Eureka Street.

Not every Central City saloon has been reincarnated as a casino. Dillon's Saloon, located in an 1874 building at 161 Lawrence Street, once advertised itself as "The First Chance Coming Up, and the Last Chance Going Up." In 1994 it was remodeled as the Central City Police Department. Since the town's law enforcers spend much time in saloons one way or another, their move into Dillon's Saloon struck locals as hunky-dory.

The Glory Hole
129¹/₂ Main St., (303) 777-1111

In the Glory Hole, you can find a few crumbling walls and the original bar of the famous old saloon. Reflecting the shifting fortunes of a mining town, this structure saw many uses over the years before it was entombed in a huge four-story gambling palace. Its 2-foot-thick stone sidewalls survived Central City's 1874 fire, although the rest of the structure was gutted. Various restaurants, a funeral parlor, the post office, and the *Gilpin County Observer* were here before 1897, when Ignatz Meyer added a second story to the building, put his name on the cornice, and reopened it as a saloon.

When Prohibition arrived, Meyer's saloon became Cash Harper's Grocery. Emily "Emmy" Wilson, a recently liberated graduate of Mrs. Porter's Finishing School in Connecticut, converted the grocery in 1947 to the Glory Hole. She installed old barroom furnishings, but she was herself the main attraction, entertaining customers by lowering herself through the ceiling trapdoor and swinging her legs to wake up the barflies. She also posed for Margaret Kerfoot's backbar reclining nude, *Mother,* and *The Fanny on the Barroom Ceiling.*

Sid Squibb, an elegant swell of toothpaste fame, came to Central City in 1949 as a piano professor. He rented a room upstairs at the Glory Hole and played the piano downstairs. "We were packed," Sid told me in 1988. "Emmy's quiet little cocktail club for her theater friends became a madly popular piano bar." Dick Hicks painted the suggestive Victorian stenciling, which kept tipplers studying the south wall of the saloon for hours. The Glory Hole became a favorite place, noted even in winter for its stiff drinks, lavish barbecued ribs, lively piano, and warm potbellied stove.

All that vanished in 1992. The old hole was enveloped inside a four-story brick building that opened as Colorado's largest casino. The Glory Hole restored the Main Street façades and built a new brick-and-stone rear entrance on Pine Street opposite St. Mary's Church. The old backbar was preserved and doubled in length, while the tiny upstairs living quarters were rehabilitated as private dining rooms. New pressed-tin ceilings, Victorian wallpaper, heavy velvet drapes, and fake palm trees adorn this gambling haven, where the saloon's old potbellied stove reappeared with perpetual cellophane flames. Amid all the Victoriana, an escalator and two elevators carry customers to their gambling stations.

On the casino's opening day in 1992, I found Chocolate Dan Monroe at the Glory Hole Bar on his old stool in what used to be a tiny, near-empty bar. As a boy, Dan had been rechristened on that stool after regularly asking for hot chocolate. Amid the jingle-jangle of slots and the crashing of coins, thousands of strangers came and went. Chocolate Dan did not even look up anymore to see if he might know anyone. A few passersby stared at him, wondering if he was part of the Victorian decor. Dan has the thickest, blackest beard in the Little Kingdom of Gilpin. He used to run Central City Liquors before it, too, became a casino. He is president emeritus of the Gilpin County Historical Society and the town's champion barstool historian.

Chocolate pointed to the backbar, which used to be lined with murky bottles wearing ambitious labels. "That was the finest collection of booze in the county. Now look at it. They even moved *Mother* over to make room for the ice machine. And they promised they would preserve this place!"

"At least," I tried to console him, "they kept the old doorway and Sid's piano bar and stage."

We started looking for other ancient and holy fixtures in this desecrated sanctuary. The "All Hope Abandon Ye Who Enter Here" sign by the door was gone. Doubtless the casino czars did not appreciate that warning from Dante's *Inferno*. Dick Hicks' wall murals, with their trompe l'oeil erotica hidden amid Victorian foliage, had disappeared. We searched high and low for *The Fanny on the Barroom Ceiling,* Emmy's reply to the *Face on the Barroom Floor* over at the Teller House Bar. That fanny is gone—the fanny that inspired Sid Squibb to write his masterpiece, "Bottom's Up at the Glory Hole."

And so to this day, in her own unique way
She is very much to be seen,
With her face in one place,
And her base up in space,
And a block and a half in between.

Wild West Development, a corporation including United Artists and United Cable Television moguls, spent more than $13 million to casinoize the Glory Hole. Developers are required to maintain exterior walls in the Central City National Historic Landmark District. In the case of the Glory Hole, however, they argued that the enveloped exterior walls had become interior walls and removed most of them.

Chocolate and I returned to the barstools. He shook his head slowly and painfully. "Emmy's gone. All the good stuff is gone. And you can't even find a liquor store, or a gas station, or a laundry in this county anymore. You can't even buy an aspirin!" We settled for another drink, and it wasn't hot chocolate.

Gold Coin Saloon/Casino
120 Main St., (303) 277-1900

"This bar," longtime Central City mayor William Carroll Russell Jr. told me, "sits on top of the Mountain Lion. That gold mine kept people from building here until the 1890s, when three Eye-talians erected this two-story red brick joint. Bart Partelli opened it as the Gold Coin. After his death, Bart's wife, and then his daughter, ran the Coin. It's always been open, and always been the favorite of the old-timers."

Beyond the golden oak swinging doors, past the foyer with its cigar case and shoe-shine chair, lies one of Colorado's most authentic old-time watering holes. The inner sanctum is warmed by an ancient pot-bellied stove on a pine plank floor. Notes from a player piano bounce off the tongue-and-groove wooden ceiling. The neoclassical backbar, made in 1897 (the same year the saloon was built) by the Brown Furniture Company in Denver, is fronted by a brass rail and high, round, oak barstools. The saloon interior was preserved as the centerpiece of the three-story casino, which opened in 1992.

Investors paid $3.9 million for the Gold Coin, once a dirty old saloon that couldn't be given away. They spent millions more building the new casino around it. In the basement of this casino, the old Mountain Lion stope was roped off, covered with clear plastic, and made into an exhibit. Gamblers, however, are discouraged from throwing their money down the shaft, as so many mining stock investors did. Slots and gambling tables have been banned from the interior of the old Gold Coin Saloon, a refuge from the eternal casino din. At this bar you can find people who actually make eye contact and even talk. And they often talk of old Jack Brown, their legendary bartender.

The Gold Coin has refined the ancient art of "treating" with its alcohol futures board, where you could buy someone a drink in advance. Smiling Jack Brown took your money and you wrote the name of the recipient (say, Lew Cady) and the type of drink (say, a bottle of Coors) on the Alcohol Futures Chalk Board. Such heartening acts of friendship and faith have made the Gold Coin a beloved shrine. Outside, everything is colder and less certain. And apprehension is not lessened by the sign you'll see over the swinging doors as you depart: "Watch your step! It's 8,496 feet to sea level!"

Teller House Bar & Casino
110 Eureka St., (303) 582-3200

President Ulysses S. Grant stepped out of a stagecoach on April 28, 1873, to find the Teller House walk paved with silver bricks. Townsfolk quickly took up the $12,000 silver carpet after the cigar-chomping Civil War hero left. The hotel was named for one of its builders, Henry Moore Teller. As Colorado's most distinguished politician, Teller served the state's first and longest senatorial term and as U.S. secretary of the interior. Teller and his partners spent $107,000 on the site and its four-story, red brick hotel.

The pride of the Teller House was not its plain brick exterior, or its 150 small unheated rooms with one toilet per floor emptying into Eureka Gulch under the hotel, but rather its magnificent public spaces. Besides the lobby, with its elegant mineral display cases, the first floor housed a bank, bar, library, post office, and skylit dining room.

Anne Evans bought the deteriorating, largely abandoned hotel in 1933 and began restoration. Herndon Davis, a Denver artist, painted a woman's face on the barroom floor in the summer of 1936, drawing inspiration from Hugh d'Arcy's poem. This barroom is also graced by *Apollo, Venus with Apple, Leda and the Swan,* and five other murals of life-size Greek gods and goddesses. The murals, found underneath layers of wallpaper during the 1930s restoration, are the work of Charles St. George Stanley as restored by Paschal Quackenbush, who added two figures.

Evans arranged for the Central City Opera Association to operate the hotel as a bar, restaurant, and museum. In 1991 the Teller House underwent a $15 million restoration and the installation of 361 one-armed bandits, 82 video poker games, and 6 blackjack tables. A Swiss casino firm assumed a lease to restore and operate the Teller House.

Mixologist Louis Spies presided in 1937 as the Teller House Bar reopened after the long Prohibition dry spell. To this day, barflies spend hours studying the mural of Leda *and the* Swan *to discover her anatomical quirks. Tom Noel Collection.*

Accustomed to rehabilitating European casinos, the Swiss eagerly took on what they described as "the youngest building we've ever restored."

The Teller House had originally opened with mirrors brushed with diamond dust so that "women could see themselves in all their glory," Henry Teller supposedly said. Mae West, one of the celebrities who stayed at the Teller House in 1949, gloried in the role of Diamond Lil. She requested that all women be cleared from the building. Mae, according to local legend, wanted only men to wait on her.

The bar is blissfully free of Central City's ubiquitous slot machines. It retains its old decor, from the unforgettable face on the barroom floor to the ceiling mural of unclad women priestesses offering communion chalices.

Critics claim that legalized gambling enacted in 1991 has shamefully commercialized the historic mining towns of Black Hawk, Cripple Creek, and Central City. They would have found the 1970s signage even more brazen, as in this Central City shot of the Toll Gate Saloon. Photo by Glenn Cuerden.

Toll Gate Saloon & Casino
108 Main St., (303) 582-1204

Robert Harris's Furniture Store and Undertaking Parlor first occupied this handsome brick edifice constructed in 1878. Over the years the building also housed the Knox Mining Machinery Company, a drugstore, and the Knights of Pythias Hall. The second-story balcony overlooks a large first-floor hall used for everything from basketball to movies.

In 1940, Earl Peterson converted the Harris Block into the Toll Gate Saloon and installed a dance floor and bandstand in the main hall. The Toll Gate had a persuasive doorman who dressed in cowboy garb to lure tourists inside for, among other things, "authentic barroom gunfights." Live rock-and-roll music made the Toll Gate Central City's hottest honky-tonk. Among the Toll Gate stars were "The World's Oldest B-Girl—the one and only Mattie Mausche." This octogenarian banged out piano tunes and swished through vaudeville routines. The Toll Gate attracted bikers, fighters, lovers, and sensation seekers with its brazen signs: "Buffalo Bill Drank Here" and "Vaudeville Is Dead and We've Got the Acts That Killed It." Banana- and peach-eating contests, striptease, and pinups of local male "Gunslingers" instead of the usual female nudes in Madame Gail's basement bar helped make Central City what historian Robert G. Athearn called "the Coney Island of the Rockies, a tired old painted up bawd."

In spite of all the signs and the shenanigans, the Harris Block has never lost its splendid plate-glass storefronts between decorative cast-iron columns, pedimented and scrolled second-story windows, and large pressed-metal cornice.

Gambling is nothing new for the Harris Block, where Cicero's Pool Hall was once ruled by "The Judge." This 1898 floor-model slot machine, a splendiferous, claw-footed, golden oak monster, is on exhibit at the Gilpin County Historical Society Museum in the old stone high school on the hill at 226 East High Street.

Saint Monday is as duly kept by our working people as Sunday; the only difference being that instead of employing their time cheaply at church they are wasting it expensively at the ale house.
—Benjamin Franklin

Clifton

Elevation: 4,710 feet

lifton sprang up around the 1890 D&RG depot and was named for the nearby Book Cliffs, which Hayden Party topographer Henry Gannett named for "the characteristic shape of the cliff, which, with its overhanging crest and slight talus, bears considerable resemblance to the edge of a bound book." Long a tiny hub for surrounding orchard tenders, Clifton emerged in recent decades as Grand Junction's fastest-growing suburb. Its peach orchards were bulldozed for the Coronado shopping mall and residential subdivisions.

The Cross Orchards Museum (1909) at 3073 F Road is on 243 acres acquired by heirs of the Red Cross Shoe fortune. They turned it into a demonstration orchard. A huge stepped-gable barn, a blacksmith shop, a bunkhouse, and packing sheds have been preserved in a 24-acre museum, which exhibits vintage farm machinery. The farmhouse was razed, but the summerhouse stands, a branch of the Museum of Western Colorado hemmed in by new subdivisions. Another relic of old Clifton is a landmark tavern usually surrounded by motorcycles and pickup trucks.

Triple Tree Tavern
**201 2nd St. (nw corner of Orson Ave.),
(970) 434-9428**

This large, two-story, stuccoed IOOF (Independent Order of Odd Fellows) Hall built in 1905 houses an old-fashioned tavern and pool hall in the corner storefront. Twelve-foot-high ceilings and high walls are smothered with antiques: a 5-foot-long rattlesnake skin, a longhorn steer skull, beer ads, a dartboard, a framed *National Geographic* magazine map of Vietnam, and old photos of this place as the First National Bank. A bronze wall plaque erected by patrons salutes the owner: "Congratulations to John Krosky for Hanging Around Ten Years. From the gang at the Tree, January, 1997."

This locals' bar is filled with blue-collar types, including card players, old duffers reminiscing, and bikers. Both the beer hall and the corner pool room are lit by large plate-glass storefronts and central transomed double doors. The men's room has a 6-foot-high antique porcelain urinal. Amid the sprawling new suburbs of Grand Junction flooding Clifton, the Triple Tree is a treat, a retreat into the past.

"I never could see liquor drinking as a bad habit," said the Old Soak, *"though I admit fair and free, it will lead to bad habits if it ain't watched."*
—Don Marquis, The Old Soak

Colorado City

Elevation: 5,800 feet

El Paso County's first Anglo-American settlement rivaled Denver and was briefly the territorial capital. Colorado City later lagged behind Colorado Springs, which annexed it in 1917. The town became a smelting center, processing much of the gold ore pouring out of Cripple Creek. The last of the four local gold mills, the Golden Cycle, was dismantled in 1949. Mountains of smelter waste and the smokestack remain Colorado City's most massive monuments. The Old Colorado City Historic Commercial District—Colorado Avenue between 24th and 27th Streets—has some notable watering holes, including a spirited reincarnation of the town's old opera house. While Colorado Springs put on airs, Colorado City remained a working-class community with down-to-earth taverns.

Bambino's Pizzeria
2514 W. Colorado Ave., (719) 635-1212

Barbara Megyeri and her three sons and daughter opened this Italian restaurant in 1978. The bar features a pool table, a Technicolor jukebox, and big-screen television. The adjacent dining room is dripping with plastic grapes, a floral print rug, and fruity plastic tablecloths tinted by the orange and purple stained-glass windows. The food is inexpensive, good, and also available by free home delivery, giving rise to other Bambino's in the Colorado Springs area.

Henri's Authentic Mexican Restaurant
2427 Colorado Ave., no phone available

Henri and Ventura Ruiz started the first Mexican cantina in the Colorado Springs area in 1946. Ventura still lives upstairs and with her children and grandchildren, who keep this place lively and well staffed. The two-story pink stucco edifice sports turquoise trim and outrageous decor. Paintings on the glass storefront, like the murals within, feature comfortable Yankee stereotypes of Mexico—bull fights, pink plastic flamingos, and flirting señoritas. Huge ceramic parrots perch in the life-size plastic palm trees in a place that does not take itself too seriously. Exotic, colorful surroundings and good, cheap food may keep you waiting for a seat at the Spanish-tile bar. Purple plastic tablecloths with turquoise place mats provide background for exotic Mexican fare and thirteen different margaritas. A strolling mariachi delights both adults and children with her attentions and bilingual song.

Meadow Muffins
**2432 W. Colorado Ave.
(ne corner of 25th St.),
(719) 633-0583**

Painted people in the second-story windows may make you wonder about the 1901 red brick edifice, first built as the Waycott Opera House. It is now a theatrical bar and restaurant adorned with antiques, including two buckboard wagons suspended from the ceiling of the first-floor saloon and an Egyptian barge over the front bar. A maze of rooms jammed with antiques and bric-a-brac make this a museum/bar with basement game rooms, a dance floor, and one room labeled "Pick Up Male Here." Before its 1985 rejuvenation as the Meadow Muffin, the opera house hosted the Isis Theater and Ku Klux Klan meetings upstairs.

Colorado Springs
Elevation: 6,012 feet

General William J. Palmer laid out Colorado Springs with broad, tree-lined streets and no saloons. For this model town, he sought "moral, temperance-minded" colonists. Saloons were confined to the nearby working-class town of Colorado City. Alas, some of the aristocrats Palmer recruited fancied champagne, and soon drinking resorts arose—just outside the city limits—at places such as the Broadmoor Casino. Drinking did not officially become legal in the Springs until 1935, but the town was not exactly dry before that.

During Prohibition, mining millionaire Spencer Penrose bitterly opposed the Noble Experiment. Penrose, an ardent Republican whose brother was Boise Penrose, the rock-ribbed Republican U.S. senator from Pennsylvania, even broke with President Herbert Hoover and the GOP to support the Democrats and happy days. Before Colorado became legally dry on January 1, 1916, Penrose acquired a vast cache of fine spirits, which he hid under the swimming pool at his Broadmoor resort. Some of these cases were not discovered until the 1990s. Penrose built Colorado Springs' Broadmoor Hotel with its most elegant bars: the Golden Bee Pub and the Tavern, with its palmy Garden Room. As a noble experiment in sober town planning, Colorado Springs has gone awry.

The Broadmoor Hotel Tavern
1 Lake Ave., (719) 577-5776

Like a pink wedding cake, the nine-story Broadmoor Hotel sits on the eastern shore of the lake of a former dairy farm. Spencer "Spec" Penrose, the black sheep of a prominent Philadelphia family, bought the site in 1916 for $90,000 in cash. He hired the firm that designed New York City's Ritz Carlton and Biltmore hotels to do an Italian Renaissance–style palace. Penrose lavished $4 million on his hotel, including the seventeenth-century Venetian sculpture fountain in the entry garden and Maxfield Parrish's 1921 painting of the hotel in the main lobby.

Broadmoor guests never went dry, even during Prohibition. Penrose stocked the Broadmoor Drugstore with alcohol for "medicinal purposes." He celebrated Repeal in 1933 by selling whiskey and scotch wearing the Broadmoor name. Since its 1918 grand opening, The Broadmoor perennially outshines competitors, earning five diamonds from the American Automobile Association and five stars from the Mobil Oil Company.

The Colorado Springs Company Office, a landmark at the northwest corner of Kiowa and Nevada Streets, housed the firm that started this once boozeless model town. Plans for a temperance utopia went awry and the Underground Pub now occupies the basement. Photo courtesy of the Penrose Public Library, Colorado Springs, Pikes Peak Library District.

Its tavern is a wood-paneled retreat with thousands of liquor bottles lining the walls. Penrose bragged that he helped empty many of them. The Tavern occupies what was once the Broadmoor Stock Exchange, where Penrose got news of his Utah (now Kennicott) Copper Company profits, which funded construction of The Broadmoor and kept it open during the early decades when the hotel was often nearly empty. Beyond the Tavern, the Garden Room (1953) is a glass-roofed, stone-floored dining patio profuse with plantings. Evenings bring a small band to the Tavern, where you can see Ike look-alikes dancing with their Mamies.

There are only two ways to get ahead today— sell liquor or drink it.

—*W. C. Fields*

Clubhouse Restaurant & Underground Pub
130 E. Kiowa St (nw corner of Nevada Ave.), (719) 633-0590

In his search for an appropriate local style, the Dutch architect Nicholas Van Den Ahrend gave this five-story, buff brick structure exotic window shapes and vibrant dark green terra-cotta trim patterns reminiscent of Art Nouveau. He built this showy edifice to house the Colorado Springs Company, which was created in 1871 by town founder William J. Palmer to sell lots in the 2,000-

acre original town site. Buyers had to be "of strict temperance habits," unlike modern bar patrons. Gothic arches lead to the basement pub, café, and game rooms. This smoky subterranean dive has a maze of spaces, including many dark corner nooks and crannies. Live music makes this a favorite hangout for younger folks.

Giuseppe's Old Depot Restaurant & Pub
10 S. Sierra Madre St., (719) 440-8857

This rambling Queen Anne–style passenger depot has been deliciously restored as a restaurant and bar decorated with railroad artifacts. Outside, the stone structure rises to a roofline bristling with gabled train sheds, dormers, porches, and a cupola. Additions on either end of what was already a long, narrow depot make this Colorado's longest tavern.

Inside, the original hexagonal tile and oak floors, oak waiting benches, marble-topped oak ticket counter, stained-glass windows, and high wood-paneled ceiling survive. Besides many railroad photos and memorabilia, plenty of real rail action takes place on the seven tracks just outside the many window seats. You'll see Burlington, Santa Fe, and Union Pacific trains, but no D&RG rolling stock—that grand old Colorado line was swallowed by its old nemesis and rival, the Union Pacific, in 1997.

The old depot serves good, inexpensive Italian meals, with a popular salad bar, pizza, prime rib, and full bar service. High ceilings, well-padded captain's chairs, and railroad memorabilia galore make this a rail fan's heaven. The parkside dining room contains the original depot cornerstone and a view of preserved D&RG Engine 168 in Antlers Park. The north-end bar is wrapped around a four-sided fireplace. In a second bar, the Pullman Lounge, sit in one of the wheeled captain's chairs, order one of their special cocktails served in a Rio Grande glass, and keep your eye on the steam pressure gauge on the backbar.

Golden Bee Pub
1 Lake Ave., (719) 577-5776

Colorado's finest English-style pub is a terrific nightcap for the state's grandest hotel, The Broadmoor. Fixtures from a nineteenth-century London pub transplanted to the basement of the Broadmoor's International Center include a magnificent African mahogany backbar with matching sidebars. The ornate woodwork rises into wreathes and human faces. A plank oak floor, a brass bar foot rail, a pressed-metal ceiling with antique chandeliers, a piano, and nightly sing-alongs add ambience. Ancient grog barrels line the entry. Inside, customers can sample imported English beers by the yard, tankard, or pint. This dim, cozy bar with its exquisitely carved wood, sparkling crystal, and frothy beverages boasts its own songbook with 110 favorites, ranging from "America the Beautiful," inspired by a visit to Pikes Peak, to "If I Were a Rich Man." Prices are steep here, but there are free

Golden Bee stick-on souvenirs. If the free cheese pots and crackers don't fill you up, try The Broadmoor's versions of traditional pub meals. Ever since its 1971 opening, this antique tavern has been a fanciful escape from the modern convention center on top of it.

Murphy's Tavern
2729 N. Nevada Ave., (719) 634-9196

Look for the revolving, green neon shamrock fronting this streamlined tavern in green and white stucco. Inside, Murphy's curved plate-glass front window is echoed by the horseshoe-shaped bar. Bartenders have to be short and skinny to work inside that horseshoe. Kelly green vinyl covers the wall booths as well as the barstools. In front of each stool, the Formica countertop has dark depressions where innumerable drinks have rested since opening day in 1954.

An Irish immigrant converted an old diner into Murphy's. His son, Thomas Murphy Sr., also ran the bar until he died in 1994 after having ten heart attacks and losing 100 pounds. Thomas Murphy Jr. now runs the bar, where he can be found nightly.

The decor has changed very little since Grandpa Murphy's days. It is still a tiny blue-collar place with the proud motto

"Where Friendly People Meet." Every Christmas they bring out the now-antique Coca-Cola portrait of Santa Claus (with the Coke ad cut off), the same little blinking plastic Christmas tree, and beer mugs full of red and green candy. The leprechauns and "Cead Mile Failte" (10,000 welcomes) plaques for St. Patrick's Day, however, stay up all year. Bing ("Too-ra-loo-ra-loo-ra") Crosby still lives on the jukebox. On St. Patrick's Day, the bartender reported, "We have to lock the front and back door, and let one person in as we let another out. Cops are pretty fast to come pick up troublemakers. But then they get even by calling us from downtown and telling us to come pick up people who claim that Murphy's is their home!"

Cheap drafts from 10 A.M. to 6 P.M. make this a popular place to get an early start on the happy hour. Murphy's is also a terrific place to eat, thanks to a tiny appendage next door, Trivelli's Philadelphia Style Steaks and Hoagies. Mama Barbara Trivelli opened this tiny lunch stand in 1976 with inexpensive, heroic hoagies, sandwiches, barbecue, grinders, steaks, and hotdogs wrapped to go in butcher paper. Order and pickup lines often extend out the door, but they will deliver to your barstool next door at Murphy's.

Murphy's Tavern has been a rallying point for the Irish of Colorado Springs ever since this tiny place opened in 1954.

Navajo Hogan
2817 N. Nevada Ave., (719) 634-3865

A 9-foot-high neon Navajo Indian bust advertises this prize piece of roadside Americana, a restaurant and bar inspired by a traditional Navajo dwelling. In 1935, Caesar and Dorothy Gheno used hand-hewn native pine logs to build the hogan and its twelve-sided roof. The Hogan thrived and two years later the Ghenos added an eight-sided hogan and pentagonal office, all cloaked in stucco. The Gheno family ran the place until 1952, when they leased it out. Once fashionable for dining and dancing, it began a long descent.

A 1981 arson fire left two black humps that sat vacant for seven years. To the rescue came a reformed Texas oil man, C. Cagg Eubanks, who bought the ruins in 1987 and did a first-rate restoration that won it designation as a National Register landmark. The Hogan reopened in 1988, serving mesquite-cooked Tex-Mex specialties, fresh fruit margaritas, Mexican beer, and fried ice cream desserts. Eubanks added an outside dining area and brought in live bands on weekends, when "shooter girls" circulate with bottles of tequila.

A stuffed porcupine on top of the vintage Wurlitzer exchanges glassy stares with a full-sized Alaskan brown bear and a slinking wildcat. Also watching are wall-mounted heads of deer, antelope, and jackalope. A stuffed wild turkey struts on the bar. From the high, domed log ceiling hangs a 6-foot plastic Corona bottle and piñatas. Inside and out, this is one of Colorado's finest fantasy bars.

Zigzag Moderne trim helps make the Navaho Hogan's neon sign Colorado Spring's finest piece of roadside "tavernalia."

Phantom Canyon Brew Pub
2–8 E. Pikes Peak Ave.
(nw corner of Cascade Ave.),
(719) 635-2800

Look for the Cheyenne Indian head in terra-cotta over the corner entry of this large, blond brick building. The Indian was the logo for the corner storefront ticket office of the Rock Island Line, whose "Rocket" passenger trains blasted into Colorado Springs.

After the Rock Island moved out, this neo-classical structure became the Cheyenne Hotel, a cozy family-run operation. Two weeks before its scheduled demolition in 1993, developer John Hickenlooper and his partners rescued the three-story structure for conversion into the Phantom Canyon Brew Pub.

Since its 1995 opening, this place has been hopping. It not only has a wonderfully airy main saloon but private dining rooms and an upstairs billiard hall. The pressed-metal ceiling is 16 feet high and huge plate-glass windows offer a fine view of downtown Colorado Springs and Pikes Peak. The unusual 1902 Brunswick backbar came from the Depot Bar in Pueblo's Union Station. Besides oak arches framing its mirrors, the bar has stained-glass Art Nouveau panels that are electrically backlighted, giving it a holy glow. The front bar has a fine, cool, smooth limestone top ideal for sliding beer glasses.

Resident brewmeister Eric Jefferts is called "Hopalong" for his aggressively hoppy beers. Try Zebulon's Peated Porter, which has won two national prizes. It wears a label mug shot of the explorer who failed to climb Pikes Peak and the slogan "He would have made it to the top with this one." The beer is available to go in reusable half-gallon jugs. The food is reasonable, trendy, and tasty, especially the sandwiches and pizza.

Ritz Grill
15 S. Tejon St., (719) 635-8484

Colorado's largest martini can be found at this Art Deco watering hole. Bright neon lights, marble counters, and chrome fixtures are nifty, as are the sandwiches, pizzas, martinis, and local microbrews. At the U-shaped island bar, happy-hour libations are two for one, and you can make a meal of the appetizers and/or Nabisco's Ritz Crackers. The large glass storefront frames downtown Colorado Springs with its easy, diagonal, on-street parking. This bright, high-ceilinged space in the turn-of-the-century Carlton Building retains its Roman tile floor from its former life as a music store. Nowadays the crowd makes their own music here, enhanced with live weekend jazz.

Craig

Elevation: 8,133 feet

The Moffat County seat was named for the minister who started the handsome First Christian Church at 601 Yampa Avenue. Churches notwithstanding, Craig became a "yee-haw" Saturday-night town for cowboys, railroad workers, and oil-field roughnecks, with stops such as the rowdy White Horse Inn and Popular Bar.

Golden Cavvy
Restaurant & Lounge
538 N. Yampa Ave., (970) 824-6038

This old foursquare residence now houses a cocktail lounge wrapped around a remarkable fireplace made of stones from the Bonanza Mine, the old Hahns Peak Jailhouse, the old Routt County Courthouse, and other noteworthy local edifices.

Popular Bar
24 W. Victory Way, (970) 824-9938

A longtime fixture previously known as the Office Bar, this well-named place located on U.S. 40 features beer, burgers, and pool behind a neon sign boasting "Good Food and Fine Folk." Wagon-wheel chandeliers illuminate the knotty pine walls.

White Horse Inn
476 Yampa Ave., no phone available

Despite the name, this is a blue-collar bar. It is also a pro-union place where the United Mine Workers of America Local 1799 holds rallies supporting its members who labor in Moffat County's huge strip mines. Bruce Castine opened it in 1935 as the White Horse, complete with a neon stallion. His daughter, Wanda Cury, and her husband, Bill, now own what is the county's oldest bar.

We found it hopping on a Friday night with a female deejay playing loud rock music and working up the crowd: "Come on, you guys. Dance and shout! It's so quiet in here! Is this a bar or a church?" Besides the dance floor, there are two pool tables and a shuffleboard. Some two hundred ceramic liquor bottles on the wall have somehow survived errant cue balls, bottles, and bullets.

Creede
Elevation: 8,852 feet

Nicholas C. Creede struck a silver lode on Willow Creek 2 miles above its junction with the Rio Grande in 1889. His discovery lured some 10,000 fortune seekers into this remote canyon and led to the establishment of Creede.

This silver city, squeezed into a narrow chasm between towering basalt spires, was scorched by fires and drowned by several major floods. But nothing stopped the eternal hubbub of mining and ore processing, of gambling and carousing in some thirty saloons strung out along Willow Creek. Creede attracted a rogue's gallery of western characters: Poker Alice Tubbs, Bob Ford, Calamity Jane, Bat Masterson, and Soapy Smith. Cy Warman, editor of *The Creede Candle,* wrote of the frenetic frontier boomtown, "It's day all day in the daytime, and there is no night in Creede." Nowadays Creede's nightlife is greatly enhanced by the Repertory Theater, as well as two memorable groggeries.

Creede Hotel Bar
120 N. Main St., (719) 658-2608

Philip Zang of Denver's Zang Brewing Company built this place in 1892 as Zang's Hotel. It still has four quaint rental rooms off the second-story porch, complete with rocking chairs overlooking Main Street. At the rear of the hotel, a stone and brick structure that once held five tiny brothel cribs now houses the proprietors.

Creede was sewerless until 1978, and this hotel, like other Creede buildings, had a metal trough outside to take waste from the bar and hotel into Willow Creek. When the open flume froze or became slushy, the stench drove many into the bar for strong drink. Refugees found the hotel saloon decorated with ore specimens and wooden plaques carved with the names of leading local mines. A few softer, frilly, feminine

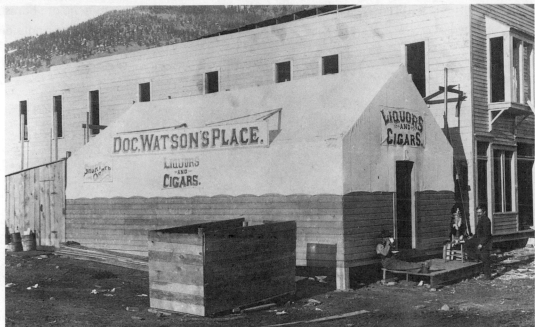

Tent taverns, such as these in Creede, sprang up overnight in new mining towns. If mines panned out, the town and its saloons graduated from canvas-and-frame buildings to brick and stone structures. Photos courtesy of the Colorado Historical Society.

Victorian touches are lost on old codgers gabbing around the stone fireplace by a reassuring ore bucket full of firewood.

Ed Hargreaves, one of the old-timers around the saloon fireplace, told me in 1994: "I bought this hotel for $7,000 in 1946, when it was open, but barely. We filled all twelve rooms with miners who got room and board for $80 a month. I ran the bar, which got pretty wild. We had to shove a lot of Saturday-night fistfights out into Main Street. Chester Brubaker played the piano and a beautiful gal from Denver jumped up on the bar for volunteer stripteases until my mother stopped her."

Old Miners Inn
107 N. Main St., (719) 658-2767

Creede's oldest edifice, a fireproof, brick edifice built after the fire of 1892, originally housed the Miners & Merchants Bank and Post Office. For decades the bank vault has chilled beer instead of cash in Creede's most notorious and long-lived haven for miners. Venerable carvings in the stout wooden front bar sluice spilled beer into golden pools. The ore-car track used as the foot rail is supported by horseshoes, and miner's pick heads are used as door handles. Exposed ceiling rafters and a hardwood floor add to the underground feel of this dim, smoky, steamy dive with the backbar mirror slogan "We only cheat tourists and drunks." Truly objectionable customers, unless they are miners, are banished to the church pew outside on the front sidewalk.

Coors Brewery in Golden and the Neef Brothers and Zang Breweries in Denver staked their claims in the 1890s boomtown of Creede. Raw, thirsty new mining towns proved to be bonanza beer markets. The Colorado Sun, *February 25, 1892, reported that the one-year-old silver city had "thirty saloons in full blast night and day [with] every species of deviltry." Photo courtesy of the Colorado Historical Society.*

Crested Butte
Elevation: 8,885 feet

Once a grungy coal-mining town, Crested Butte reawakened in 1963 as one of Colorado's slickest ski resorts. Tourists helped revive some of the fifteen saloons that sustained coal miners, whose tavern homes away from home, according to one minister, were gateways to hell. Cradled by the Elk Mountains, this town is named for the most prominent of many nearby peaks, a flattened mountain with a distinctive crest. Crested Butte still crows about its numerous bars, especially some crackerjack hangovers from the coal-mining era.

Crested Butte Brew Pub
226 Elk Ave., (970) 349-5026

Gary Garcia and his family erected the town's first brewpub in 120 working days in 1991, using large peeled logs. They topped the river-rock fireplace with a mountain lion 7 feet long, measuring from its whiskers to the tip of its tail. Even after several pints of the home-brewed stout, few can outsnarl this big cat. Red Lady Ale, this pub's pride and joy, is as luscious as the label lady. The White Buffalo Peace Ale is also popular, as is their chunky elk stew.

Crested Butte Club B & B
512 2nd St., (970) 349-6655

Known as Croatian Hall, this 1885 lodge was once a respite for Croatian coal miners. It provided not only food, drink, and lodging, but also sick benefits, burials, and prayers of the St. Barbara Society, named for the patron saint of miners. Such consolations were needed in the accident-prone coal industry; frequent tragedies included an explosion in Crested Butte's Jokerville Mine, which killed sixty men. The restored false front incorporates the original storefront and recessed entry to what remains a first-floor saloon. The upstairs has been converted to elegantly furnished guest rooms with such amenities as a racquetball court, an aerobics room, steam baths, and a giant hot tub.

Forest Queen Hotel Bar
129 Elk Ave., (970) 349-5336

"One-Eye" Ruby, the original "Forest Queen," ran this as a brothel. Room 4 is still reportedly haunted by a prostitute who jumped out the window into Coal Creek, killing herself. The brothel became a grocery, then a general store, and is now a bed-and-

Kochevar's Saloon & Gaming Hall typifies mining town saloons. This Crested Butte landmark sports an ornately crested false front echoed by the cornice of the neoclassical backbar inside.

breakfast. The parlor doubles as a bar, which is usually full because the rental rooms upstairs are too tiny for anything but sleep. The 1880s building has a false front outside and a fine backbar inside. Decorated with burlap-bag curtains and a jungle of plants, this pub resembles a library, with guests reading, playing cards and board games, sipping, dining, and talking quietly. Rowdier, randier types head for Kochevar's next door.

Heg's Place
310 Elk Ave., (970) 349-5304

J. Dial's Mortuary now offers embalming fluids of another kind. This antique false-fronted 1900 building also served as Crested Butte's first movie theater, as a roller-skating rink, and as the post office from 1925 to 1964, before its reincarnation as a watering hole.

Kochevar's Saloon
127 Elk Ave., (970) 349-6745

A little-altered antiquity, Kochevar's retains its transomed plate-glass storefront, vestibule entry, and high-ceilinged saloon with gaming tables, antique slot machines, and potbellied stove. With its cornice puffed out proudly, the antique backbar is as stacked as the false front outside with its decorative brackets. Beneath the clapboard skin of this three-story edifice lie hand-hewn square timbers. Jacob Kochevar, a skilled carpenter, constructed this saloon and ran it until 1917. It has withstood Crested Butte's winter blizzards since 1890. History, ambience, and good Mexican food make this a hot spot.

Cripple Creek
Elevation: 9,494 feet

Bear Creeks, Coal Creeks, Deer Creeks, Dry Creeks, and Sand Creeks abound, but Colorado has only one Cripple Creek. Pioneer settlers might have given it another name if it weren't for their numerous misadventures along this stony little stream.

Levi Welty homesteaded along the creek on the west side of Pikes Peak in 1872 with his sons George, Alonzo, and Frank. While roofing the cabin, George fell off and injured his back. Some accounts say he fell on the family dog and crippled it. Around the same time, Alonzo's axe slipped while he was chopping wood; the gash in his leg left him laid up for months. Frank only sprained his ankle. Folklore has associated many other lame burros, cattle, horses and humans with the stream called Cripple Creek. With relief the Weltys sold their spread to a family of cowboys from Kentucky, the Womacks. The stream had little water, a bad reputation, and more gold than any watershed in the Rockies.

Ever since the Pikes Peak gold rush of 1858–1859, prospectors had been poking around Cripple Creek. Dr. Frederick V. Hayden, the U.S. Army surveyor who first mapped Colorado, noticed that the area west of Pikes Peak was a huge sunken volcano. He predicted that volcanic water laced with gold had been forced up into the faults and fissures in the peak's granite and other formations. Yet Hayden and hundreds of others never found pay dirt. Not until thirty years after the Pikes Peak gold rush began did "Crazy Bob" Womack, a cowpoke on his father's ranch, find the richest strike of all just west of the mountain that gave the gold rush its name.

While herding cows, Bob kept his eye open for gold ore specimens to take to the assay offices down in Colorado Springs. When some of the ore pieces assayed rich in gold, folks began to realize that Crazy Bob might just be "Brilliant Bob." His golden rocks sparked the 1890s Cripple Creek gold rush. By 1900, Cripple Creek had become a city of more than 10,000. Some 475 mines and a dozen other towns sprang up in the 25-square-mile Cripple Creek District. It produced more than $15 million a year during the 1890s, making it the richest gold district in the world. Not until after World War I did mining centers in South Africa, Canada, and the Homestake Mine in Lead, South Dakota, surpass Cripple Creek's gold output. This last and greatest of Colorado's golden cities has produced more than $500 million. That total keeps climbing as mining companies are still extracting gold, reworking old ore with colossal cyanide heap leaching operations that have buried the old towns of Altman, Anaconda, and Midway, and endangered Victor.

Cripple Creek gold bought a lot of booze. At its peak, the city had almost one hundred saloons. It still has some twenty-five watering holes—but watch out for the burros. These descendants of pioneer mining burros delight tourists, so the town tolerates the resident pack of hee-hawers, which cut the grass and fertilize it. Like the tourists in this high, dry, often blustery town, the burros have been known to wander into watering holes.

Johnny Nolon's Saloon & Gambling Emporium still thrives on booze and betting, despite Carry Nation's vicious attempts to close one of Cripple Creek's most notorious gambling hells.

Johnny Nolon's Saloon & Gambling Emporium
301 E. Bennett Ave.
(ne corner of 3rd Ave.),
(719) 689-3105

This eye-catcher has a neoclassical revival façade trimmed with festive garlands, swags, and wreaths. The windows wear pink puffy curtains lifted into enticing folds like the skirts of a bar belle. The big bright windows with leaded-glass transoms are also inviting. Usually casinos make a science of shutting out daylight and picturesque views of historic mining towns in order to keep customers focused on gambling.

Inside Johnny Nolon's, I heard—even before drinking a couple of beers—cattle bellowing and cowboys yee-hawing. It was only recorded sound, but a relief from the incessant chiming of one-armed bandits.

Neo-Victorian chandeliers and imitation "pressed-metal" ceiling panels in old-timey floral designs shimmer overhead. A golden oak backbar adorns the casino's soda fountain. Johnny Nolon's founder, owner and manager Bob Konczak, told me: "Marcia and I opened a gift shop here in 1984 and helped push gambling for Cripple Creek. It's worked out well—brought in at least 1,200 jobs. We've tried to keep things as Victorian as possible."

Konczak, a big, friendly Polish man from Chicago, has fallen for Cripple Creek and for Johnny Nolon, the most legendary of Cripple Creek's pioneer casino operators. He has blessed his casino with a historical shrine to

Nickel slots are very popular in Cripple Creek. Shown here through the window at Johnny Nolon's Saloon & Gambling Emporium.

Nolon, who is said to have first headed west as a Pony Express rider from St. Joseph, Missouri. Nolon arrived in Cripple Creek in 1891, at the beginning of the bonanza.

Nolon's elegant saloon and gambling emporium flourished as one of the town's most popular watering holes and gambling hells. Konczak noted that Nolon's beautiful blonde wife, Goldie, helped make the saloon a magnet for miners burdened with too much money. Nolon, according to Konczak, was a soft touch for the homeless, never denying them a meal or a pool table to sleep on.

Bob Konczak took me up to Nolon's third-story ballroom to see his prized possession: a grand copy of Sandro Botticelli's famous Renaissance painting, *The Birth of Venus*. With glee he told me the story behind it. A similar painting had been Johnny Nolon's favorite treasure. He fancied it as the finest saloon-hall nude in the Rocky Mountains and made it the centerpiece of his joint—before Carry Nation came up from Colorado Springs.

Nation, the hatchet-faced old lady mascot of the Woman's Christian Temperance Union, specialized in invading saloons with her hatchet, smashing up booze bottles and any items that displeased her. As she strolled down Bennett Avenue, saloon after saloon closed in front of her, in fear of her hatchet. Nolon, however, refused to close, saying he "was not going to let Carry Nation buffalo me!"

Carry marched into Nolon's groggery and began preaching against "Demon Rum" and companion vices. When she saw *Venus* on the wall, she screamed: "Hang a blanket over that trollop! If that naked wench ain't covered up, I'll chop her to shreds." Hatchet uplifted, Carry dashed at *Venus* and chopped her to pieces. Nolon leaped over the bar, picked Carry up, spun her around until she dropped the weapon, and called the sheriff. She was jailed for disturbing the peace. When no one would pay her bail, Johnny did so—with the proviso that Carry Nation take the next train to Colorado Springs, a haven—even back then—for militant Christians.

Cripple Creek's Palace Hotel is haunted by Kitty Chambers, owner of the hotel from 1908 to 1918. She was found stone dead in Room 3.

The Palace
172 E. Bennett Ave., (719) 689-2992

Among Cripple Creek's liquid landmarks, one of the oldest and coziest is The Palace. This three-story, red brick hotel had been boarded up for several years when Bob and Martha Lays, greenhorns from Rochester, New York, bought it for $55,000. With the help of their five children, they refurbished it and reopened it in 1976. Five of the upstairs rooms were made into bath-

rooms, so all the guests no longer had to share a single bathroom on each floor.

Today the hotel houses a restaurant, a casino, and a ghost. Robert Lays Jr. believes this feminine apparition is Kitty Chambers, owner of the hotel from 1908 to 1918, who was found stone dead in Room 3. In 1993 the Lays family opened a first-floor casino, but preserved the façade, floor plan, and upstairs hotel rooms, making this one of the least prostituted examples of preservation in a casino conversion.

One of Colorado's few mom-and-pop family casinos, The Palace is owned and operated by a theatrical clan who once produced many dinner-theater musicals here. Brothers Bob, Martin, and Rick have turned it into a folksy, friendly little casino that is also noted for fine meals. Bob Lays Jr. has been known to leap up on the bar to welcome customers with a brief lecture on casino etiquette in a rumbling bass baritone:

"You can swing from the chandelier, but don't jump on the bar!"

The Red Rooster Bar
133 N. 3rd St., no phone available

Wayne and Dorothy Mackin purchased the boarded-up, run-down hotel for $18,000 in 1946 and outfitted the rooms with brass beds and antique furnishings. Over the years they acquired the adjacent two-story, red brick Pittsburgh Block with fancy fleur-de-lis trim fronting Bennett Avenue. The Mackins converted it to additional hotel rooms, offices, and commercial space that became the Imperial Casino in 1991. Melodramas have been performed since 1948 in the basement Gold Bar Room Theater, including revivals of antique plays staged under the supervision of Dorothy Mackin, author of *Melodrama Classics* (1982).

The Red Rooster piano bar occupies what was originally the hotel sample room where salesmen displayed their wares. The original red rooster—the one with the broken tail on top of the backbar mirror—has been joined by more than one hundred other paintings, statues, and assorted red roosteriana. The more you drink, the more red roosters you'll see. Not to mention one reclining female nude—the prettiest little hen you ever saw.

Denver

Elevation: 5,280 feet

Denver was wet from the beginning. Even before the town's birth on November 22, 1858, liquor was sold out of wagons and tents. By 1859 more substantial saloons arrived with Uncle Dick Wootton's Western Hall. This two-story log tavern boasted the first glass windows and first shake-shingle roof in town. Uncle Dick's stood at 11th and Walnut Streets, on what is now the Auraria Higher Education Center campus.

The Western Hall doubled as a political center where Jefferson Territory was formed on April 15, 1859. Territorial delegates, perhaps after some of Dick's Taos Lightning, created a new territory carved out of Kansas, Nebraska, Utah and New Mexico. They were cheered on by the May 7, 1859, *Rocky Mountain News:*

> Shall it be the government of the knife and the revolver, or shall we unite in forming here in our Rocky Mountain Country, among the ravines and gulches of the Rocky Mountains, and the fertile valleys of the Arkansas and Platte, a new and independent State? Shall the real keystone of the Union be now set on the summit of the arch, and a republic inaugurated that can from her mountain aerie cast her eye to the Pacific on the one hand and the Atlantic on the other ... she at once becomes the real center of the Union.

Such high sentiment carried the day and the territory was born. All hands adjourned, presumably, to toast the new territory. Although the federal government did not sanction Jefferson Territory in 1859, it did establish Colorado Territory in 1861. After its creation, a thirsty territorial legislature moved around to wherever they could find free drinks. They met in Golden from 1862 to 1864, where William A. H. Loveland offered them libations at his stone inn. Next, the legislature traveled to Colorado City, testing the hospitality there before returning to Denver, which had far more saloons than any town in the territory—some thirty-five watering holes by 1866 when the territorial government moved to Denver for good.

Meanwhile, Denver city dads had convened in Libeus Barney's Apollo Hall in 1859 to create the People's Government of the City of Denver. Denver city officials met in various taverns until 1889, when a city hall was built at 14th and Larimer. Numerous saloons surrounded City Hall, just as the Capitol Grill, Congress Lounge, Senate Lounge, General Assembly, Pierre's Quorum, and similarly named bars have clustered over the years

G. N. Woodward wrote home from early Denver: "We have 6 stores, about 12 to 15 saloons, 1 hotel … . There is more drinking and gambling here in one day than in Kansas City in six—in fact about one-half of the population do nothing else but drink whiskey and play cards." 1867 Harper's *magazine drawing, Tom Noel Collection.*

around the state capitol. To this day, considerable political activity revolves around taverns, where lobbyists lubricate and enlighten lawmakers.

By 1890, Denver had 319 saloons, according to the *City Directory*. By 1916, when Colorado began statewide Prohibition, the city had more than four hundred. After Prohibition was repealed in 1933, taverns quickly redecorated the cityscape. In recent decades Denver has harbored around five hundred places licensed to sell alcohol for consumption on the premises. Unlike me, you probably do not have time to visit them all, but the following are memorable.

Bonnie Brae Tavern
740 S. University Blvd., (303) 777-2262

Carl Dire was adding a garage to his gas station when Repeal came in 1934. He celebrated by converting his tile block garage to a tavern. Initially it had four booths and a bar with eight stools. Dire's wife, Sue, did the cooking. A hamburger cost a dime. So did a beer or a shot of whiskey. Sue's popular spaghetti dinners cost a little more but sold well too. The Dires built living quarters upstairs for their growing family of children who worked downstairs after school.

The Dires' sons, Michael and Henry, have enlarged the place twice to accommodate crowds. They come for pizza, prime rib, spaghetti, and other standbys in inexpensive, generous portions. They don't come for the decor—well-scrubbed linoleum floors, acoustic tile ceiling, and brown and turquoise leatherette booths. Growing old with the neighborhood, the Dires expelled the jukebox when pop music turned loud and obstreperous. They catered to families and to old folks, some of whom have been coming here for six decades.

A few things have changed since 1934. In the 1960s, this tavern became one of the first places in Denver to make and serve pizza. Two grandsons, Michael Dire II and Rick, Henry's son, still run this neighborhood classic. Over the mahogany bar, Carl and Sue live on in portraits beaming down on the little gas station that became Denver's most fabled pizza place.

Buckhorn Exchange Restaurant
1000 Osage St., (303) 534-9509

Denver had no museum of natural history until 1900, but saloons offered some astonishing natural and unnatural history. The best of the tavern museums, the Buckhorn Exchange, has more than three hundred stuffed mammals and birds. Not even the Denver Museum of Natural History has some of these specimens, such as the two-headed calves and the albino jackalope.

Upstairs at the Buckhorn, the white oak front bar is adorned with handcarved oak leaves and acorns. Old Henry H. Zeitz Jr. told me years ago that it came from his great-grandfather's tavern in Essen, Germany. Four generations of Zeitzes, he claimed, made a living behind that bar. I believed him, as he sat beady-eyed on his barstool with a holstered pistol on his hip. He claimed that his father, H. H. "Shorty Scout," was a hunting buddy of Buffalo Bill, Sitting Bull, Horace Tabor, and President Theodore Roosevelt. He pointed to some of Buffalo Bill's weapons and an autographed photo of President Teddy Roosevelt as proof.

I asked Zeitz about the Prohibition era, when the Buckhorn was listed in the Denver *City Directory* as a "soft drink parlor" and a "grocery." He denied ever having sold illegal libations, as well as the stories that brides of the multitudes worked upstairs and that their panties had been seen on the windowsills. For its good behavior, he noted, the Buckhorn received, after the Repeal of Prohibition in 1933, Colorado Liquor License Number 1. That trophy is still showcased behind the upstairs bar.

Like a lot of old-timers, the Buckhorn understates its age. It was not established in 1893, but in 1871, when Theodore Zeitz opened a tavern at 2672 Market Street. His son, Henry H. Zeitz Sr., moved that business in 1893 into the two-story brick building at 1000 Osage Street. Decorated with exterior wildlife murals by Noel Adams as well as with many interior marvels, the Buckhorn has garnered Denver and National Register landmark designations.

Originally called the Rio Grande Exchange, it courted railroaders at the Denver & Rio Grande's (now Union Pacific) Burnham

The Buckhorn Exchange originated with Theodore Zeitz's 1871 saloon on Market Street before moving in 1893 to 1000 Osage Street. Would-be cowboys gather at this designated Denver and National Register landmark for the Buffalo Bill look-alike contests.

Shops just across Osage Street. They ate and drank downstairs and rented rooms upstairs. H. H. Zeitz Jr., who was born in the family quarters at the rear of the Exchange in 1896, grew up working the bar. He could be found there until he retired in 1977. After Zeitz died, his place was boarded up until Roi Davis and Steve Knowlton put together a coalition to restore, update, and reopen the establishment in 1978.

"Mr. Zeitz kept seventeen items, like the so-called Custer sword, Sitting Bull's Colt 45, an elk's-tooth vest, and the chair made out of longhorn horns," Roi explained over a copious Dutch lunch at the Buckhorn. "We bought just about everything else, including the elk penis and the barbwire they found around the neck of the North Denver gangster pulled out of Sloan's Lake."

Grease and cobwebs, some claimed, had held the Buckhorn together. The new owners gave it a long-overdue cleaning and airing. They hand-shampooed the mounted animals, reblackened their noses, and polished the glass eyes. The artifacts and the Buckhorn sparkled anew for its 1978 reopening with a new kitchen, air-conditioning, electricity, and plumbing.

"For decades, Zeitz offered steaks and pork chops," reported manager Bill Dutton. "Now, we also offer alligator, buffalo, elk, rattlesnake, and saucy, sliced Rocky Mountain oysters."

The far-famed Buckhorn Exchange was operated by Henry H. Zeitz Sr. and Jr. (behind bar), of a German immigrant clan. The Buckhorn proudly displays Colorado Liquor License Number 1, together with some three hundred species of animals and birds that make it a museum as well as a saloon and steakhouse. 1937 photo courtesy of the Denver Public Library, Western History Collection.

Although vegetarians and animal-rights activists call it a nightmare, the Buckhorn is a dream come true for aficionados of wild game—on the wall or on your plate. The food, the decor, and the old songs of house musician Roz Brown are heavenly for fans of western history and the old-time saloon. The Roofgarten, with its chuck-wagon service, overlooks the railyards, the downtown skyline, and RTD's light-rail line. This spiffy new streetcar stops right in front of the Buckhorn at 10th Avenue and Osage Street for an easy trip into Denver's liquid past.

Casino Cabaret
2625–2633 Welton St., (303) 292-2626

For two decades, peeling paint identified this onetime pride of Five Points. It became a shadowy, lifeless structure along Welton Street amid the bright new, old-fashioned streetlights, new street trees, and RTD's spiffy new light-rail line. Not until 1997 did the place return to life as a jazz club. Passengers zipping by on light rail can now stop at the place once famed for Colorado's hottest jazz, barbecue, craps, and dancing.

Only a few old-timers in Five Points remember that during the Great Depression and the four decades thereafter, this was Benny Hooper's club, which provided food, drink, rooms, and entertainment. Benny took money from those who could afford it, and treated thousands of others.

Along with the now-restored Rossonian Hotel Lounge across Welton Street, Benny Hooper's old club was the best known of

perhaps two hundred African-American taverns to have served Denverites since Isaac Brown opened a pioneer black bar in 1871. Most have been in Five Points, the traditional black neighborhood named for the intersection of East 26th and 27th Avenues, and Washington and Welton Streets.

I first visited the two-story, red brick complex in 1973, when it was labeled "Deluxe Recreation Parlor and Ex-Servicemen's Club." It was no longer deluxe, but shabby both inside and out. The old oak backbar held trophies and plaques honoring Benjamin Franklin Hooper as the "Unofficial Mayor of Five Points." Two homemade cardboard signs on the backbar read "No Profanity" and "No Profanity Please." Although the afternoon crowd was raucous, it was not profane. Of course, Benny's was always primarily nocturnal, opening at 2 P.M. and closing at 2 A.M. High-back wooden booths with hat racks filled the other side of the long, skinny barroom. In the dim light, two white bandages shone on green-felt pool tables. An elderly gentleman with a kind smile and a neat suit caught my eye.

"Benny Hooper?" I asked.

"Benny Hooper," he said almost reverently. "There's nobody I'd rather be. He's an awfully fine man. But he's not me."

He then introduced me to a slight, short, light-skinned, plainly dressed man in his seventies. Benny, I found, wore a demure expression like a mask; when he took it off, his eyes became keen and mirthful. He seemed to take everything in, and he still moved fast, attending to customers and breaking up scuffles. When some big bad cats, the Black Panthers, rioted in Five Points after Martin Luther King, Jr.'s assassination in 1968, Benny even patrolled his street front to ward off potential looters.

When we were alone, Hooper spoke rapidly. He was born in a house at 23rd and Welton, just a few blocks away, on May 2, 1893, one of seven children of a janitor and his wife. He quit Ebert School after the sixth grade, bellhopped at the old St. James Hotel downtown, and served in World War I. Army pay seemed like a fortune to Benny, who saved it for the day he returned to Denver in 1920.

"Those days," Benny told me, "colored people couldn't stay in the downtown hotels, so I used my Army money to open a place. We called it the Ex-Servicemen's Club and welcomed colored soldiers. It started out in 1923 as a little place down on 23rd and Arapahoe. But Mayor Stapleton came by, put his around my shoulder, and asked me, 'Why don't you get a new location?'"

In a primarily white town, finding a new location for a black bar was not easy. Denver, like other cities, felt threatened by a growing black population, and took the usual step of restricting them to one neighborhood. Five Points, which was Denver's first streetcar suburb, had originally attracted wealthy white families. Later, as the upper classes moved on to Capitol Hill, Cheesman Park, and the Country Club, Five Points became a German and Jewish neighborhood. By 1900, blacks were moving in, and by the 1920s the Five Points triangle bounded by the South Platte River, 23rd Street, and Downing Street was the specified area for blacks, although a considerable number of whites, Asians, and Hispanics lived there then and now.

During the relatively flush 1920s, Benny added a bar, a billiard room, and a basement jazz joint to his Ex-Servicemen's Club. Veteran reporter Alberta Pike, in the August 17, 1932, *Rocky Mountain News,* profiled Benny's Deluxe Recreation Parlor and Ex-Servicemen's Club. She found it "a swell place" where "business is good. The noisy black-and-tan crowd is the sporting, fun-loving, easy-going element …. Benny at the front counter gives you a shrewd once-over from enormous soft brown

In the 1940s, African Americans, unwelcome elsewhere, gathered at Benny Hooper's Ex-Servicemen's Club and Hotel.

eyes … . At Benny's you are likely to find almost the entire personnel of the White Elephant ball club, the team of colored boys that pretty regularly cleans up the other clubs in the City League." The baseball team went to Benny's for "the most succulent barbecue sandwiches … five tables where the balls click merrily all day long" and "lots of room for smoking and plain sittin' around."

In the 1930s, Benny opened the Casino next door to the Ex-Serviceman's Club. By 1948, the Casino had evolved into a two-story hall with balcony seating for one thousand, a 40-foot-long bar, and a huge hardwood dance floor. Five Points in those days drew whites and blacks from all over. While the Casino was basically black, the Rossonian Lounge across the street, which had a doorman and required customers to wear ties, attracted many whites for big-name jazz bands. Morris "Knock-Out" Brown, an ex-prizefighter, operated a club known for music and barbecue a few doors down Welton Street. The Crap House at 2440–2550 Welton, Fern Hall at 2711–2719 Welton, the Roxy Theater at 2549 Welton, the Porters & Waiters Club at 2627$^{1}/_{2}$ Welton, the Apex Recreation and Social Club at 2645 Welton, and the St. Louis Barbecue at 29th and Welton were all memorable Five Points nightspots. The last of these legendary Welton Street jazz joints was the Voter's Club, which operated until the 1980s at 2617 Welton. Since then, the jazz scene has focused on El Chapultepec at 20th and Market.

The fact that Runyon drank other than water in those days need not mean that he was alone in this respect.

—Gene Fowler

The Casino, the largest and most luxurious of the Five Points jazz joints, was dressed up for Christmas, Easter, and other holidays, when Benny donated the hall to churches and charities, including the NAACP, the American Legion, Zion Baptist Church, and the YMCA, all organizations of which he was a member. During World War II, black soldiers with weekend passes flooded Benny's place. "They got real hot," Benny told me, "when they couldn't find anyplace to stay and my rooms were all full. So I cooled 'em down with a few beers and let 'em sleep on the floor."

Brook Benton, James Brown, Ray Charles, Fats Domino, George Morrison, Muddy Waters, Flip Wilson, and other entertainment legends played the Casino over the years. It had been little used since the 1970s, when blacks, taking advantage of the civil-rights acts of the 1960s, began to use finer, fancier downtown facilities. The Casino was mostly memories and cobwebs when Benny showed me around the huge, dim, abandoned hall. Its 1997 restoration and reopening are a welcome revival of a venerable community institution.

The last time I saw Benny, he said: "It's dangerous here now. You be careful when you go outside. I've seen 'em take a white man's shoes off just to see if there's any money in them." The street life outside remained vibrant: small girls on tricycles, junkies, nattily dressed young blades with crazy hairdos, strutting streetwalkers, and gossiping old men.

Benny's ninety-one years in Denver began in Five Points in 1893, when Denver had a tiny black community of fewer than 4,000. By the time he died, the population was more than 40,000. In 1991, Denver would elect its first African-American mayor, which was unthinkable during Benny's lifetime.

"Once colored town was just Five Points," Benny told me, shaking his head. "Now I've got sixty empty beds upstairs and the one room where I live. I've put fifty years and everything I own into this place, and it's probably not worth anything. People have moved all the way out to the airport."

Seeing Denver's black community grow, prosper, and become better integrated was bittersweet for Benny. For making it in Denver meant leaving Five Points. Many Five Points nightclubs are moribund, as younger African Americans go to integrated clubs in other parts of town, but some of the past glory has been resuscitated in the reborn Casino Cabaret.

Cherry Cricket
2641 E. 2nd Ave., (303) 322-7666

The Cherry Cricket is in the Zim's Building, named for the Zimmerman family, who ran the pioneer beer joint in the Cherry Creek bottoms. Alois Zimmerman, a German immigrant, opened Zimmerman's Saloon at the corner of East 2nd Avenue and Clayton Street in 1896. After his death, his wife, Caroline, and then his daughter, Mary, ran the bar at various locations on this block.

Mary sold out to Bernard J. Duffy, who converted her old place to Duffy's Cherry Cricket after selling Duffy's Shamrock Tavern downtown in 1963. Duffy expanded and modernized, making the Cricket chirp with good inexpensive food, libations, and lively pool tables. The Salturelli boys, Tom and Richard, kept the name and kept it a great eating and drinking place before moving on to open the Bay Wolf Restaurant, which also became a Cherry Creek legend.

After that, the health department closed the bar—not only crickets but roaches were thriving here. To the rescue came Elizabeth "Eli" Peck McGuire, who grew up a few blocks north on 7th Avenue Parkway. She attended two of Denver's best private schools, Kent and Graland, and then majored in philosophy at Scripps College. She dropped out and came back home to purchase Colorado license plates reading "No Tofu," and the Cherry Cricket. "The Cricket had a terrible reputation and we bought it for a song," Eli reminisced. "Since 1990, we've brought it back to what Duffy and the Salturellis made it."

Eli installed eighteen draft-beer handles and began offering some of Denver's best hamburgers, with twenty-four different options (try the grilled Bermuda onions). Spiffy watering holes come and go in and around the Cherry Creek Shopping Center, the city's poshest shopping on what was once Denver's old dump. Yet the Zimmermans' dumpy little tavern, reincarnated as the Cherry Cricket, remains a perennial favorite. As Eli McGuire put it, "Even our wines must be good—they have corks in them. Our non-smoking area is the best of Cherry Creek."

The Church
12th Ave. (se corner of 1160 Lincoln St.), (303) 832-3528

Early Sunday morning, about 1 A.M., I saw lightning flash through the stained-glass windows. Then came pounding thunder. The building seemed to be rocking. A mob of young people lined 12th Avenue and Lincoln Street, waiting to get into one of Denver's oldest churches. Upon investigating, I found St. Mark's Episcopal Church reborn as a steamy new nightclub—with a $10 cover and rigorous I.D. card inspections. At the red Gothic door a sign warns, "No hats, tee-shirts or athletic apparel." If you pass scrutiny, the wardens take your cash and anoint the back of your hand in Gothic letters, "Church."

Inside, hundreds of celebrants jammed the main sanctuary for rituals of techno-rock. The music was so loud you couldn't hear it, but feel it. It rattled even the stained-glass window of the Sermon on the Mount. Revolving mirrors splashed colored strobe lights on the hot dancing bodies and cold stone walls. Smoke rose in mini-clouds from many smoking customers. The creamy sandstone walls highlight the pink stone columns whose capitals are carved into grape clusters. These columns support dark wooden beams that flower in shamrock patterns as they soar upward into airy Gothic arches toward the high, vaulted ceiling.

Two great European narcotics, alcohol and Christianity.

—Friedrich Nietzsche

Minimal alterations scar the magnificent interior of St. Mark's. A new sprinkler system has been installed for what is now a very hot nightspot. The pews are gone to make way for dancing. So is the altar and its exquisite gold-leaf painting, *The Ascension and the Angels* by Albert Byron Olson, an artist from Montrose, Colorado. Above where the altar once stood, the sanctuary end wall still has seven tall window slits shaped like lit candles.

These red glass candles shed crimson light on what is now Candles VII, one of seven bars and dance floors in a maze of side and subterranean rooms. Each area offers different recorded music (jazz, retro rock-and-roll, alternative, blues, big band, disco, funk, even Gregorian chant) as well as a live band stage. The quietest place is the cigar bar in what used to be the Chapel of the Holy Comforter for the deaf. The south-side parish hall has been reborn as the Japon Sushi Bar with a fireplace artistically lit with seven candles.

Regas Christou (Christ the King), a local nightclub owner, rehabilitated this 24,000-square-foot designated landmark. He reopened it on December 31, 1996, and it has been attracting thousands of pilgrims on Friday and Saturday nights ever since.

This corner of Capitol Hill first rocked in the 1880s when Sister Eliza Barton's Mission of the Holy Comforter staged gospel singing in an old house. The current church was built in 1890, embodying a daring design from one of Colorado's great pioneer architects, William Lang. Working with a partner, Marshall Pugh, Lang used his typical eclectic mix of High Victorian elements— both miniature and huge Gothic windows, slender spires, and a chunky Romanesque tower. A huge, square, corner bell tower dominated this edifice until the 1950s, when it crashed onto the sidewalk below. Only a stubby base survives amid the protruding buttresses, bays, gables, and spires, all made of whitish Larimer County sandstone.

A small band of Episcopalians struggled to keep St. Mark's alive during the 1970s and 1980s. As traditionalists, they heroically fought adoption of the new *Book of Common Prayer* with its bland, modern prose. After a bitter religious war of words, the diocese evicted the congregation and sold the church. In 1987 a tearful, tiny congregation celebrated St. Mark's last mass, using the grand old Elizabethan language they clung to stubbornly. For seven years, the church sat empty.

"We worked three and a half years fixing this place up," said Christou. "We reopened every room and even put in a rooftop garden bar. The idea of a church is to bring people together for a great time, especially on Sunday. Now I'm looking for a gospel band to do Sunday brunch. I believe God is still in here. Every night at closing, we leave a glass of Chivas Regal for Him. Next morning it's always gone!"

Cruise Room
17th & Wazee Sts., (303) 628-5400

The best Art Deco decor, the best martini, and the oldest LoDo bar all happen to be in the same place: the Cruise Room of the Oxford Hotel. This 1935 redesign of an 1890 Victorian saloon by architect Charles Jacka and artist Alley Henson introduced streamlined decor and wall panels of world leaders with toasts in their native tongue. Although Hitler was removed, Stalin survives along with other world leaders of the mid-1930s. England's King Edward VI, who abdicated to marry the American divorcée Wallis Warfield Simpson, occupies the

"Cheerio" window, while an Indian and the California Zephyr occupy the "Bottoms Up" U.S. panels.

The downstairs boasts a grand old lavatory with marble stalls and porcelain urinals big enough to shower in (which I once saw derelicts do during the Oxford's down-and-out 1970s). Charles Calloway and Dana Crawford restored the hotel for a 1983 grand reopening. The Governor's Room sparkled anew with its stained-glass, monogrammed transoms and stained-glass skylight. McCormick's, the noted Seattle fish house, opened a first-rate restaurant and bar, whose backbar sports the fabulous large, stained-glass window from Denver's legendary old Dutch Mill, a now defunct German restaurant and tavern at 1535 Champa.

"Cruising" does take place here, but the Cruise Room is named, according to Lisa, the landmark bartender, for the saloon on the cruise ship *Queen Mary*. Among the many ghosts to gather here are those of Mother Jones, Big Bill Haywood, and the poet Thomas Hornsby Ferril. He held cocktail-hour seminars here to discuss bawdy limericks, play the mandolin, and pass out free samples of his poetry such as these closing lines from "Stories of Three Summers":

Dare I believe more dreams than I can prove?
We never never know until long after
If even then
For centuries are only flicks
Of dragonflies
Over the granite mountains.

Denver Chophouse & Brewery
1735 19th & Wynkoop Sts.,
(303) 296-0800

For a cool $2.3 million, the old Union Pacific Freight Depot was reincarnated in 1994 as a brewpub, restaurant, and museum of railroadiana. The Union Pacific Museum and Archives in Omaha provided a wealth of photographs, art, posters, and artifacts evoking the golden age of crack UP trains like the "City of Denver." Inaugurated in 1936, this dreamy streamliner made the Chicago-Denver trip overnight. Framed wall art includes Otto Kuhler's futuristic locomotive designs. The "chophouse" theme of a railroad dinner is reflected in railroad-style equipment, linen table napkins, and good, reasonably priced food.

The Chophouse men's toilet room has been acclaimed as the best in Denver, even by Denver's longtime, beloved ex–U.S. Representative Pat Schroeder, whose testimonial hangs on a wall over a urinal. The men's bathroom is resplendent with wonderful black-and-white photos of women smoking, chatting, and sprucing up in the ladies' lounge car of the "City of Denver."

The Chophouse is adjacent to Coors Field and shares the baseball park's public square, featuring the *History of the Ball.* This is perhaps the most playful public sculpture in Colorado, with its comical snowball, goofball, meatball, debutante ball, and a hundred other spheres, even a high ball.

Denver Press Club
1330 Glenarm Pl., (303) 571-5260

Carousing newspapermen kept this place lively seventeen hours a day after it opened in 1923. Nowadays it's quieter, although you can still play pool in the basement poker room in the company of famed journalists of the past, who appear in the wall murals and portraits. This room is also storied for who slept on the pool table—alone and/or coupled. The bar and dining room, basement pool hall, and second-story meeting hall are haunted by the ghosts of prominent journalists such as William Barrett, Paul Conrad, Thomas Hornsby Ferril, Jack Foster, Gene Fowler, Pat Oliphant, Damon Runyan, Lee Casey Taylor, and—after women were admitted in 1970—Sandra Dallas and Marjorie Barrett.

Although it was founded in 1884, the Press Club lacked its own home until completion of this cozy clubhouse, discreetly described by the late cowboy columnist Red Fenwick of *The Denver Post:* "Back in a lustier but unlamented era of journalism, the Press Club was a friendly island of threadbare public rectitude."

The Union Pacific Freight Depot at 19th and Wynkoop Streets was reincarnated in 1994 as the popular Denver Chophouse & Brewery. Photo by Tom Noel.

Duffy's Shamrock Restaurant & Bar
1635 Court Pl., (303) 534-4935

If you're ever lost in downtown Denver, duck into Duffy's, which is open every hour that it legally can be. The placemats provide a fine map of downtown, complete with arrows showing the one-way streets that befuddle visitors.

Above all, this is Denver's Irish bar and the birthplace of the city's modern St. Patrick's Day parade. Celebrations were first organized in 1885 by Father Joseph P. Carrigan of St. Patrick's Church. These galas, which included costumes and bagpipers, song and dance, ended not in a bar but at St. Patrick's Church with a High Mass and sermons on topics such as "Ireland's Loyalty to Patrick's Faith."

St. Patrick's Day festivities went out of style during the 1920s, when the anti-Catholic, anti-immigrant Ku Klux Klan stepped on any such displays of "un-American" behavior. Not until March 17, 1962, did Bernard Duffy and the "Evil Companions Club" (a hard-drinking group that included many journalists) meet at Duffy's to revive this religious observance. Duffy talked the Adolph Coors company into greening its beer for his bar. After several rounds of the green sudsy inspiration, the Evil Companions paraded out of Duffy's Shamrock, around the block, and back into the bar.

No one lost the way.

Bernard Duffy opened Duffy's Tavern on January 1, 1950, in what had been the Brass

Duffy's Shamrock Restaurant & Bar has comforted Denverites since 1950. Tom Noel Collection.

Rail Restaurant at 1515 Champa Street, a few doors down from the old Denver Post building. This strategic location guaranteed a steady flow of customers at all hours and plenty of publicity. Man-in-the-street reporters often settled for barstool interviews at Duffy's.

In 1956, Duffy's moved into a storefront of the Colorado Hotel at 1635 Tremont Place. There, journalists found themselves joined by businesspeople, doctors, lawyers, and other uptown types. Duffy's next move came in 1974, to its current home, 1635 Court

Place. Bernard Duffy reconfigured the Court Place Hotel to look like his Tremont barroom with a 72-foot-long bar—Denver's longest—and thirty-four barstools. Because the same type of interior decor was used in a similar midblock location, some customers did not realize that Duffy's had ever moved.

Duffy sold his downtown bar to Joseph T. Lombardi in 1963. Lombardi appreciated its name, traditions, and lively business. Joe's sons, Joseph Francis "Frank" and Kenneth "Kenny," maintain Duffy's name and traditions to this day.

"Dad bought Duffy's for $245,000," Frank Lombardi told me in 1997. "Who would guess that Republic Plaza would offer us $3.5 million? But they were contemptuous, treated us like we weren't worth dealing with. Besides, we like this bar and our customers." The Lombardis became national heroes when *The Wall Street Journal* headlined the story in 1984. "We're kind of an eyesore for them," Kenny Lombardi told the *Journal,* "but we're happy where we are. Why should we leave?"

After making two earlier moves to accommodate downtown developers, Duffy's said no to developers of the fifty-six-story Republic Plaza, the coldest and tallest of down-town's skyscrapers. That colossal, granite-clad shaft now shares the block with Duffy's dignified, two-story brick building with its fancy cornice.

Duffy's is something of a miracle, a thriving vestige of the past. Some say St. Patrick spared this bar. Others wonder. Public tipsiness, mob scenes, and battalions of policemen with their paddy wagon made Duffy's on and around March 17 one of Colorado's great wonders. Celebrants sometimes stood in lines two blocks long waiting their turn to get in. Cops patrolled the lineup but usually looked the other way when someone passed a bottle to fight the chill. Duffy's let one person in for each person they let out.

"It was crazy inside," recalled Kenny. "We took out booths to make more room but it was jammed. In 1974, do you remember when streaking was popular?" Yes, I was there on that St. Patrick's Day, wearing one of the dogtags Duffy's used to provide: "I'm out for the night at the Best Irish Place in Denver .... If I get drunk, tie this tag to my buttonhole and send me home to_____" I filled in my address and tied one on right away.

Kenny continued: "That year, Duffy's was struck by two streaking young men. The two somehow undressed in the men's room, rolled up their clothes, slung them over their shoulders, and proceeded leisurely toward the front door. Unbelievably, they passed most of the way unnoticed by the crowd. When they were finally spied, cheers and applause broke out. They sprinted past the

Souls of poets dead and gone.
What Elysian have ye known,
Happy fields or mossy cavern
Choicer than the Mermaid Tavern?

—John Keats

CHRISTOPHER COLUMBUS HALL,

A CHOICE LINE OF

Wines, Liquors and Cigars,

ALSO DEALER IN

Imported Maccaroni, Cheese and Olive Oils.

2219 Larimer Street,

DENVER, - - COLORADO.

I drink at Christopher Columbus Hall.
SIRO MANGINI, Prop.
I don't, but will.

An advertisement for Siro Mangini's Columbus Hall strongly implies that patrons are more "prosperous" than noncustomers. Tom Noel Collection.

policemen at the front door. Outside, they ran into a wall. As luck would have it, just at that moment a police car happened by and picked them up."

Duffy's caters to both the white- and blue-collar crowds, and offers an appetizer menu until 1:20 A.M. The long "Stag Table" is for single men and, since 1993, single women, who find this a club of sorts tended by high-spirited waitresses who treat them like lords and ladies.

El Bronco Bar
2219 Larimer St., CLOSED

On upper Larimer, where they still call it "Larm-er" Street, a saloon rests between Charlie's Second Hand Store and the Burlington Hotel. Only the delicately arched sec-

ond-story windows and fancy metal cornice suggest the once-elegant building buried under boards and beer ads. The front-door transom—now covered by plywood—may still carry the sign "Christopher Columbus Hall." Siro Mangini gave his saloon that name in the 1870s, thinking that Columbus was one Italian whom Americans knew and respected. Mangini knew that many Coloradans had little love for the first Italians who came to the state in the 1880s as cheap mine and railroad labor.

"The hardest labor is reserved for the Italian laborer," wrote one nun working with Denver's poor. "There are few who regard him with a sympathetic eye, who care for him or remember that he has a heart and a soul; they merely look upon him as an ingenious machine." That nun, Mother Frances Cabrini, founded Denver's Queen of Heaven Orphanage, directed Mount Carmel School, and became the first U.S. citizen to be canonized as a saint. She was right about her countrymen. Italian immigrants did much of the hard work in Colorado, as the Chinese did in California, the Irish did in the Northeast, and African Americans did in the South. They lived in tents and hovels down in "The Bottoms," as Denverites called the trashy South Platte Valley floodplain. For these poor newcomers Mangini established the first Italian tavern. There his countrymen could find pasta and Chianti, as well as a place to socialize, organize, and look for better jobs and a better life. Hoping to build up goodwill for his people, Mangini hosted lavish spaghetti dinners. He invited the cops on the Larimer Street beat, the councilman, and the neighboring Jewish, German, and Irish shopkeepers.

"Papa had lots of friends and they all came for those dinners," his daughter, Mrs. Adelina Mangini Joy, told me in 1977. She was the last of ten children born and raised over the saloon. "Everybody came. Oh, so many to cook for and it went on all day!"

In the 1880s, Denver's Italian immigrants found a haven in Siro Mangini's Columbus Hall. Tom Noel Collection.

After the feast, Italians found themselves more welcome on Larimer Street. Mangini, who had fought with Garibaldi's Red Shirts to unify Italy before coming to the United States, continued to work for Italian solidarity in his new country. After his death in 1907, however, Columbus Hall passed into other hands. A succession of taverns, restaurants, cafés, and the Acme Sheet Metal Company occupied the building until the 1960s, when Pete Bonney Sr. opened El Bronco Bar. The Bonneys were from Mora, New Mexico, and brought many New Mexican customers to the bar.

Pete Bonney Jr. lived upstairs and ran the bar below, as his father did, as a family bar: "We have baptism parties for Sacred Heart [Denver's oldest operating church] at 28th and Larimer. We provide free Thanksgiving and Christmas dinners and we take up collections to send flowers to sick or bereaved customers. This is a bar where just about everybody knows each other. We don't have many strangers come in."

Spanish songs, talk, and laughter invitingly drifted out of El Bronco's front door. On one drizzly evening in 1978, I found welcoming plastic flowers in an old mayonnaise jar at the doorway and went in. Neatly dressed women and children sat talking and playing in the front booth. One small girl skipped over to a cowboy-hatted geezer at the bar and tugged on his overalls. He bought her a bag of popcorn and 35-cent beers for the tableful of women. Laughing, the girl ran to the front door and tossed handfuls of popcorn into the Larimer Street darkness.

Para los pichones y los pobres, she yelled back to her mother. Beside her on the windowsill, St. Martin was cutting his cloak in half to share with a naked beggar in a Mexican holy picture.

The earth is grown puny and pallid,
The earth is grown gouty and grey,
For whiskey no longer is valid
And wine has been voted away.
As for beer, we no longer will swill it
In riotous rollicking spree:
The little hot dogs on the skillet
Will have to be swallowed with tea.
                                    —Christopher Morley

Father Phillips, the phony priest who has been working downtown for decades, came in next. He is a clean-cut, quirky fellow with a Roman collar. After repeatedly busting him, the cops decided to let him do his thing so long as he wears a beggar's photo I.D. around his neck. Even he was rewarded here in the poorest and most generous part of town.

A dapper old man wearing a fine white Stetson hat shot a scholarly game of pool with young Chicanos, while an antique lover in a nearby booth told his señorita, "I'm definitely going back. You come with me? I'll take good care of you." A tremendous Indian in a sleeveless cotton dress chased after her young ones. Fragments of soft Spanish floated about. I heard one happy ending in English: "... and this went on for three years, and then one day the cockroach was gone."

Beneath mounted cattle horns, the mustachioed bartender patrolled the mahogany, stopping to swat a sleeping patron with a newspaper. The dozer flinched, ordered another *cerveza,* and slid back to sleep. The barkeep fed the cash register, which had its own guardian angel, a kneeling nude statue clutching her bosom. She and other angels kept this bar open a long time.

The 1873 Denver *City Directory* lists Siro Mangini, fruit peddler, at this address, but does not list his saloon here until 1882. Denver Water Department records show that a saloon water tap was issued in 1881. The 1887 *Robinson Real Estate Atlas for Denver* shows the two-story brick tavern here.

Time has brought changes. The second-story balcony for the Mangini apartments is gone, along with other Italianate-style façade gingerbread. Inside, Pete Bonney used a flashlight to show me the old tin ceiling through a missing panel of the lowered acoustic-tile ceiling. Brass doorknobs still dangled from the closetlike bathrooms with a single coed washbasin between them.

Hispanic patrons found this antique saloon a welcome refuge from the sometimes cruel city that has grown up around 2219 Larimer Street. El Bronco lasted until 1995, when repeated drug busts and fights led Bonney to close its doors.

El Chapultepec
1962 Market St. & 20th St., (303) 295-9126

After Prohibition was repealed in 1933, this bar opened on July 4 to celebrate. Since the 1970s, it has been Denver's great jazz joint, serving bebop, burritos, and beer. Jerry Krantz started working here in 1958 as a bartender for his father-in-law, Charlie Romano, who had started out tending bar for his father, Tony Romano.

After Krantz took over, he renamed it "El Chapultepec" and brought in the jazz. He made it the hottest spot in LoDo before the Lower Downtown Historic District was created in 1989, before Coors Field and the Rockies arrived in 1995, and

El Chapultepec has been Denver's coolest jazz joint since the 1970s.

before some fifty liquor licenses made this the wettest neighborhood in Colorado. Krantz can still be found at the corner front door, which is nearly always open. Nowadays, he's usually shaking his head. Yuppies. Sports fans. Microbrew buffs.

"Ya got any microbrews?"

"Any what?" Krantz says with a shake of the head. "Look, we got places down here now that make their beers right there where you can see 'em. We got places that get their beer from as far away as possible. Most of mine just comes from Golden or Fort Collins."

After all the slick new places opened around him, Krantz was told to shape up, to at least get decent rest rooms. He still has tiny closet toilets and a communal urinal in the men's room. Krantz said, pouring a Coors, "Changing 'em would ruin the atmosphere." El Chapultepec has a loose, lively atmosphere that other places are striving for with their studied, million-dollar interior designs.

El Chapultepec's decor consists of old auto upholstery and a broken lighted mural of El Chapultepec Park in Mexico City. You have to get down on your hands and knees and crawl between the barstools to see this amazing 30-by-4-foot photograph on the front bar.

This is a tiny, unrehabilitated joint with no cover charge and no reservations, whose crowds, jazz, and mystical vibes often spill out into the sidewalk.

Although many legendary jazzmen have played here, the longtime favorite is Freddie Rodriguez. Born just a few blocks away, Rodriguez plays "brown jazz," a spiced-up music that reminds people that jazz lovers in Colorado are as often brown as black and white.

Gaetano's Restaurant & Pizzeria
3760 Tejon St.
(se corner of W. 38th Ave.),
(303) 433-3172

The Smaldone clan still operates this legendary North Denver relic of mobster days. Flip Flop, Checkers, Fat Paulie, and Chauncey are gone now, but the stories linger of the shotgun blasts, bulletproof Cadillacs, the Leavenworth pen, and the era when the Smaldones ran bootlegging and gaming in this town. Gone are the days of car bombings in the parking lot, extortion, bookmaking, loansharking, machine guns in violin cases, and

The Smaldone clan still owns and operates Gaetano's, on Tejon Street, a legendary North Denver tavern and pizzeria that would probably still honor this beer token. Tom Noel Collection.

silencers hidden in desk drawers.

Gaetano's has not survived just on memories, however. Old-fashioned Italian dishes smothered with rich red sauces, the deep-dish "Terrorizer" pizza, and the nostalgic decor are perennial draws. Don't miss the downstairs bar with its bottle collection. Thanks to personal experience, I've learned to avoid playing dollar-bill poker with the bartenders or asking too many questions. During the course of a long, leisurely, Chianti-soaked dinner here, the ghosts will probably reappear without anyone asking.

Gaetono's is also a shrine to the late Frank Sinatra, who monopolizes the jukebox and the wall decor, along with Italian flags, classical nudes, and reminders of the Roman Empire. Like the empire, the tavern, founded in 1947, is lingering long after the demise of its founding heros.

If I ever met a girl with kisses like wine, I'd marry her on the spot.

—W. C. Fields

La Coupole Cafe
2191 Arapahoe St. (corner of 22nd St.), (303) 297-2288

One of Denver's finest French cafés and nightclubs was a different place when I first visited it in 1973. The Club 21 Bar & Grill, as it was then called, was landscaped with winos, broken bottles, and "No Loitering" signs. Black, brown, and white customers loitered inside, trying to scrape up funding for the Club 21 specials: a 70-cent shot and beer and $1.35 plate lunches. The place was so poor it didn't even have a television. Spanish jukebox tunes competed with the pinball machines and pool table.

Today, fashionably dressed people jam this place for exquisite French food and cool late-evening jazz in the basement. Brothers Philippe and Pierre Muraz transformed the old Club 21 into a place where people come to see and be seen. Not only the first floor but also the entire three-story Hamburger Block, rechristened the Paris Hotel, shine as they did on opening day in 1891. Lofts, studios, and apartments occupy the upstairs of this landmark, with its handsome arched windows and cast-iron storefront. Inside, instead of stale beer, the aromas are from delectable cheeses, chocolates, wines, and French delicacies galore.

Micky Manor
2544 Federal Blvd., (303) 458-0043

One of Denver's roughest bars has learned manners, thanks to a North High School wrestler and ex-Marine. Ron Bay, who still looks like a toughie in his sixties, bought the tavern in 1986. He grew up in North Denver, where the Micky Manor opened in the 1930s. It was a respectable restaurant and bar run by Mike Philaposo, who later changed his name to Phillips and had his wife, Madelyn, run the bar. By the 1980s, as Bay put it emphatically, "this place had become a damn toilet, a trash can."

When I first visited the Micky Manor in 1973, its primary merit was 25-cent beers, but the sullen clientele, who were belligerent and well armed, gave the cheap beer a bad taste. In 1985 I sat at the bar as a cockroach scurried across the pink Formica counter and into an overflowing ashtray. Another bar bug looked bold enough to use a straw to pole-vault into my beer glass. That night, someone pushed another customer and his chair over. Nobody did anything, as if this were a common occurrence. A sign behind the bar read "This Property is Protected by a double barrel shotgun 3 nights a week. You guess which 3." The sign didn't do much good. One night, someone even knocked the framed photo of Dominic Coloroso and Vice President Hubert Humphrey off the wall.

Today, this venerable 1897 building, supposedly built as a horse stable for the fire station across the street, is stuccoed and painted a cheerful yellow. The rounded front windows form Art Deco chrome frames for the pink neon mice wearing aprons and serving drinks labeled "Micky" and "Minnie." Although Micky's name was misspelled to appease Walt Disney, Bay said that Disney forced him to take the rodent off his card and logo. Some Denver lawyers, he added, make a fast buck by reporting even the slightest possible trademark infringement to giant corporations like Walt Disney, Inc.

"Sorry, we're open," said the sign on the front door, but Bay heartily welcomed most visitors, and he loved to tell one and all how he brought manners to the Manor. "I kept telling troublemakers, politely, 'No more fighting. No more peeing on the bathroom floors.' I fined customers a quarter every time they used the 'F' word." "If you want to use foul language," said a sign Bay posted, "go to the park and talk to the ducks." "I kicked out over fifty people, a third of them ladies. And I put up another sign, 'The first punch you throw in here will be the last.'" In the bathroom, Bay installed another sign, "Welcome to the MEN who can hit the target."

When men drink, then they are rich and successful and win lawsuits and are happy and help their friends. Quickly, bring me a beaker of wine, so that I may wet my mind and say something clever.

—Aristophanes

The pool table in the back of the bar caused much of the trouble. Bay put a life-size Santa Claus dummy in a chair to guard the pool table and promote goodwill. He also installed year-round Christmas lights and tinsel. By the front door he hung a huge American flag and a Marine Corps flag. Bay, who served in the Korean War and still looked like a Marine, whipped his customers into shape. Then he bought the business in 1986.

Sergeant Bay transformed one of the scuzziest bars in town to one that consistently earned "100" ratings from city health inspectors. Inspector John Cohen couldn't recall another bar ever making such a comeback. But neither health department nor police department scores were the Micky Manor's main claim to fame. It was the Rockyburgers and Rockydogs that Bay resurrected. He said he acquired the secret formula for the sauce that made now-defunct Rockybilt Colorado's most famous hamburger chain. The first Rockybilt opened in 1936 with 5-cent hamburgers flavored with gobs of onions and fabulous sauce. The last of twenty-two Rockybilts closed at Federal and Speer in 1980. Bay specialized in $1.39 Rockyburgers and Rockydogs, but he also sold other sandwiches, Mexican food, and even a flan for dessert. The food and drinks were inexpensive, tasty, and served quickly in a friendly atmosphere, where trouble seemed to be in the past tense.

Jerri Sanchez and her husband, Richard, bought the Manor in 1996 from an exhausted

Bay. The Sanchezes have kept the Rockyburgers and the behavioral standards while spicing up the place with steak tacos, fiery green chili, and free menudo on Sunday morning.

Mori Sushi Bar & Tokyo Cuisine
2019 Market St., (303) 298-1864

For decades following World War II, intense prejudice against the Japanese led this place to call itself the Cathay (i.e., Chinese) Dining Room. Although they began serving Japanese food in 1948, it was not until the 1990s that Mori's finally came out of the closet. Mori's offers superb Japanese cuisine. The nineteen-page menu is the cleverest in town: The selections are the names of stops on the Tokyo transit system, so customers get a tour of Japan's largest city along with all possible combinations of sushi, starters, entrées, and fried ice cream desserts.

Besides Mori Sushi Bar & Tokyo Cuisine, the first floor has a classic dark, smoky bar behind a large, red-lacquer gateway inscribed, "It's Your Responsibility to Cut Yourself Off Before We Do." Hideki Mori has transformed this dim refuge for persecuted Japanese Americans into one of the best and brightest of Denver's ethnic inns.

Mori's is on the first floor of a brothel that in the 1950s became Nisei (first-generation Japanese) Post 158 of the American Legion. Many of these Japanese Americans served in the 442nd Regiment, which had more casualties and decorations than nearly all other

U.S. units fighting in World War II. In the upstairs hall where the veterans meet, framed photos of aging Japanese-American veterans in decorated military uniforms adorn the tiny rooms where whores once plied their trade. Both the 2015 and 2019 Market buildings were erected around 1887. Mrs. Leah J. Woods, the alias of Madam Jennie Rogers, moved into 2015 with her girls in 1887. In the 1892 "Red Book" guide to Denver brothels, Madam Jennie B. Holmes advertised that 2015 Market had "23 rooms, 3 parlours, 2 ball rooms, pool room, 15 boarders, choice wines, everything correct."

After the Market Street red light district was shut down by reformers in 1912, 2015 Market became a Chinese store run by Quong Lee. No trace of the store or the laughing ladies of easy virtue is left at 2015–2019 Market, although the Mattie Silks brothel, next door at 2009 Market, is a designated landmark. Now 2015 and 2019 are united by corrugated metal paneling, a new mansard roof, and new windows and doors that hide their naughty antiquity.

My Brother's Bar
2376 15th St. (corner of Platte St.), (303) 455-9991

This is Denver's oldest saloon still serving booze on the original site. It was opened by M. A. Capelli in 1873 as the Highland House, a block from today's Confluence Park.

I found R. G. Dun credit reports on "M.A. Capelli" at the Baker Graduate Business School at Harvard University in their Dun & Bradstreet collection. Dun's confidential reports, intended for eastern creditors, bankers, and suppliers, first cryptically assessed M. A. Capelli on September 5, 1873: "Commenced with nothing, now worth $3,000, doing fair business, pays prompt." A year later, the Dun agent reported that "M.A. Capelli is a woman, wife of Angelo Capelli who failed in St. Louis before coming here … worth $5,000–$6,000 clear … owns property called 'The Highland House.' " Next to this

---

When the hoary Sage replied,
"Come, my lad, and drink some beer."
—Samuel Johnson

---

saloon and boardinghouse, Maria Anna and Angelo Capelli had a butcher shop, restaurant, and fruit business, forerunners of other Italian meat markets, restaurants, and produce companies that thrive to this day in Denver.

The Colorado History Museum has an 1870s photo of the Highland House as one of the few buildings in then mostly undeveloped North Denver. As the first Italians to reach Denver, the Capellis fed and housed their compatriots—mostly poor immigrants. At the Highland House, Italian day laborers, railroad workers, and miners were welcomed with pasta, vino, and songs of the old country. According to the *Rocky Mountain News* for June 7, 1874, "The anniversary of the independence of Italy, which occurs today, is to be celebrated by our Italian fellow-citizens in style. Mr. Capelli of the Highland House always takes the lead in these patriotic demonstrations and today his premises will be gorgeous with the flags of all nations. There will be a banquet this evening. Everybody is invited."

By wining and dining German merchants, Irish cops, and American politicians, the Capellis strove to build up goodwill for the struggling Italian community first concentrated in the Denver's South Platte River bottoms. In 1880, Angelo was appointed Italian consul to assist the growing number of Italians streaming into Colorado. When Colorado became the first state to proclaim October 12 as Columbus Day, the Capellis held a grand gala. Angelo and his three brothers and their collective families operated the Highland House until about 1907, when it became the property of the Schlitz Brewing Company.

In subsequent years, the two-story, red brick building successively became Paul's

Paul's Place, as the ancient bar at 15th and Platte Street was called from 1929 to 1951, has become My Brother's Bar, owned by Jim and Angelo Karagas. The brothers made it famous for neoclassical hamburgers and classical music. Tom Noel Collection.

Place, Whitie's Restaurant, and the Platte Bar. Jim and Angelo Karagas bought it in 1970. They renamed it My Brother's Bar and made it the legendary tavern it is today, noted for its lack of television, its exquisite hamburgers, a wide variety of tap beers, and a vast selection of classical music.

Jim Karagas explained: "Our first bartenders—Charley Sampson and Jake Williams—also worked for KVOD, the classical music station. Whenever I wasn't looking, they turned the radio to KVOD. I'd say, 'What are you trying to do, put us out of business?' Then one day, Jake says, 'Look,' and he points to a railroader and a truck driver. They were listening to the music."

For neoclassical repasts, classical music, a beer garden, and the antique ambience of Denver's oldest bar, try My Brother's Bar. There, with the ghosts of the Capellis, you can still celebrate Colorado's rich and spicy Italian heritage.

Nallen's Irish Pub
1429 Market St., (303) 572-0667

Colorado's finest Irish pub is the work of John Nallen. "I left Ireland on holiday and couldn't afford to go back. I opened Nallen's on California Street in 1992, moved down here in 1995. Now we're between two popular restaurants with take-out, so we can concentrate on wet goods." Handsome John Nallen holds court at the front table of his long, skinny bar. There I found him with the honorable Dennis Gallagher, Denver city councilman and Regis University professor.

I intend to die in a tavern; let the wine be placed near my dying mouth, so that when the choirs of dying angels come, they may say, "God be merciful to this drinker."
—Walter Map

"John," Gallagher confided, "is a Gaelic-speaking entrepreneur from a tiny town in County Mayo. He's a fine fellow, but not perfect—he joined the Republican Party! Maybe he confused 'em with the IRA."

Nallen's is a haven for Irish people, who hold most of the jobs here and do much of the storytelling and singing. A sign outside reads "Parking for Irish only. All others will be towed." Kelly green walls are smothered in Irish farm implements, Irish travel posters, a large map of Ireland, a clock giving the time in Dublin, and a leprechaun's buckle shoe. Behind an old-time 25-foot-wide glass storefront, the floor is hardwood, the foot rail brass, and the tables a stout 2 inches thick.

John Nallen is wary o' the green, even on St. Patrick's Day. "Never heard of green beer in Ireland," he said in a rich brogue. "And never heard of corned beef and cabbage in all my life. We serve Guinness, not green dishwater. Indeed, we're the biggest seller of Guinness in Colorado." John sticks to the thick black stout. "Beware whiskey," he added. "God made whiskey to keep the Irish from ruling the world."

Patsy's Inn
3651 Navajo St., (303) 477-8910

Since its 1927 origin as a speakeasy restaurant, Patsy's has been a liquid landmark of North Denver. Owner "Chubby" Aiello, whom you could always find behind the bar next to his prized liquor cabinets, knew Little Italy upside down: "North Denver has always been Denver's melting pot," he recalled with a sage grin. "Even on this corner there were four different businessmen: a Jew, a German, an Irishman, and us. Now the Mexicans are moving in. Some Italians don't like it, but they don't remember that this neighborhood wasn't always Little Italy. When we Italians began moving in, the Irish didn't want us any more than the English and Scots had liked the railroad Irish moving in during the 1880s.

"I saw what happened to the Germans during the First World War. When the Second War came with Mussolini and all that, I changed our name from the Italian Inn to Patsy's. Patsy was my kid brother." Although Chubby is retired, Patsy's sails on, looking much as it always has: classical statues, plastic grapevines, red plastic tablecloths, red plastic roses, and red swag drapes. The food and

Beginning in the 1920s speakeasy age, many women learned to drink and smoke as a rite of passage. When bars became legal again, they joined men at the bar to celebrate the return of "Happy Days," as in this 1943 view at Patsy's Inn in North Denver. Tom Noel Collection.

drink are also generally red and served in inexpensive, generous portions. Dean Martin and Frank Sinatra still monopolize the jukebox and wall murals still take one back to Italy, with copies of Michelangelo's creation scene on the dome of the Sistine Chapel, the Leaning Tower of Pisa, Ponte Vecchio in Florence, and the Grand Canal in Venice.

Pint's Pub
221 W. 13th Ave., (303) 534-7543

The royal red British phone box and Union Jack outside make Pint's Pub easy to find. Inside you can savor ales, bitters, and stouts galore; fish and chips and other pub fare; as well as copies of the *London Times* and *London Telegraph*. An old Mission-style apartment house has been converted to a cozy home away from Mother England for Anglophiles. It has a fireplace, hardwood furnishings, photos of English pubs, painted English scenes, and dartboards galore. Specialty beers include standbys (Guinness, Newcastle, Watney's) and some exotics such as Felinfoel, a Welsh ale. Pint's brews its own beers as well as serving British imports. From an astonishing array of alphabetically arranged bottles atop the backbar, Pint's pours more than 150 single-malt scotches.

Owners Scott Diamond and Lance Nonding reward regulars by giving them Imperial Pint glasses (20 ounces) reserved behind the bar. The music is British, be it popular or traditional. And late at night, when the crew is deep into their cups, they have been known to sing "God Save the Queen."

Chubby Aiello checks his liquor supply at Patsy's Inn, as he renamed his Italian Village Inn, a pasta palace, to duck anti-Italian prejudice during World War II. Photo by Roger Whitacre.

Punch Bowl Tavern
2052 Stout St., (303) 295-7974

"Chief Sundown painted these during the Great Depression," saloonkeeper Carl Greer told me in 1972, pointing to the dark, romantic, mountain landscapes on the high, wooden-back booths. "He used a 4-inch brush, painting a whole spruce tree with one slash. He painted for drinks, and the more he drank, the better he painted."

The snowy cross on the Mount of the Holy Cross is wobbly and Pikes Peak looks shaky, but most of the murals are sharp enough to be recognizable Colorado scenes.

Decades of dirt and booze have formed a varnish on these venerable and little-known public art treasures. Chief Sundown's work is reminiscent of the dramatic storm-and-sunlight mountainscapes of Albert Bierstadt. But while Bierstadt's work hangs in Washington's National Gallery of Art, the Denver Art Museum, and the Denver Public Library, the work of Chief Sundown (a.k.a. Noel Adams) has been a backrest for customers of the Punch Bowl.

Of Denver's five hundred taverns, the Punch Bowl is one of the oldest—and looks it. Unlike new franchise taverns built to look old, the Punch Bowl is an old tavern that long ago gave up trying to look new. It is located in an 1885 cottage—from the front sidewalk you can see the old roof and gutter behind the storefront addition tacked on around 1900. This tiny, 18-foot-wide barroom would inspire claustrophobia if it weren't for the 12-foot-high ceiling.

Inside, the cherry backbar has unusual, illuminated, colored-glass corners and a border of naked electric lightbulbs. They date to the early days of electric lighting, when no

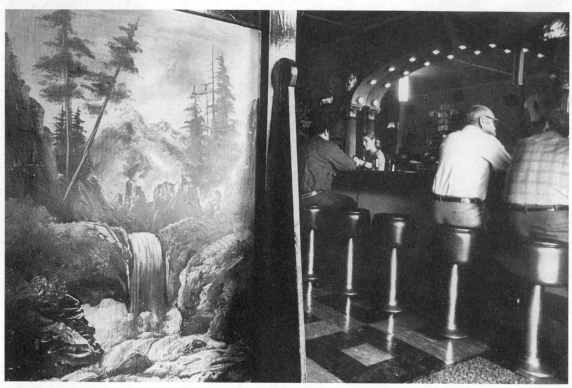

Noel "Chief Sundown" Adams painted murals in and on various Denver saloons. Supposedly he worked for shots and beers, explaining, "The more I drink, the better I paint." Most of those saloons have evaporated, but his colorful Colorado mountain scenes survive on the booths in Denver's Punch Bowl Tavern. Photo by Kenn Bisio, courtesy The Denver Post.

one wanted to hide the magical new invention under a lampshade. Old-fashioned, string-pull lights hang from the pressed-metal ceiling. In the rear, where the living quarters of the old house were once located, are an antique wooden phone booth and a huge wooden walk-in icebox. To slip into the Punch Bowl's high-backed, private booths is to return to a nineteenth-century saloon.

Back in the 1970s, when I wrote about the Punch Bowl for the *Rocky Mountain News,* it was owned by Carl Greer. He seemed as old as the bar, serving shots and beers in slow motion. The Punch Bowl, he explained, was named for boxers and their fans who once patronized the bar. Many of Carl's customers moved with the help of canes, walkers, and wheelchairs. The Punch Bowl offered cheap beers for elderly indigent downtowners. For many of them, dim bars such as this were the day's bright spot. "Friday" Murphy dressed up in a top hat and his best cane for his visits to the Punch Bowl. At the far end of the bar, another regular was usually asleep, chin to chest, in his wheelchair.

On one of the round, red, vinyl-and-chrome barstools sat an old man with yellow hair holding a white puppy. Everyone in the crowded bar seemed to know the old man and dote on the puppy. Fritz ordered his regular red (tomato juice) beer and the puppy, Skip, got his usual "white port" (water) in a Coors ashtray. Fritz told me that he dined at the Punch Bowl every night. "If the bar doesn't see me by six, someone will telephone my apartment to see if I'm sick. If I don't answer the phone, someone'll walk over the way I always come to see if anything has happened to me. And things do happen to us old-timers on the street alone at night here in Five Points."

"I come here to cash my Social Security check," another regular told me. "Carl has known me for years and will always cash a check for me. When I was down he loaned me $500—no questions asked and no interest, either. Know of any bank that will do that for you? Of course, I spend a lot of money here, but the beer is cheap and so's the food."

Jimmy Spinelli and Paul Kakavis, two Denver natives, bought the Bowl in 1975. "We inherited eight regular customers," Spinelli said with his trademark grin. "Among them, two were capable of walking to the men's room unaided, three could get shot glasses to their lips without spilling, and two were usually asleep on the bar."

Jimmy and Paul introduced terrific burgers and lavish onion rings. Benny Roy Lisenby bought the Bowl in 1980 and added Cajun food from his native Vidor, Texas, on the Louisiana line. Benny married Shirley,

the most beautiful waitress of all. Together they have run the bar happily ever after.

This onetime geriatric bar now attracts downtown office workers, slinky secretaries, studly judges, lawyers, and FBI agents from the nearby Federal Building. The Punch Bowl became the place to celebrate federal court victories or cry over losses. FBI agents who drop in here have been known to break up fights, arrest a fellow trying to sell a gun, and try to arrest beautiful women.

Benny has left the walls with much of their original decor— pink-cheeked Coca-Cola nymphs, a Brooklyn Dodgers pennant, old-fashioned Art Deco nudes, old Denver theater programs, and visual art that makes the Punch Bowl an art museum to this day, as well as downtown Denver's least-altered old-time saloon.

Rocky Mountain Diner
900 18th St. (corner of Stout St.), (303) 293-8383

This Old West–style diner occupies one of Denver's finest, oldest, and ghostliest structures: the 1889 Ghost Block, named for its developer, Allen M. Ghost. Originally located at 15th Street and Glenarm Place, it evolved from a fashionable office building into a flophouse—the Graystone Hotel—with first-floor tenants such as a secondhand magazine shop and a corner greasy spoon serving coffee and chili. A monstrous old shoe stuck out of the façade with a neon plea for Lord's Shoe Repair.

The Ghost Block almost became a ghost. It nearly vanished forever after Public Service Company next door bought it in 1979 to demolish it for a parking lot. Preservationists placed it on the National Register, but doom seemed imminent until architect Brian T. Congleton persuaded the giant utility to let him salvage the Ghost Block in 1979. Congleton carefully disassembled the building, numbered each of the stones, and put them in a warehouse. There the building slept for a decade before its reincarnation as the Rocky Mountain Diner in 1990.

An antler chandelier at the entrance lights one corner of the bar, which has an antique Wurlitzer rockabilly jukebox. David Parker's saucy western art on the walls in bright colors resembles the Sunday comics. A buffalo head and western movie posters add to the decor. Two rows of tongue-and-groove-paneled and upholstered booths rise from the plank floor. The glass storefront offers inviting views of the old main post office across 18th Street, a white marble Greek temple guarded by sculptor Gladys Caldwell Fisher's bighorn sheep.

The diner's home-style buffalo meatloaf, Yankee pot roast, hot turkey sandwich, chicken-fried steak, and many other items come in cheap, tasty, generous portions with cornbread. Ever since its opening, this place has been lively seven days a week with no ghosts reported. At night it becomes a great bar specializing in Cactus Juice cocktails.

Ship Tavern/Brown Palace Hotel
321 17th St. & Broadway,
(303) 297-3111

Landlocked Denver has one port that draws the thirsty and curious. Where else

The Ship Tavern, Denver's most splendiferous saloon, started out as the original 1892 café of the Brown Palace Hotel. 1900 photo by C. M. Graves, Tom Noel Collection.

in the Rockies can you find a crow's nest with rigging? Ships in bottles line the walls. Solid chestnut paneling, a Honduran mahogany bar, brass and rope trim, and nautical artifacts adorn this Yankee clipper grounded in Denver's grand old hotel, the Brown Palace.

To celebrate Repeal, the Ship Tavern was installed in 1938 by Claude Boettcher, whose father bought the 1892 hotel built by Henry C. Brown. Claude wanted a place to drink and to display his nautical artifacts. In this museum saloon, don't miss the 1830s Staffordshire Jamaican Rum barrels on the backbar and Montague Dawson's painting, *Picking Up the Pilot—The Cutty Sark*. The priceless ship models portray the history of sailing from the 1600s to 1900s. In addition to the clipper ships, note the yacht *America* and the Spanish galleon.

For decades the Ship Tavern was the stuffiest tavern in town. To enter, men had to don a tie and coat, which the solicitous bartenders could provide. Single women were excluded until Denver journalist and novelist Sandra Dallas staged a one-woman

protest in 1974. "Why do you have guys in drag in here, and male prostitutes," she fumed, "but not real women?" Sandra won the day. Nowadays, any and all are welcome to this fantasy bar in a prowlike corner of the Brown Palace.

Ship Tavern Ale is a sweet brown elixir that should cure anything ailing you. Other favorites are the Brown's clam chowder, macaroons, and a high-class pizza. Of an evening someone usually finds the piano and songs drift toward sea chanties. Since 1995, Churchill's Cigar Bar also occupies the Brown Palace with a sumptuous lounge of easy chairs, sofas, and elegant company for puffing and sipping.

Even if fine cigars and bars aren't what you fancy, savor the hotel lobby with its nine-story, skylighted atrium. High tea with harp or piano music is a lobby tradition. Be sure to sample the water fountains—the Brown's naturally purified H_2O is drawn from two 850-foot artesian wells. Whatever your thirst, the Brown Palace and its storied Ship Tavern are most refreshing.

Soapy Smith's Eagle Bar
1111 14th St., (303) 534-1111

Jefferson Randolph Smith is a Coloradan to be celebrated. Outdoing both Texans and Californians, he earned the title "King of the Western Con Man." He gained the nickname "Soapy" for his soap sales on Larimer Street. Unpacking his carpetbag, Smith brought out a display of soap—not just ordinary soap, he assured the crowd that gathered. They

watched as he inserted dollar bills between the soap and its wrapper and began a pitch that went something like this:

Step right up, pards,
and flirt with lady luck.
When you raise your arm,
do you loose your charm?

You can't lose with soap.
Cleanliness is next to godliness,
And the feel of a crisp new greenback
is heaven itself.

This soap is made in my own factory
with my own special formula.
It will cure everything, even baldness,
and wash away the gray.
Enhance your manhood, charm the
ladies, amaze your grandchildren.
Wash away your troubles,
wash away your sins to-day.

Soapy never missed a scam, be it gambling or selling phony mining stock. Ultimately he graduated to the biggest scam of all: politics. After he was caught rigging Denver elections, Soapy was chased out of town. He wound up in Skagway, Alaska, where a public-minded citizen shot and killed him.

As its list of three hundred shots suggests, this spirited saloon perpetuates the hard-drinking, boisterous era of Soapy Smith, who supposedly died with booze on his breath and a smile on his lips. The building originally housed Dr. Byron A. Wheeler and his medical offices in the late 1870s. During the 1880s it became Euclid Hall, a meeting place used by Masons, Populists, Minute Men, the Colorado Women's Relief

It [drink] provokes the desire, but it takes away the performance.

—William Shakespeare, Macbeth

Corps, and, most memorably, the Cootie Club of World War I veterans.

In 1977, Euclid Hall became Soapy Smith's Eagle Bar. To furnish the antique building Soapy's owners installed a fantastic mahogany backbar from Leadville, a stained-glass rose window skylight from a Greeley church, and many other historical artifacts.

Soapy's is still unreformed, notorious for its strong shots, local bands, rambunctious crowds, and grand decor. Note the noose at the entry and the warning "Caveat Emptor." That was Soapy's motto, as he suspected most suckers didn't know Latin.

Dick Bacon, a former University of Kansas and Pittsburgh Steeler football star, has been a guiding light of Soapy's since its 1977 opening. "If you find a prettier bar in Colorado," he requests, "come in and tell us about it! We'd like to see it too!"

Triangle Lounge
2036 Broadway (corner of Stout St.),
(303) 293-9009

Some 150 gay bars have come and gone in Denver since the 1950s. Somehow, one of the raunchiest and most controversial has survived. Beware: This place is not for the squeamish. The patio and basement bar are also scenes of sex acts, according to affidavits made after a 1995 undercover police raid that led to the temporary closing of the Triangle in 1995. Undercover agents also testified that the Triangle television sets showed how-to pornography. Little wonder that this gay landmark keeps a low profile outside. Inside it is filled with macho decor: a cement floor with sawdust, raw plank wall paneling, and gay art.

Wazee Lounge & Supper Club
1600 15th St. (corner of Wazee St.),
(303) 623-9518

Of three dozen LoDo bars and restaurants, this was the first stylish reincarnation in what was Denver's Skid Road. Jim and Angelo Karagas of My Brother's Bar bought it in 1974.

They kept the old name but redid the interior in Art Deco style. The chandeliers were once Milwaukee streetlamps and the benches once graced the old downtown Elks Lodge.

The chairs are chrome on a classic black-and-white checkerboard tile floor framed by boxcar-wainscoted walls. A veneer of bleached mahogany burl enhances the unusual Art Deco–style backbar, which was salvaged from the American House bar at 16th and Blake Streets shortly before its demolition. The Karagases opened up a balcony section and rigged up a dumbwaiter, powered by a 1934 garage-door opener, to hoist pitchers of beer and thick pizzas up there. Another of the Wazee's mechanical wonders is its 1932 G.E. refrigerator.

The Wazee Lounge & Supper Club became one of the first and liveliest of LoDo's revived saloons in 1974.

Bubbly John Wright Hickenlooper, a literature major from Philadelphia, came west to open, with five partners, Colorado's first brewpub on October 18, 1988. Since then, more than 100 other Colorado brewpubs and microbreweries have appeared. Hickenlooper's Wynkoop Brewing Company claims to be the "largest brewpub in North America." 1989 photo by Thomas Arledge, Tom Noel Collection.

This friendly, funky place specializes in beer, pizza, wine, sandwiches, conversation, folk music, and art. The Karagases attracted artists and art lovers by using the high, bare brick walls to showcase a different artist each month.

The Karagases made it a trendy hot spot before selling it in 1998 to John Hickenlooper of the Wynkoop Brewing Company. John said he can think of only one improvement: bringing in Wynkoop beers. Otherwise he promises to keep things the same.

Wynkoop Brewing Company
18th and Wynkoop Sts., (303) 297-2700

Even before the ale and stout started to flow at our heavy wooden table, the thin, boyish entrepreneur poured out his story, on the Wynkoop's opening day. Like many pilgrims, Philadelphian John Wright Hickenlooper Jr. headed west to run away from failures: an aborted love affair and a collapsed renovation project. Armed with a B.A. in literature, he had written several short stories and a screenplay about Damon Runyon. Rejections buried his literary efforts.

Hickenlooper came west in search of black gold. He jumped into the oil industry just in time for the bust of the mid-1980s, when the price of crude oil sank from $40 to $9 a barrel. Hickenlooper and some other ex–oil sidekicks, Jerry and Martha Williams, used their severance pay to start Colorado's first brewpub. The partners raised $935,000 to buy John S. Brown's mercantile warehouse, a five-story stalwart at 18th and Wynkoop Streets.

"Brewpubs then were going gangbusters on the West Coast, and we thought they might catch on in Colorado," Hickenlooper told me. Colorado at that time still had an old law forbidding the manufacture and sale of alcohol on the same premises—a leftover from the Prohibition-era fear of brewery-owned saloons that pushed more and more consumption, regardless of the state of the clients. "Fortunately, Senator Dennis Gallagher, who represented northwest and downtown Denver, helped to change that law. We named one of our beers after him—it's witty and stout like the good senator."

Hickenlooper, who wears secondhand clothing, scrounged around to find discarded china from the Brown Palace Hotel, a walk-in cooler from an expired Safeway store, and cash registers, chairs, and other fixtures from failed restaurants and bars. He found a backbar from the old Tivoli Brewery that is

I,
Being dry,
Sit, idly sipping here
My beer.
—*George Arnold*

now the centerpiece of the Wynkoop's Mercantile Room. To qualify for tax credits, Hickenlooper and company obtained a National Register of Historic Places designation for their Wynkoop Street warehouse, a fine design by Aaron Gove and Thomas Walsh, who also worked on Union Station across the street and the Cathedral of the Immaculate Conception on Capitol Hill. A $575,000 restoration brought the sparkle back to this 72,000-square-foot warehouse, a post-and-beam structure rising from a quartzite base into pressed red brick walls trimmed in red sandstone and culminating in a fancy brick frieze and cornice.

The grand opening ocurred on October 18, 1988. Overnight, the Wynkoop Brewing Company became the hottest spot in town. As many as one thousand people a day flow through the casual, hardwood-floored, reborn warehouse with it shiny, stainless-steel beer vats. They wash down tasty, moderately priced pub food with a full spectrum of home brews.

"For the Wynkoop to prosper," Hickenlooper told me, "the surrounding Lower Downtown Historic District has to work. We donate a lot of time—and thousands of gallons of beer a year—to the community. To reintroduce housing, we converted the top three stories of our building to lofts, which sold out by the time they were completed in 1993. We've converted the second story to Denver's largest pool hall, and the basement to a jazz club and meeting hall. People wondered about living above a crowded restaurant and a noisy pool hall. But the pressed tin ceilings are more than gorgeous—they reflect noise downward, keeping the upstairs lofts peaceful."

Hickenlooper took another sip of his Railyard Ale and grinned. His eyes slitted into smiles behind the round wire-rim glasses and his furry-tongued voice rose. He began gesturing expansively toward the high pressed-tin ceiling, golden oak wainscoting, and sturdy fir beams of his brewpub. "Old buildings and brewpubs are a great fit. Strong masonry walls, sturdy timbers, high ceilings, and structures saturated with history are perfect. We've helped quite a few other brewpubs get started in old buildings around Colorado. ... There must be over a hundred in Colorado by now."

Brewpubs, Hickenlooper bubbled, are heavenly. "Our beer is fresh, wholesome—liquid bread—from the finest grains. It's unpasteurized, naturally carbonated, and without preservatives. The alcohol content is moderate, generally under 5 percent. And we make this elixir in recycled old buildings, creating a labor-intensive product while helping to revitalize urban neighborhoods by tapping into history."

Zang Brewing Company
2301 7th St. (corner of Water St.),
(303) 455-2500

Denver's oldest sports bar originally housed workers of the Zang Brewing Company. Of the huge brewery complex once surrounding this remnant, the only other

> *Drink no longer water, but use a little wine for thy stomach's sake.*
> *—The Epistles of St. Paul*

survivor is the Brewmeister's House, another National Register landmark a half block up the street at 2345 West 7th. Zang was the largest brewer in the Rockies until it dried up during Prohibition.

For house teamsters who carried Zang beer to saloons, Wilhelm Weigle built this hotel in the 1880s. Upstairs you can still see the twelve small sleeping rooms. Teamsters ate, drank, and socialized downstairs before hitching up horses and wagons and loading up kegs, bound for saloons throughout the Rocky Mountains. Zang's is a big place with many rooms on the first floor, as well as basement space and a rear beer garden. The Weigle family owned and operated it until the 1920s. I first visited it in 1972 when it was the Rocky Mountain Bar & Hotel, a gay establishment. The proprietor told me it had been a flophouse before lesbians took a shine to it in 1970.

Dave Pike and Lyn Ilg bought the place in 1975 and installed a $10,000 satellite television system, a video recorder, and a soundboard. They transformed an ancient school bus into the Zang shuttle to take patrons to and from sporting events. Nowadays the old inn is alive with techno-sports amid much Zang's memorabilia in a rejuvenated landmark.

Durango
Elevation: 6,512 feet

The Denver & Rio Grande Railroad founded this town on the Animas River, which the Spanish named for lost souls (Río de las Ánimas Perdidas). William J. Palmer, Alexander C. Hunt, and other D&RG town promoters named Durango after the city in Mexico, which they hoped the railroad would someday reach.

The Durango-Silverton narrow-gauge steam train still operates every summer, attracting some 200,000 customers. Like railroaders since 1881, many of these passengers head for Durango's watering holes. Seventeen rip-roaring saloons kept downtown hopping during the flush times before the 1893 silver crash. Some of the old-timers, like the grandiose Italianate-style Kern Saloon at 1015 Main and the Coors Building at 643–645 Main, are now recycled for drier uses. Others, like the Strater Hotel Saloon and the El Rancho, are still wet. Although the original Durango Brewing Company evaporated decades ago, it was reborn as a microbrewery under the same name in 1990. Durango also has two notable brewpubs, along with two of Colorado's finest antique saloons.

Carver Brewing Company
1022 Main St., (970) 259-2425

Bill Carver opened this brewpub in 1988 in an old two-story, Art Deco–style building, where he also runs a bakery, restaurant, and health foods store—something for everyone. Bakery goodies make this one of Durango's favorite breakfast spots, while the hundred-seat beer garden in back draws late-afternoon and nocturnal patrons. Carver's makes its own beer, bread, and fine food in this saloon filled with interesting art and reading material.

Diamond Belle Saloon
699 Main St., (970) 247-4431

"Work is the curse of the drinking classes" is the slogan of the Diamond Belle, a splendiferous nostalgia parlor tended by waitresses wearing ostrich feathers. A bar, a drugstore, and then a real estate office occupied this strategic corner storefront of the grandiose Strater Hotel. In 1946 a bar reclaimed its rightful place: The Diamond Belle has sparkled ever since with red and gold wallpaper; a Corinthian-columned, mirrored backbar; and a balcony for bird's-eye people-watching. Fancy chandeliers swing from plaster ceiling fixtures sculpted to resemble the mouths of lions. Plaster is also used for the bare-breasted caryatids supporting the balcony. Evelyn, a primitive nude reclining over the entry, winks at departing customers.

Of many fine pianists to perform here, Dick Kreckel is a devout train buff who worked on the Durango-Silverton train as a brakeman. Dick's specialty at the honkytonk piano is imitating steam trains with the help of his cigar.

After a toot in the Diamond Belle, treat yourself to a night in the Strater Hotel. Like a fancy wedding cake with sugary trim, it has a fabulous façade. Inside, it is gorgeously adorned and appointed, a far cry from the humble hotel Henry Strater opened in 1888. Since 1926 the Barker family has owned and enhanced it as the grandest hotel in southwestern Colorado. Besides the Diamond Belle, don't miss the Columbian Room with its naughty 1890s photographs of plump ladies of the night.

El Rancho Bar
975 Main St. (sw corner of 10th St.), (970) 259-8111

The mural on the north wall of the 1892 Central Hotel with its distinctive mansard third story recalls the days when Kid Blackie strode into the bar and shouted: "I can't sing. I can't dance. But I can lick any son of a bitch in the house!" Kid Blackie, better known as Jack Dempsey, grew up in the San Luis Valley town of Manassa. As a youth he went to work in the mines of Cripple Creek. There he became a barroom brawler who

found he could make a living by appearing in bars and betting that he could knock out any and all challengers. He fought around the state in bars like El Rancho, where in 1915 he knocked down Andy Malloy in the tenth round. The reference librarian at the Durango Public Library pronounced this a fictional event, but they don't believe her down at the El Rancho. At any rate, the "Manassa Mauler" went on to the world heavyweight championship.

And malt does more than Milton can
To justify God's ways to man.
Ale, man, ale's the stuff to drink
For fellows whom it hurts to think.
                                    —A. E. Housman

Real cowboys and Indians fancy the Old West decor of wagon-wheel chandeliers and backbar souvenirs such as a pair of boxing gloves, branding irons, a bridle, and rodeo posters. The main attraction is three pool tables in back under a large mural that immortalizes legendary locals, all men and women of enviable dimensions. The mural is worth studying, especially the barefooted old-timer slipping a jack to another gambler while the bar harlot eyes a tipsy card player fanning the air with his winnings.

Steamworks Brewing Co.
801 E. 2nd Ave. (nw corner of 8th St.), (970) 259-9200

The old Pittman Motor Company (1921), a Nash dealer, graduated to a higher and better use in 1996, when it opened as a brewpub and wood-fire-oven pizzeria. The old concrete floor showrooms now showcase handcrafted beer instead of new Fords and Lincolns. Beneath a high, open-rafter ceiling, the industrial decor has been retained and augmented in this cleverly designed space. The Italian food and fine brews are equally well designed. From the bar, with its railroad-track footrest, you can monitor brewing operations behind the glass backbar.

A new concrete deck overlooks Durango, and new stainless-steel siding enhances this old bunker of an automobile shop. Corrugated metal siding is the motif, repeated on corrugated cardboard menus, corrugated panels of interior decor, and even corrugated (striped) blouses and shirts on the waitpersons.

Empire

Elevation: 8,601 feet

New Yorkers named Empire for their native state with great expectations. But the frenetic mining center soon peaked and became a quiet town of about 400, little affected by modern developments. Pioneer buildings include the Mint Saloon at 13 East Park Avenue, and a Carpenter's Gothic–style cottage (1881) at 167 Park Avenue (U.S. Highway 40). The Town Hall on Park Avenue (U.S. Highway 40) is a two-story clapboard building with a cupola and siren on top, but much city business is conducted in the downstairs Hard Rock Cafe, which has been here since 1932. Although its Park Avenue doesn't rival the one in New York City, Empire does boast the oldest inn in Colorado.

The Peck House
83 Sunny Ave. & U.S. Hwy. 40,
(303) 569-9870

Colorado's oldest still-operating tavern dates to 1862, when James Peck arrived in Empire and struck it rich with the Pay Dirt Mine. He built the two-story clapboard hotel with its full-length front veranda overlooking the town of Empire. The original four-room house (now the reception, bar, and kitchen area) is on the west side of the current hotel. The large, two-story east addition (c. 1881) contains twelve bedrooms and a downstairs billiard room, library, office, and women's lounge.

The hotel doubled as a stage stop on the Georgetown–to–Middle Park run over Berthoud Pass. During the quiet decades following Empire's brief mining boom, it became a boardinghouse that was often vacant. In 1958, Louise C. Harrison and Margaret Collbran reopened it as The Hotel Splendide. They rehabilitated the bar and restaurant after installing central heating and plumbing and carrying out an extensive restoration and refurnishing. Harrison, the granddaughter of brewer Adolph Coors, tells the story in her book *Empire and the Berthoud Pass* (Denver, Colo.: Big Mountain Press, 1964).

Sally and Gary St. Clair took over in 1981 and have made The Peck House famous for food and lodging as well as the bar, which has a picture-window view of this picturesque mountain town in place of a backbar. In the sedate library, parlor, and music rooms, antiques galore include portraits of bushy-bearded James Peck and his prim-looking wife.

Estes Park
Elevation: 7,522 feet

his town at the main entrance to Rocky Mountain National Park is named for Joel Estes, who settled in this broad mountain valley in 1859. An abundance of game attracted sportsmen, most notably Irishman Thomas Wyndham-Quinn, fourth Earl of Dunraven, who attempted to make Estes Park his private game preserve.

By 1876, the village of Estes Park had emerged where the Fall and Wind Rivers join the south fork of the Big Thompson River. A tourist town from the beginning, it blossomed with the establishment of Rocky Mountain National Park in 1916.

Riverfront Plaza (1988) and Riverwalk (1990), along the Big Thompson and Fall Rivers, are adorned with well-landscaped parking lots, waterfalls, pools, native plants, boulders, and life-size outdoor wildlife sculptures. Elkhorn Avenue, the main street, underwent a $1 million streetscaping in 1987 that introduced trees, rock gardens, Victorian lighting, and new patios and rear entrances on the Riverwalk. Some historic businesses remain, including Grubb's Livery (c. 1890) at East Riverside and Elkhorn Avenue, and MacDonald's Book Shop (1909) at 152 East Elkhorn Avenue, which started out as a family home and general store. The Continental Hotel (c. 1890) at 110 West Elkhorn has become Lonigan's Saloon, a romper room filled with electronic games, pool tables, televisions, and even a basketball hoop.

Dunraven Grille
333 Wonder View Ave., (970) 586-3371

Freelan O. Stanley and his twin brother, Francis, developed a photographic dry-plate process that allowed film to be sold in rolls, which they sold to George Eastman. They also invented the steam-powered automobile named for them: the Stanley Steamer. After contracting tuberculosis, Freelan moved to Colorado in 1903 for the climate cure. He bought 1,400 acres from Lord Dunraven to build his summer home and the magnificent Stanley Hotel, one of the finest examples of the Georgian Revival style in Colorado. To commemorate Dunraven's pioneer role, the hotel tavern is named in his honor.

If the tavern is stuffy, take your drink out to the generous veranda, relax in the easy chairs, and gaze across Estes Park to Longs Peak. Adjacent to the Dunraven Grille are the MacGregor Dining Room, a music room, and the Piñon Billiard Room. The latter was the original hotel saloon and still has elegant mahogany woodwork, including built-in racks for billiard sticks and balls, and an enormous stone fireplace.

After Stanley sold the hotel in 1926, it weathered hard financial times when its frame construction made it difficult to maintain and insure. Closed during World War II, it opened intermittently afterward during the summers. Following a 1980s renovation, it is now open year-round and enjoying a renaissance. Stephen King's horror story *The Shining*, which was filmed here, attracted national attention. Despite protests, a 1980s shopping center was constructed at the base of the 125-acre hotel site, compromising the view of the hotel and obscuring its entrance. Inside the hotel, however, the elegant Dunraven Grille and Piñon Billiard Room offer consolations of a more pristine character.

> While pure as a spring
> Is the wine I sing,
> And to praise it, one needs but name it.
> For Catawba wine
> Has need of no sign,
> No tavern-bush to proclaim it.
> **—Henry Wadsworth Longfellow**

Evergreen
Elevation: 7,040 feet

Founded in the 1870s at 7,000 feet, this mountain community was named for its abundant spruce, fir, and ponderosa pine forests. Originally, logging attracted settlers, who operated a half-dozen sawmills along Upper Bear Creek. Governor John Evans and other prominent Denverites built rustic summer homes in this picturesque mountain valley. Tourism began to boom after the Denver Mountain Parks Department built Evergreen Dam in 1927 to create Evergreen Lake, the centerpiece of a park noted for fishing and ice-skating. Since World War II, Evergreen has boomed as a year-round home for some 20,000 people who have displaced much of the forest. Many of them work downhill in Denver, but find some worthy saloons up amid the surviving evergreens.

Keys on the Green Restaurant, Bar & Golf Club
29614 Upper Bear Creek Rd.,
(303) 674-4095

A rustic saloon lies inside this octagonal log building. Tipplers, diners, and golfers needing consolation after play on the adjacent course find a haven in this tavern wrapped around a massive, circular stone fireplace. Chandeliers made of gnarled tree branches hang from a hoganlike, conical log roof. An antique dating from 1925, this clubhouse is a friendly, inexpensive place with good service, a sundeck, and appreciation of "well-behaved children."

Little Bear
28075 Main St. (Colorado 74),
(303) 674-9991

Among Colorado's mountain bars, the Little Bear growls the loudest. Located on Colorado 74, its loud live music and large noisy crowds make it the place to be Friday, Saturday, and Sunday nights.

In this large, old, two-story building, be sure to check out the upstairs pool tables and

Many a man who thinks to have found a home discovers that he has merely opened a tavern for his friends.

—Norman Douglas

the double row of wooden benches overlooking the stage. Raw plank walls are decorated with old skis, road signs, license plates, and other trash and treasures. From rustic stools wrapping three sides of the bar, regulars speculate on the bras hanging from the rafters. Both management and the live bands customarily encourage female patrons to add to the collection and make themselves more comfortable.

The Little Bear is famous for its live musicians, who have included such celebrities as Ringo Starr, Willie Nelson, Taj Mahal, Leon Russell, Firefall, and Canned Heat, as well as local rock, blues, and country-and-western bands who regularly fill this mountain hot spot to its 350-person capacity. One of the seats is occupied by a big stuffed bear that presides over an often sweaty, hopping, dancing clientele. "If you can't get picked up at the Little Bear," as someone wrote on the women's room wall, "you can't get picked up anywhere!"

Frederica "Freddie" Bellamy Lincoln, an Evergreen resident since 1919, told me that the Little Bear was originally McCracken's Drug Store. During the 1920s, Prince McCracken added a second floor and enlarged the first for a tavern called the Roundup. "Evergreeners used to ride their horses down to the Roundup for dances, movies, and socials," Freddie recalled. "It and Keys on the Green were the only bars in town then. The Roundup became the Red Ram and then the Little Bear, which attracted motorcycle gangs from Denver. On Sundays, of all times!"

A 1997 fire destroyed the adjacent Stewart Hotel and almost cooked the Little Bear. Since then, the place has reformed—somewhat. The bras were still flapping the last time I checked.

Florence
Elevation: 5,187 feet

Florence was founded in 1873 by James McCandless, who named it for his daughter. Eleven years earlier, oil bubbling to the surface of Oil Creek had inspired Alexander M. Cassidy to dig a well. He found the first oil field in the Rocky Mountain West and supposedly the second in the country. At one time, seventy-five wells pumped 3,000 barrels of crude oil daily, and Standard, United, and other national firms had storage and processing facilities here. Continental Oil Company (Conoco), which started here as the Arkansas Valley Oil Company, still dominates the skyline with its refinery stacks. Oil wells, coal mining, smelters for Cripple Creek's gold ore, and a nearby Portland cement plant made Florence one of Colorado's major industrial centers by the early 1900s. Today, Florence boasts the largest federal prison complex in the United States, which is now the town's major employer. The oil wells are all dried up and Lil's Place, the famed brothel at 311 South Union Street, is closed. But Florence still sports several nifty old saloons.

Alibi Lounge
114 East Main St., (719) 784-4203

Glass blocks now hide the lounge's indoor activities from Peeping Toms. The bar is on an elevated platform with red plastic "leather" captain's chairs instead of barstools, overlooking a bartender in a sunken well. This is a favorite retreat for prison guards, counselors, and correctional officials.

One of them, Sonny Grass, painted the large wall mural of a 1955 Packard with huge tailfins tipped with real flashing lights.

"This is the best bar in Florence," Sonny swore. "It's friendly, with fast service. The Green Parrot is too rowdy. The Oasis is for tourists. The Capri is dingy. For decades this was the Magnet Bar, before Mary Lou Ingle took over in 1986 and renamed it the Alibi.

It's a great bar, but don't cross Mary Lou. I did once and for months I drank out of dirty beer glasses. She even trained flies to dive-bomb my beer." Sonny entertained us with endless stories of how convicts try to make booze in their cells. Most often they use their toilet bowls and throw in sugar and yeast. Especially around the winter holidays, Sonny said, the boys get really thirsty—thirsty enough for some mighty bizarre attempts at cell-house brewing.

Oasis Tavern
121 W. Main St., (719) 784-3490

Local sandstone fronts this well-preserved saloon, which reopened in 1935 as the Oasis with a palm-tree oasis mural. It occupies the storefront of the Vannest Building (1895) with plate-glass windows, a high pressed-metal ceiling, and high-backed hardwood booths with individual table Wurlitzer jukebox selectors. The 1873 Brunswick walnut and mahogany, Corinthian-columned back and front bars are a must-see.

Fort Collins
Elevation: 4,984 feet

The Larimer County seat started out in 1864 as an army post named for Lieutenant Colonel William O. Collins. The army left in 1867, but the town persisted, thanks to pioneers such as Elizabeth ("Auntie") Stone, who opened her cabin as the first hotel.

Fort Collins also welcomed the small state agricultural college dubbed "Moo-U," which became Colorado State University in 1957. Today, with more than 20,000 students, CSU is the second-largest university in the state. Giant new regional industrial plants such as the Anheuser-Busch Brewery have also made this one of Colorado's fastest-growing communities, with some 100,000 residents.

Despite its swelling population, Fort Collins has preserved much of its original commercial core, the Old Town Historic District. Local preservationists even persuaded Taco Bell to move into the old Mission Revival–style residence they were planning to tear down and replace with one of their ubiquitous "Santa Fake"–style models. Don't miss this usually fine fast foodery at 1530 South College Avenue at the northwest corner of Prospect Street. Among various liquid landmarks is the tavern at 146 North College Avenue in the old Commercial Bank & Trust Company, with its distinctive Greek Revival façade. After a visit here and to the following noteworthy old-time saloons, hop a ride on the restored streetcars of the Fort Collins Municipal Railway.

Coopersmith's Brewpub
220 E. Mountain Ave., (970) 498-0483

Scott Smith and his son, Cooper, opened Colorado's second brewpub here in 1989. It has overflowed with business ever since, adding a pool hall in what was once a children's clothing store, as well as a beer garden. The brewpub occupies the Hohnstein Block, a handsome, two-story Italianate edifice built in 1904. You can purchase beer for take-out in half-gallon growlers, kegs, or barrels. Besides their legendary Pedestrian Ale, Poudre Pale Ale, and Horse Tooth Stout, Coopersmith's produces many seasonal and specialty brews.

Jefferson Street Station
200 Jefferson St., (970) 493-4348

The old Union Pacific Freight and Passenger Depot at the foot of Jefferson Street in Old Town has been restored as a terrific tavern, specializing in many local brews as well as Railyard Ale from the Wynkoop Brewing Company of Denver. A sunroom and a beer garden have been added on the back, track side. Railroad memorabilia and old photos of this building when it opened in 1911 as "the finest station in proportion to its size of any town on the entire UP system" make it advisable to fire up your engine and get your caboose down to the old depot.

Old Town Fort Collins, shown here in the 1940s, has been restored and now boasts memorable saloons such as Coppersmith's Brewpub, the Northern Hotel Bar, and the Town Pump. c. 1940 photo courtesy of the Denver Public Library, Western History Collection.

Northern Hotel Bar & Bar Bazaar
180 N. College Ave. (se corner of Walnut Ave.), (970) 493-4437

How often we bar-goers feel uncomfortable, no one knows. It is so difficult to find just the right noise and interaction level. All too often, a bar is either too dull and quiet or too noisy and obnoxious. The Northern Hotel resolved this problem by installing a polite hotel bar and a rude bar at opposite ends of the large first floor. To get precisely the noise and wildness level you want, simply move closer to your choice of the two antithetical nodes.

Even one of the shiest and rarest creatures in Colorado has found a home in this den of diversity. On a counter near my barstool, I saw the creature created by the marriage of a jackalope and a Chinese pheasant, descended from those liberated from the Denver Zoo years ago.

On the tattered fringes of the Fort Collins Old Town Historic District, the Northern remains unrehabilitated. Besides the "jackapheasant" in the bar, don't miss the grand Art Nouveau–style, stained-glass skylight in the lobby.

The Town Pump
124 N. College Ave., (970) 493-4404

This is the oldest bar in town—and looks its age. Located in the Avery Building, a downtown landmark erected in 1897 by Franklin C. Avery, who platted Fort Collins, it's a tiny, dark, old-fashioned saloon. An armadillo greets customers from atop the miniature backbar, and numerous other stuffed animals watch glassy-eyed from the walls. In a bit of one-upmanship with the nearby Northern Hotel Bar and its famous "jackapheasant," the Pump has a horned bobcat on the backbar.

During Prohibition this was a drugstore with a speakeasy in the basement. Booze came out of the closet for good in 1936, when the drugstore was reborn as The Town Pump. Because Fort Collins was a semidry town until 1969, this place was allowed to serve only 3.2 beer.

The Pump collects nothing but the best slogans and graffiti:

> "Good girls go to heaven, bad girls go anywhere."
> "I'm not dead, I'm just ignoring you."
> "It's not pretty being easy."
> "Jesus is coming. Look busy!"

Although the front-door sign says, "Sorry, We're Open," this is a very congenial little joint with nine barstools and a few booths. Entry sign notwithstanding, they seem very happy to be open and most visitors are tickled pink that Fort Collins's oldest tavern is still alive and kicking.

Fort Morgan

Elevation: 4,330 feet

Strategically sited at a bend in the South Platte River, Fort Morgan has long been a watering hole for travelers crossing the Great American Desert. The town started in the early 1860s as a sod-and-adobe fort named for Colonel Christopher A. Morgan, a Union officer. Abner Baker, a member of the Greeley Union Colony, platted a town near the abandoned fort in 1884. The community grew slowly as a livestock, truck-gardening, and irrigated-farming center.

The skyline is dominated by the giant, gleaming white sugar canisters of the Great Western Sugar Plant (1906), one of the last operating plants among a dozen refineries that once hummed in the Platte Valley between Brighton and Sterling. Fort Morgan is also perfumed by a major meatpacking plant and various feedlots. Extensive oil and natural gas development has augmented the agrarian economy to make this a perkier town than most on the High Plains. While most agrarian towns in eastern Colorado have been shrinking, Fort Morgan has been growing into a town of some 9,000.

The Fort Morgan Museum at 414 Main Street is a superb, small-town institution, whose many attractions include a reconstructed soda fountain from the Hillrose Drug Store. An unusually intact Main Street with some splendid Art Deco–style buildings heads north to Riverside Park and the town wonder: the reconstructed Rainbow Arch Bridge. This Art Deco–style concrete-and-steel landmark with curving lines and elegant built-in lampposts was recently restored as a pedestrian walkway crossing the South Platte River.

Club Tap Room
212-214 Main St., (970) 867-5423

Despite the colorful Art Deco façade on this 1930 gem, the most exciting attraction of its nondescript interior is the large goldfish aquarium built into the backbar. The long, narrow bar, trapped between a lowered chipboard ceiling and a linoleum floor, is filled with real flies and a few barflies watched by that huge frilly goldfish. In an attempt at sexual egalitarianism, this bar offers a Men's Night (Monday) as well as a Ladies' Night (Wednesday) with half-priced drinks. It also has some notable graffiti: "Drive like hell and you will get there" and "I didn't realize he drank until he came to work sober."

The Queen Lounge
112 W. Kiowa St., (970) 867-9945

At the Queen Hotel, they still remember the man who stopped time. Painted-over storefronts and a shuttered exterior make this place look suspect from the street, but a congenial waitress reassured us and told us The Queen's story. The yellow brick building opened in 1911 as a hardware and farm implement store. The second and third stories were added in 1929, when the old store was remodeled as a grand hotel. The splendid lobby, with its 16-foot-high, pressed-metal ceiling, is now The Queen Lounge. The most striking decor items are portraits of the queens of Fort Morgan—framed in old-fashioned wooden toilet seats. These dignified ladies, who look like they might be the local D.A.R. chapter, are even illuminated so they can shine all night.

The Queen's decor, cannibalized from upstairs rooms, includes a front bar made of old, numbered bedroom doors with the Queen of Hearts and other memorabilia shellacked into them. One old sign boasts, "The Hotel Queen, Largest and Leading Hotel in the Sugar Bowl of America."

Fort Morgan, the waitress explained, has one of the biggest sugar-beet plants—and the only one still operating. "Once, The Queen had fifty rooms and twenty-five baths. And no prostitutes! Or booze. You couldn't even buy booze in Fort Morgan until 1965."

The once-grand lobby retains its Art Deco chandeliers, coffered ceiling, mosaic tile floor, and forlorn grand piano. Old parking meters form the posts of the grand stairway. "We took the meters off Main Street to make Fort Morgan more tourist friendly," the waitress explained.

We settled into the stout captain's chairs for kraut dogs and shrimp, the house specialties. After lunch and a few beers, I noticed the clock, which hadn't marked the passage of time. "Oh, yeah," the waitress sighed. "When Bill finally got out of jail— he's the town drunk—he came in here to celebrate. 'When you drink as much as I do,' he joked, 'you've got to start early and stay late.' Finally, I had to tell him—'last call for alcohol. I've got to close. It's two o'clock.'"

"No, it ain't," Bill fired back, whipping out a pistol. He shot the clock, stopping it at two minutes to two. Bill went back into Fort Morgan's spiffy new jail, and the bar is still open at the Queen Hotel, where it is still two minutes to two.

Franktown
Elevation: 6,120 feet

James Frank Gardner founded Frank's Town as a stage stop and sawmill along the Cherry Creek route into Denver. Frank's Town, the original (1861–1874) seat of Douglas County, was bypassed by the railroad, and the county seat moved to Castle Rock. Later renamed Franktown, it was later again bypassed, this time by Interstate 25. Its fame rested on a gas station renowned for its café, bar, grocery store, and country music.

Stagecoach Restaurant & Lounge
2077 Colorado 83 & Colorado 86,
(303) 660-3773

During the 1960s, Bill Shea, a trucker, acquired a cinderblock gas station and turned it into a legend. He put in a long bar and a stage, which the Shea family mounted on weekend nights. Bill blew on a corn-liquor jug while his wife played the washtub fiddle. He also sang and his son sometimes joined in, belting out country-and-western hits deep into the night. Whenever a car or truck pulled up to the fuel pumps, the band would take a break to go out and pump gas and wash the windshield.

The Sheas gave this haven its current name, the Stagecoach Restaurant & Lounge.

During the 1970s, the Stagecoach became a notorious biker bar and the hangout for Douglas County drunks. The county wisely set up an alcoholic rehab center next door so the customers would not have to drive to it.

Reform came in 1995, when Stephen and Debbie Rice took the reins and converted the north end of the complex into their home and a farm for their son's sheep, ducks, rabbits, and chickens. Steve explained: "We let the kid and the animals run around to encourage the family trade, to show that this is now a wholesome country place. We even have a horseshoe pit. I've fixed up a little corral and watering trough out back so folks can park their horses outside. We don't allow people to ride their horses into the bar

drinks and meals. She painted Debbie Rice with long blonde hair and one red-gartered leg dangling out the stagecoach window. The bemused stage driver is shaggy-bearded Steve Rice. The eight horses pulling the stage-coach are Clydesdales cut out of a Budweiser billboard and glued into the mural.

Steve added, "We've chased off the bad bikers and kept the good ones. We've added a dance floor, music stage, and outdoor seating. Debbie and I have made this not only a swell bar, but the best and most reasonable place to eat. We have a 16-ounce T-bone special, family hotdog and hamburger cookouts, and specials galore. And on weekend nights we bring in bands, sometimes country-and-western in honor of the Sheas, who got this place jumping."

anymore. It's only cute the first time. Now, I even say no to the gals who want to ride in naked."

Annie Miller, an itinerant artist, arrived in the spring of 1995 and painted the huge mural in the dining room in exchange for

Fraser

Elevation: 8,550 feet

The people of Fraser once bragged that it was "The Icebox of the Nation," ignoring the other claimant, International Falls, Minnesota, not to mention Alamosa and Gunnison, Colorado. That was before iceboxes were replaced by refrigerators and chamber of commerce types began downplaying Fraser's frigidity. Founded in 1905, this railroad town was named for its river, which in turn was named for a pioneer settler, Reuben Frazier, whose name was misspelled by post-office officials.

As Fraser's frigid air flows down from the surrounding peaks after the sun sets, it is wise to find a warm saloon. The first tavern in town, Cozens Ranch House, is now a nifty museum at 77849 U.S. 40. William Cozens, the fearless pioneer sheriff of Central City, married Mary York, the first white woman in these parts. She insisted that they leave the wild mining town for a better place to raise a family. Across Berthoud Pass, in then-unsettled Grand County, the Cozens clan started this pioneer cattle, hay, and potato ranch.

The original hewn-log house under board-and-batten siding was enlarged in 1876 with a rear stage stop and a small post office on its south side. Travelers used the six tiny, windowless rooms over the stage stop as a hotel and inn. Cozens welcomed stagecoaches but not railroads. He is said to have fired on the railroad survey crew from his rocking chair on the front porch, shooting out the stakes they planted in his hay meadow. According to this tale, that is why the railroad tracks are still out of firing distance from the Cozens Ranch, hidden across the valley in the woods. Visitors and Cozens consoled themselves in his inn with libations and vows to fight progress. Cozens Stagehouse is a grand museum today, but you have to look elsewhere for libations.

Byers Peak Inn
U.S. Hwy. 40 and County Rd. 72,
(970) 726-8256

This 1885 stage stop was first known as the Gaskill Inn for early proprietor Clinton Gaskill, who also built the original 1876 Berthoud Pass Inn. The two-story stagehouse had few doors and windows, probably a defense against the cold air and howling snowstorms that beset "The Ice Box of the Nation."

In 1975, Bill Faraklas and his Bavarian wife, Liesel, bought the dilapidated stage stop, removed the sagging front porch and balcony, and transformed it into an Alpine Bavarian inn. The Faraklases added a shed-roof dining room bright with windows and views in 1987, along with an outdoor beer garden. The snow white plaster walls and wood trim are decorated with German platters and baskets of dried flowers. Lace curtains, heavy German silverware, blue-and-white floral china, embroidered floral tablecloths, and Liesel's lovely accent add to the Bavar-

ian ambience. More recently they erected a two-story chalet, which they operate as a bed-and-breakfast.

"This was just an old run-down residence when we bought it," Liesel said. "We tried to fix it up. People need a warm inn here. It gets awfully cold. I can remember 60 degrees below zero. Our water pipes froze and did not thaw until June."

In the tiny, five-stool bar and in two dining rooms, German beers and wines are a specialty. "We never run out of Oktoberfest and Rhine-Ruhr-Mosel wines," Liesel laughed, "because those are my favorites!" Along with Wiener schnitzel, bratwurst, potato salad, and apple strudel, the inn offers local trout and prime rib. Service can be slow in this popular family restaurant, but customers wait while listening to classical music. We heard Beethoven's entire *Moonlight Sonata* while waiting to order lunch. Savor the grand views of North Park and surrounding peaks, of which the most prominent is Byers Peak. This handsome, 12,804-foot mountain was named by the Hayden Survey for William N. Byers, the founder and indefatigable editor of the *Rocky Mountain News*. Byers joined the Hayden party in 1873 for the first recorded ascent of Longs Peak. He explored many other nearby mountains and was a great promoter of North Park and the upper Colorado River, whose Byers Canyon commemorates his work. He also founded and promoted Hot Sulphur Springs, the county seat. To the northeast lies a rocky erection on the Continental Divide, Devil's Thumb, which was originally named for another part of the devil.

Gardner

Elevation: 7,000 feet

On the upper Huerfano River amid the Greenhorn Mountains, this isolated, unincorporated ranching town is the shrunken hub of a large mountainous chunk of northwestern Huerfano (Spanish for "orphan") County. Gardner's roots, however, lie in a predecessor Hispanic town, according to tales I heard in the Gardner Tavern.

Gardner Tavern
CLOSED

After putting a pinch of salt on the rim of his sweating beer can, Augustino Garcia nodded a welcome. I mounted the barstool next to him in the dim tavern. He was the first person I had seen in Gardner, where this tavern was the only sign of life. This dusty, sleepy village on the upper Huerfano River seemed to be a ghost.

Glad to find another human being, I bought Tino a beer. Bertha Trujillo, the owner and bartender, stuck another piñon log in the old potbellied stove to keep the low-ceilinged, adobe-walled saloon toasty. After a few more beers, Tino grew talkative. "A long time ago, before Gardner, there was another town here. My father told me about it. It lay down in the valley next to the old riverbed. My great-grandfather lived and died there."

Augustino told me some of the stories he had heard as a boy. He seemed to remember the Chavez Town church the best. It had a flat dirt roof so leaky that it rained indoors for days after the rain stopped outdoors. The church seemed wet and cold for years, until a stranger appeared one day and offered to repair the roof.

"He was a man so strong that he needed no ladder," Garcia said, jamming a lime wedge into a fresh can of *cerveza*. He shook his head. "He just threw shovelfuls of mud high up on the roof. After that, it did not rain inside the church anymore. Some of the people thought it was a miracle. They thought this man must have been José, the carpenter, come to help his people."

St. Joseph may have saved the chapel, but he did not save the town. Garcia had no idea what year Chavez Town drowned. Every spring, the Huerfano River swells and sometimes floods. One year, the river rose over its banks and into the town. The people rushed to higher ground. Looking back, they saw their village sink under the rising waters.

The orphaned residents of Chavez Town moved uphill to a new town 2 miles away that the gringos called "Gardner." Herbert Gardner, the son of a governor of Massachusetts, had amassed land and founded the town. "He named it for himself, not for one of the saints or for the Chavez family who first settled here," Garcia said, shaking his head.

"We hardly ever see the gringos who own most of the land around here," Garcia added, stroking his beer can. "People say they buy it as a tax write-off from those of us who have to sell off some of our land each year in order to pay taxes. My great-grandfather owned a lot of land. He gave the land for the Chavez Town cemetery." Augustino took a small pinch of salt, savored it, then washed it down with the rest of his beer. "Grandpa was buried there in 1941, and then we put my father there, too." Like Chavez Town, these pioneers lived on in the memory of a son grown old.

"Most families still left with any land have to send menfolk to find jobs elsewhere in order to survive. In the spring we start out in Wyoming, Idaho, and Montana for spring sheepshearing. There's haying work here in the Huerfano Valley in the summer. Come fall, we go to the San Luis Valley to harvest potatoes. But it's worth it to stay here. This is a better life than most places. We're blessed. The mountains stop the wind, and catch the clouds, and make the rain. We don't have the dust and the drought they have down on the plains."

The next morning, Augustino took me to the Chavez Town site 2 miles southeast of Gardner. He dug up some broken dishes along the sandy banks of the shriveled river. Then we visited the tiny cemetery with its crude wooden and cement headstones amid a few plastic flowers and much cholla. We paid our respects to Augustino's ancestors.

Back in Denver, I visited the Colorado Historical Society Library. Becky, the librarian, lugged out the oldest Colorado atlases they have. We could not find Chavez Town on Hayden's 1873 atlas, the 1877 post office map of Colorado, the giant Rand McNally maps for the 1880s and 1890s, or about seventy other early maps. Nor does the town show up in any of the ghost-town guides or Bill Bauer and Jim Ozment's *Colorado Post Offices, 1859–1989*. After a daylong search at the Colorado Historical Society Library and at the Denver Public Library, I could find no trace of Chavez Town. Both the town's life and death have gone unreported. It lies buried and forgotten under the Huerfano River that once gave it life.

Chavez Town, I am still convinced, was not a barroom fantasy. Like other Hispanic towns never put on a map and never given a post office, it is gone, except for the stories of a few old-timers reminiscing in the Gardner Tavern.

Georgetown
Elevation: 8,519 feet

In 1859, George Griffith discovered gold in what he called George's Town. The town boomed as Colorado's first silver city after the 1864 discovery of the Belmont Lode. It captured the county seat from Idaho Springs, and became the supply town for many surrounding mining districts. Population peaked at about 4,000 in the 1880s, when the town had thirteen whiskey houses.

Georgetown has an elegance strikingly different from most mining settlements. Gentrification began with town founder Griffith, who brought his wife and family to settle. Georgetown courted other families by passing an ordinance offering a free town lot to the first ten respectable women to settle. These womenfolk fancied painted houses, gardens, churches, schools, an opera house, and other refinements that made Georgetown unusually genteel. They converted one pioneer groggery, Barnes Saloon Hall, to the Woman's Christian Temperance Union and the town reading room. The women allied themselves with Father Matthews's Total Abstinence Society to wage war on Demon Rum. Taverns kept a low profile, and even the Georgetown Brewery was an underground affair, established in 1868 by a rotund, jolly Bohemian, Albert Selak. His brewery included a dancehall and wine cellar dug into Alpine Mountain. It survived for seven years.

Georgetown's population hit rock bottom at around 500 during the 1950s when it had only one bar, the St. James. Proprietor Ben Draper opened it leisurely at about two in the afternoon and kept it open as long as he had company. Draper fell in love with the town in 1921 after a ride on the Georgetown Loop Railroad. He subsequently completed a master's thesis on Georgetown and did much to restore the slumbering silver city. He bought and moved into the oldest house in town, the McClellan House at 909 Taos Street. This 1866 vertical-sawn board house has primitive tin can sheathing, but attempts elegance with wooden trim and colorful paint.

Georgetown is prim and proper today. Its vice district along Brownell Street is completely gone, wiped out by I-70. But there Mattie Silks, queen of Colorado madams, opened her first Colorado department store of vice, competing with Mattie Estes, Belle Keys, Adda LaMont, and Mollie Walker. Although the red light district has been obliterated, this unusually well-preserved town has some splendid antique taverns.

Georgetown Depot Cafe
1106 Rose St., (303) 569-2403

The original brick depot welcomed the first train of the Colorado Central at a bash on August 13, 1877. The Colorado Central, a tiny narrow-gauge line centered in Golden, was swallowed by the Union Pacific in 1880 and then became part of the Colorado and Southern in 1898. The depot closed in 1939 when the Colorado and Southern abandoned the line. Someone bought the depot for $50 and reopened it in 1951 as the Alpine Inn with considerable additions, including the large stone fireplace.

After the restoration of the Georgetown Loop as a summer rail passenger adventure in 1984, the Alpine Inn was transformed in 1990 into the Depot Cafe, complete with a large model of the Georgetown Loop Mining and Railroad History Park. Once again, the depot offers train tickets, rail information, and a large selection of railroadiana in the gift shop, and a train whistles around the depot—on a tiny maze of tracks overhead in the café. The Depot serves breakfast and lunch and local microbrews. The outside deck overlooks a locomotive, tender, and caboose display next to Clear Creek.

Hotel de Paris
409 6th St. (se corner of Alpine St.), (303) 569-2311

This once was the strangest, and finest, of Colorado's mountain taverns. The Hotel de Paris never had a saloon—that would be uncivilized—but it did have the finest wine cellar in the mountains.

Proprietor Louis DuPuy was a study in irony. He was an innkeeper who hated his guests. He built a 16-foot-high stone wall around his hotel's outdoor café, then invited people in. A woman-hater, he gave all his money to his housekeeper and was buried with her under the large stone in the Georgetown cemetery inscribed "Deux Bons Amis."

"French" Louis had big, brown, sad eyes and a droopy mustache. He was a patriot who ignored the Fourth of July, but he celebrated Bastille Day every July 14. A native of Alençon, he hope to bring French civilization to a raw, remote, American mountain mining town. He imported wines and liquors in large wooden casks and bottled them for guests in his huge wine cellar. There you can still see his stockpile of fancy French wine and liquor labels, which he slapped onto bottles he filled from bulk barrels of California wine. The labels, boasting "Cognac Vieux," "Chateau Margaux Grand Vin Brodeau," "St. Emillion Bordeaux," and "Etoile de France Grand Vin Sec Champagne," survive.

As a devout Frenchman, DuPuy took it upon himself to educate English-speaking barbarians. He strove to teach them to eat properly with a knife and fork, to use a napkin, and to linger over meals for civilized discourse. But civilizing English-speaking peoples, he sighed, was a never-ending task. Louis greeted guests in his long Prince Albert tails, then reappeared in his high chef's hat to take their orders. Yankees did not always appreciate the Haviland china, garnet goblets, and silver cruets. Smack in the middle of the dining room is a fountain—the goose boy (a cherub riding a goose)—where guests could fish for trout dinners.

Before and after his fine meals, Louis could be found in the 2,160-volume hotel library seated amid busts of Molière, Montesquieu, and Voltaire. He fancied Voltaire's

Louis DuPuy, a debonair Frenchman, opened the Hotel de Paris in Georgetown. His fine food, wines, and outdoor café attracted the genteel to what is now a museum. Photo of Louis DuPuy courtesy of the Denver Public Library, Western History Collection; exterior photo of the Hotel de Paris courtesy of Historic Georgetown, Inc., Tom Noel Collection.

Candide and other cynical observations on human nature. Yet he was less than candid about his real name, Adolphe François Gerard, and his desertion of the seminary or, some said, the U.S. Army and/or French Foreign Legion. He came to Georgetown a poor miner. After a crippling dynamite accident, he opened the Delmonico French Bakery, which evolved into this country inn.

"I love these mountains and I love America," DuPuy once told the *Georgetown Courier.* "But you will pardon me if I bring into this community a remembrance of my youth and my country—this little souvenir of France which I built in America. This house will be my tomb." After his death in 1900, the *Georgetown Courier* mourned "an eccentric, a philosopher and a student, who brought refinement to the granite slopes of Colorado."

This misogynist would smolder in his grave if he knew his hotel has been run since 1954 by the Colonial Dames, who offer neither food nor wine, but only dry, if fascinating, tours of what is now a crackerjack museum. Nearly all the original fixtures, elegant and eccentric, have been preserved, and the spirit of Louis still prevails in this vintage souvenir of France.

The Red Ram
606 6th St. (nw corner of Rose St.), (303) 569-2300

Since its 1957 opening, the Red Ram has been one of the most popular mountain bars. Après-ski libations and dancing kept the crowd going into the wee hours of the morning—when some would head back to the ski slopes. Lawrence C. Phipps III, the whimsical musician and scion of Colorado's best-known fortune, acquired and renovated the Ram in 1981, making it a fashionable hangout.

The Red Ram was preceded by a string of saloons. The original saloon on this site burned down on April 29, 1887. During the 1940s, Fitchett's Pool Hall occupied the space. The Fitchetts also built and ran the second Berthoud Pass Inn, according to Polly Fitchett Chandler of Georgetown's famous Polly Chandler Book Shop. Fitchett's was followed by the Loop Bar & Cafe, so-named for the far-famed Georgetown Loop, revived in 1984 as a narrow-gauge railroad excursion. Nebraskans Tom and Vera Spath acquired the Loop in 1952, installed a red neon "BAR" sign outside, and puffed it as "the oldest bar in Colorado."

After a day on the slopes, skiers jam the Red Ram in Georgetown for hot toddies, cold beer, and dancing. 1966 photo by Duane Howell, courtesy The Denver Post.

Tipplers familiar with The Peck House in nearby Empire, the Gold Coin in Central City, Crook's Palace in Black Hawk, and El Bronco and My Brother's Bar in Denver will find this claim hard to swallow. Pressed on this point, the bartender once told me that it is the oldest backbar. He claimed it was made in France and shipped to Georgetown by oxcart in the 1860s. Don't bet on it.

Once, during Prohibition, I was forced to live on nothing but food and water.

—W. C. Fields

Ann MacConnell threw some of us out of this bar in 1981: "You've all had too much to drink. Now go home." At the time she was a waitress, but later she became the owner of The Red Ram and a mayor of Georgetown. We protested innocence and sobriety at the time, but stumbled down from the Ram's ramshackle balcony and retreated to the cute little library across the street.

A venerable tavern with raw plank floor and walls, the Ram has huge plate-glass windows framing Georgetown's sleepy main (6th) street. Generous, tasty, and inexpensive sandwiches and light meals make it worth a stop, even if you don't fancy a stool at the magnificent backbar. Check out the dark, cavernous cellar where the "whore door" allegedly led to nearby houses of ill repute. For respectable, smoke-free dining, visit the back dining room, which fronts on Rose Street.

David Bauer, who took over in 1995, upgraded the menu and brought in oompah bands for Oktoberfest. Bauer cleaned up the trash-filled basement to install a rathskeller with sofas, easy chairs, and a fireplace. The posts and beams are painted in Alpine style with flowers and a German slogan, which my German girlfriend translated as "Old wine and young women will preserve even limp old men."

The Silver Queen
500 6th St. (nw corner of Taos St.), no phone available

Denver's legendary Windsor Hotel, a lost landmark, provided the diamond-dust mirrors and walnut frames of the backbar, while the stained-glass windows came from a moribund Denver mortuary. Such elegant fixtures helped transform what had become a machine shop into The Silver Queen Saloon in the 1950s.

The Silver Queen occupies William Cushman's imposing 1875 brick, Italianate-style commercial structure, which opened as Georgetown's finest edifice but went on the auction block after the 1893 silver crash. Originally, the building had a third-floor opera house. Although the third floor was declared structurally unsound in 1875, it did not collapse until 1969, finally relenting under heavy snow loads. The rubble was cleared away and the roof lowered, leaving this building with especially broad eaves and an oversized cornice. Since the 1950s, it has housed The Silver Queen restaurant, saloon, and wine cellar, as well as the Clear Creek National Bank.

Glenwood Springs
Elevation: 5,765 feet

Glenwood's original bar was the Cocktail Spring, a drinking fountain for the hot mineral water. Spa enthusiasts filled their cups here or took home jugs of the stuff. Besides the Cocktail Spring, a huge hot springs pool, a Victorian bathhouse, a grand hotel, rail service, and many fine taverns make this Colorado's favorite watering hole. The Yampah ("big medicine bear") had attracted the Utes for centuries before palefaces found the hot springs.

Prospectors staked out a townsite at the confluence of the Roaring Fork and Colorado Rivers in 1878. Walter B. Devereux, a mining engineer trained at Princeton and Columbia, arrived in 1883 and transformed the town into a hot springs spa with a grandiose hotel and saloon that is one of half a dozen notable local watering holes. The town's pioneer saloon, F. A. Barlow's Exchange, stood across 7th Street from the railroad station where the Glenwood Canyon Brewing Company now thrives.

Doc Holliday Tavern
724 Grand Ave., no phone available

A 10-foot, neon six-shooter was bolted to the façade of Duffy's Saloon in 1952 for its rechristening to commemorate the notorious gunslinger. Inside is a prototypical old-time saloon with a classic cherry-and-mahogany Brunswick backbar, brass foot rail, dusty plank floor, high ceiling, potbellied stove, pool tables, and plate-glass windows with lacy curtains. This saloon doubles as a shrine to John H. "Doc" Holliday (1852–1887), a pistol-packing dentist and gambler. Wall photos make a rogue's gallery of outlaws, including the corpses lined up after Doc and the Earp boys cleaned out the OK Corral. This shrine has holy garments (Doc Holliday T-shirts) and advice for those who may want to walk up the hill to see Doc's tombstone in Linwood Cemetery.

Oh, some are fond of red wine
and some are fond of white,
And some are all for dancing
by the pale moon light;
But rum's alone the tipple,
and the heart's delight
Of the old, bold mate of Henry Morgan.
                    —*John Masefield*

After a mile-long, uphill hike to the cemetery, we found a memorial stone explaining that Doc, still a slippery presence, lies "someplace in this cemetery." Belatedly realizing that Doc's tomb could become a tourist shrine, townsfolk put up this vague monument in 1958.

If you are traveling with rambunctious children or a companion you don't want to hear, Doc's is ideal, with its loud jukebox, noisy locals, tough waitresses, and the ghost of a scowling, gunslinging dentist.

Glenwood Canyon Brewing Company
402 7th St., (970) 945-1276

Thanks to this new annex, the Hotel Denver now offers "A Room with a Brew." Henry Bosco ran a bottling works here. Strategically sited across from the railroad depot, with thirteen saloons within a four-block area, Bosco's operation thrived until Prohibition. Then he and a partner expanded the building to create the Denver Hotel. He is commemorated by the Bosco Parkway, Pedestrian Bridge, and Riverwalk in front of the brewery.

On April 15, 1996, Bosco's old bottlery was reincarnated as the Glenwood Canyon Brewing Company. This is one of Colorado's better brewpubs and it has tasty, reasonably priced meals on a short menu that wisely does not stray into ethnic or gourmet realms. Handcrafted brews carry colorful, locally inspired monikers such as Strawberry Daze Ale (named for Glenwood's longtime harvest festival), No Name Nut Brown Ale, Hanging Lake Honey Ale, Shoshone Stout, and Vapor Cave Pale Ale. Fine, new plate-glass windows, hardwood floors, brass rails, stainless-steel brewing vats, four competition-size pool tables, and a mother-of-pearl train on the wall make this a popular beer haven and a great place to wait for Amtrak trains.

Hotel Colorado Palm Court Bar
526 Pine Ave., (970) 945-6511

The Villa Medici outside Rome inspired this grand hotel built with three million Roman bricks and 10 tons of Colorado Peachblow sandstone. Eighteen-foot-high windows flood the first floor with light. Sun worshippers can sit and sip in the central-court terrace garden with its Florentine-style fountain, trout pool, and outdoor bar.

The grandest hotel in western Colorado has two immense fireplaces to warm the spacious Palm Room lobby, with its elegant wing chairs, sofas, and potted palms. The fireplaces are awesome monuments of sandstone and Colorado Yule marble. The same exquisite, peachy sandstone is used for the grand staircase, which pauses at the landing below a gigantic reproduction of Botticelli's *The Birth of Venus*. Some take the stairs to avoid the lynx perched over the elevator, ready to spring on a tasty tourist.

The Palm Court Bar is in the old Aquarium Room, where the skylight once illuminated a waterfall and fountain filled with trout. This saloon offers shuffleboard, billiards, and old photos shellacked into the top of the front bar. You may still smell the cigars of Walter Devereux, the New York and Aspen mining man who built this hotel. Don't miss the free nocturnal hotel tours, which will introduce you to Devereux and other ghosts, including gangsters, murderers, and celebrities galore.

The elegant rectangular bar is governed by a huge grinning portrait of President Theodore Roosevelt, who stayed here on hunting trips in the nearby Flat Top Mountains. During his 1905 visit, the president posed on the front lawn with an enormous bear he had killed. Then and there, if local folklore can be believed, his daughter, Alice, coined the term "teddy bear."

19th Street Diner
19th St. & Grand Ave., (970) 945-9133

A jaded, hard-drinking crew lurks at the bar of this classic diner. Up front, they also serve alcohol along with shakes, malts, floats, and tasty meals. The diner has fuchsia and black vinyl tables, knotty-pine woodwork, and picture windows reminiscent of the 1950s. This place started out as Danceland, then the Joker Inn, and Gallagher's Pub before Joseph "Swanie" Schwanebeck converted it to a diner.

Our candid waitress said she much prefers the front-room diner to the back-room bar. "The bar crowd ain't rough," she confided, "just obnoxious. Town lushes who don't even stop drinking long enough to go to the bathroom. And one charming young man who asks, 'Wanna come to the bathroom with me and watch?'"

The bar is a U-shaped affair with a gruff bartender and regulars who barely tolerated my inspection of all the great diner kitsch on the walls. The closet-size bathroom has a communal urinal and a sign: "Please open door slowly … be kind to passersby."

Golden
Elevation: 5,675 feet

Tom Golden, a pioneer prospector, settled where Clear Creek emerges from the mountains, and a town grew up around him. Townsfolk used free firewood and booze to capture the territorial legislature, which met here from 1862 to 1867. Squeezed into a narrow valley between North Table Mountain and South Table Mountain on the east and Lookout Mountain on the west, Golden has remained a small town isolated from Denver's sprawl.

Beery breezes from the world's largest single brewery tease the palate for this town's liquid landmarks. If you're broke, you can drink Coors free—at the end of the brewery tour or by sneaking out early to the tasting room. Here their various brews are served at just the right temperature and freshness to taste better than they do anywhere else.

Ace-Hi Tavern
1212–1216 Washington Ave., (303) 279-1091

One of Golden's most popular bars was built in 1879 as the Golden Opera House. A grand staircase leads to the upstairs opera hall, which hosted performances of *Uncle Tom's Cabin* as well as a two-headed, 200-pound woman, and speeches by such notables as Eugene Victor Debs. The first-floor Opera House Saloon, opened in 1881, outlived the opera house.

Since 1944, Leo and Sidney Stillman have operated it as the Ace-Hi Tavern. The cheapest beer in town and the casual atmosphere attract students from the nearby Colorado School of Mines. "Some of the world's best students and greatest mining engineers hang out here," boasted Sid Stillman. "If only you could get them back to work."

Buffalo Rose
1119 Washington Ave., (303) 279-5190

A bar has existed on this corner since 1859, the year Golden was born. Initially,

Golden houses the world's largest single brewery and a host of saloons. On the western edge of Golden, the body of Buffalo Bill Cody is buried atop Lookout Mountain, but his ghost still frequents Golden taverns, as shown in this Foss Drug Store mural. Golden's oldest saloon, Kasper Hofmeister's Goosetown Lounge, was demolished in 1998 for a Coors Brewery parking lot. 1994 photo of Golden by Tom Noel; 1995 photo of Buffalo Bill by Tom Noel; c. 1890 photo of Kasper Hofmeister's, Tom Noel Collection.

I drink to make my friends more interesting.
—*George Jean Nathan*

this two-story frame building housed the International Bowling Saloon. The second story was removed in 1872 to accommodate a large organ. Today it is a popular restaurant and bar with a fancy backbar dating from the 1870s. It has expanded into the Golden Plunge Room (so named because it was the site of Golden's first public swimming pool) with a bandstand, a dance floor, and a wine cellar.

Goosetown Lounge
300 10th St. (nw corner of Archer St.), (303) 399-9703

This saloon opened in 1873 to serve brewery workers who settled here to work just across Clear Creek for Adolph Coors. Adolph's large flock of geese on the brewery lake apparently gave the community—and the tavern—its name. Another tale has it that Goldenites named Goosetown for the guttural quacking of German residents. In 1873, Julius Schultz opened this place as his home, grocery, and saloon. He sold beer by the bucket as well as by the glass, so youngsters could carry buckets to workmen or to their folks at home. To keep down the foam and keep up the liquid content, smarter bucket-carriers buttered the bucket first.

Schultz's quaint frame place with its veranda overlooking Clear Creek was stuccoed and muddled over the decades, and his beer garden became a weedy asphalt parking lot. Inside, however, the high-back wooden booths remained along with a splendid mahogany backbar with a 20-foot-long mirror.

Various Germans owned the Goosetown over the decades. In a 1908 photo on the wall, it is Kasper Hofmeister's tavern. The cash register offers another clue, with its 1909 inscription "Made for Adolph Sneller." During Prohibition it survived as a speakeasy, and during the Coors strikes it carried on offering Budweiser. Sam Wayland bought the Goosetown Lounge in 1968 and rechristened it Sam's Land. "Why did you change the name?" Dick "Mr. Beer" Kreck asked on one of our visits. "I was born with this name," said Sam.

Sam died in 1997. The old-time bar should have been renamed for longtime waitress Jeanne Sautelet, who has a sunny disposition and a voice like gravel. She refers to the chili cheeseburger specialty as "the gut buster" and put up her slogan, "If you came here to bitch, you've used up 97% of your time." Although Coors Brewing Company has made the original site into a parking lot, part of the Goosetown Lounge is still honking. The bar was demolished by Coors in 1998, but John Hickenlooper of the Wynkoop Brewing Company rode to the rescue. "We bought the furnishings and the special essence," John claimed. "We installed them in a building at 3242 East Colfax Avenue across from the Bluebird Theater and reopened the Goosetown Tavern in September 1998."

Loveland Block
1122 Washington Ave. (nw corner of 11th St.), no phone available

William A. H. Loveland, a prime promoter of Golden, built this two-story brick building in 1863. He coaxed the territorial legislature here with free use of his building while townsfolk contributed firewater and free firewood. The building, with antique decor including an old wall safe, was reborn in 1993 as a bar and restaurant recalling territorial times.

Rock Rest Tavern
16000 Mt. Vernon Rd. (corner of S. Golden Rd.), (303) 216-2895

A cobblestone tavern opened here in 1907 and became legendary as a brothel, a speakeasy, and, most recently, a biker bar. The little rear rooms, where "ladies" entertained "gentlemen," were demolished in 1997 to create a single large hall. The front barroom retains its intimate air with a small bar and a few cozy booths and signs on the knotty pine wall: "No Working During Drinking Hours," "Watch out for Pickpockets & Loose Women," and "Room Decorated by the Class of 1938."

The Rock Rest is still noted for its good, inexpensive meals and its hot dance floor. In the old days you taxi-danced (paid the girls by the dance) and could purchase other favors. During Prohibition, this was one of the most famous speakeasies in the Denver area, Gen Short, a regular, told me. "It was very popular with the younger set, especially college students. It was best to take your own hootch, though, because they often served bad booze."

Inside, they still talk about the big biker brawl of March 1972. The Sons of Silence, Hells Angels, The Deadmen, and others got into a fight. The bikers threw out the first law-enforcement officials on the scene. It took a small army of twenty-two Jefferson County sheriffs and Lakewood and Golden police to finally restore order. Twenty-six bikers were arrested and ten loaded pistols, knives, and heavy motorcycle chains were confiscated.

The bar was closed for seventy-five days, then opened on probation. The owners needed some time to replace sixty smashed glasses and delouse the joint. They never did find two pool balls. The Rock Rest is supposedly reformed and lets in only well-behaved bikers. They may come to see the waitress, who rides a purple Harley Davidson Sportster with a leather saddlebag and leather fringe on the handlebars, just like that which dangles from her bulging vest.

Goodrich

Elevation: 4,380 feet

On the north bank of the South Platte, this tiny prairie crossroads is the gateway to Jackson Reservoir, a state park noted for its fishing, camping, boating, hunting, waterskiing, jet-skiing, windsurfing, and immense sandy beaches shaded by cottonwoods. G. T. Goodrich, a pioneer and Morgan County commissioner, settled here around 1908. His false-fronted, corner grocery store, whose appendages included a now-closed garage, survives as a tavern legendary for its large round table.

Kozy Corner Bar & Cafe
24213 Weld County Hwy. 39 (sw corner of Colorado 144), (970) 645-2064

King Arthur had a round table where all were equal. So does Goodrich, Colorado, where the round table fills much of this tiny bar and café, at the junction of Highways 39 and 44. Upon opening the door, I was face-to-face with owners Art and Connie Mead and a committee of locals seated at the round table. The table looked to be 10 feet in diameter and was decorated with cattle brands seared into the heavy wood. Under the table, a trapdoor led to what they told me had been a bootleg joint. They welcomed me to the round table's unique chairs: tractor seats welded to large, metal milk cans. Seek-

ing out one of the four stools at the miniature bar or one of the backroom tables seemed impolite, for the television was off and I had the feeling these folks counted on whoever walks through that door for entertainment.

"You can have the governor's chair," Art told me. "We've had a lot of people come in, even governor Roy Romer, though not since the last election." The jokes began. Connie Mead refilled coffee mugs and beer glasses before the bottoms ever showed. The board walls and old plank floor squeaked whenever she went to the huge walk-in cooler for more beer. I asked her about the faded sign, "Squeak's," on the front of the building. "Oh, yeah. That was Howard 'Squeak' Meek, who had a squeaky voice.

He converted this store to a bar and café about 1980. And he put in the round table and these tractor seats."

She passed the bowl of hard-shelled walnuts and a pair of pliers. The round table filled as darkness chased farmers and ranchers out of their fields. They were dressed in heavy overalls or jeans and workshirts, ruddy from the outdoors, thirsty and hungry. Some eyed the chalkboard menu: Honey-dipped chicken. Rocky Mountain oysters. Chicken-fried steak. Biscuits and sausage gravy. Onion rings. French fries. Hotdogs. Hamburgers.

Connie especially prides herself on the hamburgers. She cooks them 2 inches thick and 5 inches wide—the biggest burger in Colorado, she claims. She showed me the huge kitchen with its antique stove and a separate dining room for "those who don't want to eat in a barroom."

"You city folks!" one of the more aggressive ranchers at the table said to me. "Why, a cop stopped me last time I rode into Denver with my rifle on the rack of my pickup. Hell, Denver is where you really need to carry a gun!"

"Speaking of city slickers," another crusty fellow broke in, "they're going to be invading Morgan County soon. They're converting the Union Pacific track along the Platte from rails to trails. We're going to have bicyclists and joggers and skaters from Denver wandering around out here." Connie set a large bowl of steaming-hot popcorn on the table.

"Goodrich," Art told me, "used to be a lot more than it is. Once, we had a post office, a hay mill, Kuner's pickle vats, two grocery stores, a blacksmith shop, a garage, and the Goodrich State Bank. We still have the Weldon Valley Presbyterian Church—a real pretty little white-frame church. The UP had a depot and crew boardinghouse here. I took my first train ride out of that depot, went to Weldona 7 miles down the track. Cost 5 cents. At Weldona they have a bar, the Last Stand. But it's just an ordinary beer joint. Doesn't have a round table."

"People like this table," Connie told me, "because everybody can just sit down together and chat back and forth. There's no sense changing something that works. Art and I love this business. We both like people. And people like us back."

"At this round table we discuss all the great issues of our time," a wise old farmer winked. "But I can't remember that we've ever solved any problems—except who'll buy the next round of beer."

Grand Junction
Elevation: 4,586 feet

Following the removal of the Ute Indians in 1881, George A. Crawford and others founded this town as a rail hub for the Denver & Rio Grande Railroad. Initially promoted as "Denver West," it was later named for its location at the confluence of the Grand (renamed the Colorado in 1921) and Gunnison Rivers. This site is rimmed by three large plateaus: Grand Mesa on the southeast, Colorado National Monument of the Uncompahgre Plateau on the southwest, and the Book Cliffs on the north, a rocky shelf of "books" stretching 100 miles into Utah.

With more than 100,000 residents, the Grand Junction metropolis is the largest city in western Colorado. As in Southern California, subdivisions and shopping malls are displacing fruit orchards, although vineyards are proliferating. Wine bars and cafés are now popping up to compete with the town's shot-and-beer taverns.

Pufferbelly's Bar & Restaurant
119 Pitkin Ave. (sw corner of 2nd St.), (970) 242-1600

The railroad decor of this eating, drinking, and gathering place stems from its 1906 origins as a depot for the Colorado Midland and the D&RG. A 1980s restaurant addition has replaced a diner operated by the D&RG. The depot retains its original golden oak woodwork, seating, antique fixtures, and Amtrak service.

A recent restoration removed the false ceiling and second-story office to open up the original grand lobby, with its high, coffered ceiling, for a dining room with railroad memorabilia on the second-story mezzanine. A glass greenhouse is planned to cover the historic edifice and its noble trackside façade, incorporating it into the restaurant and retail complex along with an antique railroad coach.

Quincy Bar
609 Main St. Mall, (970) 242-9633

With local liquor license number 1 on the wall, the oldest bar in town welcomes all sorts. The remarkable interior has a 14-foot-high, gilded, parquet pressed-metal ceiling and a central square bar where customers face each other. A fine mural on the boarded-over, front transom windows depicts the panorama of the Book Cliffs it hides, while the flip-side, exterior transom painting is a street scene of 1940s Grand Junction.

A female mannequin with silver skin in various states of dress is among the regulars at the mahogany bar. In the rear are pool tables, a dance floor, and giant murals celebrating the sleek, stainless-steel California Zephyr at Grand Junction's grand old depot. An unusually candid wall menu warns: "Food the Doctor Warned You About! Burrito. Pizza. Hot Pocket. Cheeseburger. Microwave Magic. Enjoy It!"

Rockslide Brewery Restaurant
401 Main St. Mall (se corner of 4th St.), (970) 245-2111

Shimmering, stainless-steel fermenting tanks shine on Main Street through the storefront windows of Mesa County's first brewpub. Inside, the big double hall has bare brick walls, bare hardwood floors, and 12-foot-high ceilings adorned with a parasail and a kayak. Opened in 1994, this popular,

Grand Junction, at the confluence of the Colorado and Gunnison Rivers, became the rail hub—and largest city—in western Colorado. The depot shown here is now a hospitable landmark named Pufferbelly's. 1910 photo by George Beam courtesy of the Colorado Historical Society.

The Quincy Bar, the oldest saloon in Grand Junction, sports a mural of the town in the 1940s on its exterior transom.

inexpensive family place offers brewmeister Clint Peterson's sweet Rabbit Ears Amber Ale, the light, popular Kokopelli Cream Ale, Big Bear Stout, and other handcrafted beers, as well as salads, sandwiches, pizza, and pasta. The dishwasher may have come up with the Tuesday "Pint Nite," which allows you to take the pint glass home. Bring it back any or every Tuesday for a discounted pint.

This building originated in 1895 as James M. and Albert R. Sampliner's clothing store, and you can still see "Sampliner's" in the blue and white floor tiles. Sampliner's was followed by two other haberdasheries, Rush-Stanford and then Brownson's, before the switch to wet goods. You can take out kegs and growlers, but not the kayak or parasail suspended from the ceiling.

St. Regis Hotel Bar
359 Colorado Ave. (sw corner of 4th St.), (970) 242-1974

Opened in 1895 as the Grand Hotel, this three-story brick hostelry became the St. Regis in 1907. Grand Junction's first radio station broadcast from the hotel ballroom in the 1930s when the Oriental Room and the Cocktail Lounge were also local hot spots. It became a flophouse that courted demolition in the 1970s before renovation reopened it in the 1980s as a pool hall, bar, and restaurant with living quarters upstairs.

Greeley

Elevation: 4,463 feet

Ironically, this college cow town with notable watering holes started out as a saloonless utopia. The "saints" of Horace Greeley's model city outlawed bars and booze and put up a fence around town to keep out bad people.

Grace Greenwood visited the new utopia and reported in her book *New Life in New Lands* (J. B. Ford & Co., 1874) that Greeley "is a model temperance town." She found some critics, such as a fellow traveler who told her: "Don't stop in that town; you'll die of dullness in less than five hours. There is nothing there but irrigation. Your host will invite you out to see him irrigate his potato-patch; your hostess will excuse herself to go and irrigate her pinks and dahlias. Every one has a ditch of his own to manage; there is not a billiard-saloon in the whole camp, nor a drink of whiskey to be had for love or money."

Colorado's first great temperance colony thrived, becoming the largest city in northeastern Colorado. The dream of a sober communal society was abandoned in 1971 when Greeley finally went wet and attracted a host of saloons. The Red Garter, Greeley's first legal tavern, is gone, but other memorable bars are worth a visit.

Fleetside Brewing Company
721 10th St. (half block west of 8th Ave. [Main St.]), CLOSED

Although the Union Colony, 1412 8th Avenue, won the race to open the first Greeley brewpub by several months, it can't match Fleetside for ambience, food, and beer. Opened July 31, 1995, in a 1920s Chevrolet dealership, this building is a swirly stucco Mission Deco affair whose entry arch now leads not to the car lot but to an outdoor beer garden. The 20-foot-high, skylighted

The state armory in Greeley has been converted to the Good Times Saloon, which boasts four bars and innumerable artifacts, ranging from a stagecoach to a B-17 bomber.

open truss ceiling and big glass windows make this place unusually light and airy. The decor consists of old dealership souvenirs, such as the garage doors, plus antiques and found objects from Denver, including benches from Union Station and railings from the 23rd Street viaduct. The 6-foot-high, neon beer glass was salvaged from the defunct Lane's Tavern in Lakewood. It took $1.8 million and six months to convert the 15,000-square-foot showroom into Greeley's largest saloon.

Pool tables, electronic darts, take-out beer, late-night food service, and a casual, pubby atmosphere are pluses, but the best part is the fine, inexpensive food and good beer, especially the Tail Gate Pale Ale and Lug Nut Stout. Meeker's Wheat Beer commemorates town founder Nathan Meeker, whose house at 1324 9th Avenue is now a nifty museum. Fleetside is a family place that also brews homemade cream sodas, root beer, and ginger ale.

Good Times Saloon
614 8th Ave., (970) 352-7424

Built as an armory in 1921, this two-story fortress now rocks with live music and large crowds. When it was an armory, it became a popular place for parties and dances. Now recycled as a restaurant and bar, it retains the armory theme with a B-17 bomber suspended over the rear dance floor, as well as numerous missiles, part of a submarine, and other weapons. Hundreds of antiques, including two stagecoaches suspended from the ceiling, and four bars make this saloon an offbeat museum.

Rio Grande Saloon
825 9th St. Plaza (catercorner from the Weld County Courthouse), (970) 304-9292

The old downtown Woolworth's five-and-dime store closed in 1993, only to reopen in 1996 as a huge bar and Mexican restaurant. This is the fourth Rio Grande in a chain started in Fort Collins, with other franchises in Boulder and Denver. The old lunch counter is now a front bar with a tile-

If all be true that I do think,
There are five reasons we should drink:
Good wine–a friend–or being dry
Or lest we should be by and by
Or any other reason why.
—Henry Aldrich

framed, Neo-Spanish Colonial Revival backbar mirror. Art Deco lamps, old Southwest-style doorways, Mexican tile appliqué, and stone accents dress up the place. With a huge outdoor patio on the downtown pedestrian mall, the Rio seats 350. They specialize in Mexican meals, margaritas, and Mexican beers, which come wrapped in a tissue. Of this novelty, our waitress said somewhat apologetically, "It's supposed to keep the bottle cooler and keep it from sweating so much."

Hillrose

Elevation: 4,165 feet

illrose is neither hilly nor rosy, but a small, flat farm hub founded in about 1900 and stuggling to stay on the map.

The Place Bar & Grill
317 Emerson St., (970) 847-3462

Coyote Heaven, the old saloon across the street, is now a café–drug–fishing tackle–grocery–laundromat–liquor–video store, so Skip Kaiser opened this place in 1989. The venerable brick storefront has housed a land office, real estate office, barber shop, and apartments.

The unusual Z-shaped front bar has room for only nine stools, but sports a handsome Formica marble top edged with golden oak elbow rests. The floor is hardwood and the walls are smothered with a fine collection of beer ad "bimbo" posters. The Quonset hut behind the storefront has been converted to a pool room. Among Skip's many entertainments are a collection of seventeenth-century, wrought-iron tavern puzzles. "Actually," Skip confessed, "these have been a mistake. People get too busy working on the puzzles and forget to order more drinks." This tiny bar has a grill, three booths, and the slogan "There ain't no place like this place anywhere near this place so this must be the place."

"Hillrose is heaven," a customer told us. "It's a quiet little town. No crime. No gangs. No traffic. No pavement on Main Street."

A trapdoor lies between the red vinyl stools and the orange plastic booths, making this the town tornado refuge. This compact, intimate bar does not have a jukebox but does possess a splendid barman who entertains with songs, stories, jokes, gadgets, puzzles, and a miniature toilet that flushes itself when you put quarters in it. The real toilet is in a tiny closet papered with a collection of Harley Davidson girls.

Hygiene
Elevation: 5,090 feet

The Dunkards (the Church of the Brethren sect, noted for their baptismal practice of dunking a person three times) founded this Boulder County farm hamlet around 1880. Still a tiny town, it has a tavern that offers immersion in Old World liquid history.

Old Prague Inn
**7521 Ute Hwy. (corner of Colorado 66),
(303) 772-6374**

Located at the junction of Ute Highway and Colorado 66, 4 miles west of Longmont, this antique, red brick schoolhouse has become one of Colorado's better country inns and the only one certified as an official Czech hospitality center. Behind red drapes with gold ropes, the mini-bar has scenes of Old Prague, Prague's famous Pilsner Urquell beer, and a portrait of celebrated Czech author and president Vaclav Havel. The Czech bartender amused us with the Old World bar trick of floating coins on the foamy head of their heaviest beer.

Red flagstone walks, huge old trees, evergreen shrubs, and windowboxes filled with red geraniums decorate the outside. Inside is a quaint stucco and dark timber house divided into various dining rooms. The large fireplace is adorned with a statuesque saint; metal-topped, porcelain beer steins; and ornamental plates. Great Czech food in large portions is heavy on the potatoes, dumplings, and butter. Owners Joaquin and Jocy Ann Armas reported that the old schoolhouse was converted to a grange hall, then to a private residence, before they opened this splendid country inn in 1977.

Idaho Springs
Elevation: 7,540 feet

In January 1859, a bar—a sandbar—in Clear Creek caught George A. Jackson's eye while he was camping at the hot springs that gave the town its name. Digging with his hunting knife and panning with his tin cup, Jackson found placer gold. A swarm of other gold-seekers soon arrived to establish mines, mills, and outlying camps for which Idaho Springs emerged as the core supply town.

In 1863, Dr. E. M. Cummings opened a commercial hot springs, which has evolved into the Indian Hot Springs Hotel and Resort. After stewing in these 100-degree springs, many folks cooled off in the town's taverns. Like the town itself, the watering holes are strung out along the narrow stretch of Clear Creek Canyon. Miner Street, the well-preserved main street, boasted twenty-two saloons during its flush times.

Fearing that their home would become just another Miner Street dive, the Underwood family donated the Underwood House in 1973 for what is now the Idaho Springs Historical Society Museum. The worst of the Miner Street saloons was the Colorado Bar, torn down to construct Citizens Park. Old-timers like Bob Bohland still recall the cockroaches and odor of the Colorado Bar. The Mountain Shadows, a den of rogues in the old opera house, was finally shut down for good in the 1970s. Surviving bars are much more reputable; the two most notable offer some of the best pizza and tastiest buffalo in the Rockies.

BeauJo's Pizza
1511–1515 Miner St., (303) 573-6924

BeauJo's is one of Colorado's most relished success stories. A hippie from Duluth, Minnesota, Franklin "Chips" Bair, took over a struggling, eighteen-seat pizza place founded by Beau and his wife, Jo, in 1973. "I used to sleep on the floor after sweeping it every night," Chips recalled in 1997, "until a customer rented me a cabin for two large pizzas a week." Since then, Chips has enlarged this place more than twenty-one times to include four adjacent buildings. He has opened additional BeauJo's in Arvada, Aurora, Boulder, Colorado Springs, Denver, Highlands Ranch, Fort Collins, and elsewhere.

BeauJo's Colorado-style "mountain pies" have thick crusts wrapping generous portions of thirty-one possible ingredients, even broccoli, spinach, chicken Cordon Bleu, fresh garlic, artichoke hearts, shrimp, and tofu. Try the barbecue pizzas and "the challenge": If any two people can actually eat all of this super-thick, 16-inch pizza, they get it free with a $100 cash prize. For dessert, BeauJo's gives you honey to put on leftover pizza crust for a sopaipilla-style treat.

Beer is served in pitchers and fruit jars in this rustic maze of upstairs and downstairs rooms. The core building is the 1879 Idaho Springs Mining Exchange, but with three adjacent structures, there is plenty of room for four claw-foot bathtubs holding the salad bars. Historic wall maps show old railroad lines and mining claims crisscrossing Idaho Springs. The imaginative decor features barn wood carved into mountains and a wooden sunset under a pressed-tin ceiling. In one of the back rooms, a nifty backbar has leaded and stained-glass cabinets and a miner's scale for weighing gold dust. The old freight elevator of the Pascoe Building has been converted to a mine-shaft exhibit, while a Model T pickup truck dresses up another back room, as do old stills from bootleggers up Soda Creek. In addition to its fantastic pizza, this place is a notable museum, but be prepared to wait for a table—even though there are seats for 750.

Buffalo Bar
1617–1623 Miner St., (303) 567-2729

A dense herd of buffalo in a huge wall mural, *The Stampede,* resembles the crowds flocking to this century-old watering hole. Among the clues to its antiquity are the communal urinal, creaky wooden floor, dusty skylights, and two potbellied stoves with piles of newspapers for reading or burning. Vintage furnishings include more than a hundred antique metal signs. The backbar in black walnut once stood in Denver's first grand hotel, the now-demolished Windsor, while the mahogany front bar carries a brass Brunswick-Balke-Collender plaque from St. Louis. Two buffalo cow heads stare at a macho buffalo sporting long and sharp horns.

The Buffalo is a combination of the Worth Saloon and John Rohner's Bar and Billiard Hall. Behind a brick storefront with a metal cornice, Rohner's large, long building was restored in the 1970s to become once again a popular bar, restaurant, and billiard hall that ultimately expanded into Worth's Saloon next door. In 1995, Will McFarlane, owner of a huge buffalo ranch and the Denver Buffalo Company ("the world's largest supplier of buffalo products"), bought the Buffalo Bar and greatly expanded its buffaloiana, edible and otherwise.

Hanson's Lodge Bar
1661 Colorado Blvd. (se corner of 16th St.), no phone available

The 1881 Club Hotel was updated with rustic-style log façade in the 1930s when the

Idaho Springs evolved from an 1859 gold strike to a popular hot-springs resort. Both miners and bathers found plenty of saloons in which to cool off along Miner Street, the town's main drag. c. 1860 photo by Joseph Collier, courtesy of the Colorado Historical Society.

Club Room bar was added to what was reorganized as Hanson's Lodge. The tavern façade features logs in vertical, horizontal, and sunburst patterns. Inside, this roomy, old-fashioned tavern has a splendid native-rock fireplace and chimney; open, round log ceiling beams; plank floors; and a rustic decor overseen by wild game trophies. The three pool tables and bar still attract local wildlife of the species *Homo sapiens*.

Indian Hot Springs Bar
302 Soda Creek Rd., (303) 567-2191

This watery resort has a bar on the front porch overhanging Soda Creek. Inside, the log swivel chairs and red vinyl, padded front bar used to be in what is now the pool room. Live country-and-western bands and dancing make the wooden floors creak and cost the upstairs hotel guests some sleep. At the adjacent hot springs, a poolside, grass-shack saloon refreshes bathers. From 1904 until the health department objected in the 1960s, this place advertised itself as the Radium Hot Springs, where "miracle waters" healed everything from rheumatism to lumbago, from heartbreak to lost manhood. All traces of the radium cure, including the abandoned wheelchairs, crutches, and canes that once stood as testimonials, are gone, but this is still a hot spot.

The stone-and-frame lodge, restaurant, and bar are attached to a plastic domed pool and baths using the hot mineral waters of Soda Creek. Water ranging from 104 to 112 degrees also feed various private bathing rooms, including some subterranean stone caverns with chest-deep pools and a mud bath.

Tommyknocker Brewery & Pub
1401 Miner St., (303) 567-2688

Brewpubs are good for what ails you—especially this one, opened by Tim Lenahan and Charles Sturdavant in 1994. It has the finest beer in town and good, inexpensive grub. The 1898 Placer Inn and adjacent bowling alley were converted into this airy brewery with multiple dining areas and three pool tables. The Mission-style façade and generous windows date from the 1920s, when this was a classy tourist lunchroom and bowling alley.

Sturdavant, a former geologist at the Henderson Molybdenum Mine, said: "I like working with chemistry and biology and my hands—and brewing pays off more steadily than mining. Rocks, however, are easier to deal with than people. I got out of mining when I began bumping into Tommyknockers—those Cornish elves that cause trouble underground—unless you leave 'em pasties and good beer. Life is too short to drink ordinary beer."

Of all the gin joints in all the towns in all the world, she walks into mine!
—Spoken by Humphrey Bogart
in the film Casablanca

The old hotel rooms upstairs are now barley storage and the offices of this large operation, which ships beer all over the state. Over half their sales are of Maple Nut Brown Ale, but the hoppy Pick Axe Pale Ale is also popular. Tommyknocker is much friendlier than the old Placer Inn, where hard-drinking locals met strangers with beady-eyed suspicion.

West Winds Bar & Grill
1631 Miner Ave., (303) 567-2029

The raunchiest saloon in town has often been renamed but never reformed. It was rechristened The Log Cabin when the round log façade was affixed to the 1881 brick building, then The Town Dump, the Spaghetti Ranch, and the Mad Hatter Restaurant & Lounge, whose decor consisted of several hundred hats. Pool and good, inexpensive beer and meals are the attraction, as well as a host of uninhibited town characters.

Kiowa

Elevation: 6,408 feet

The Elbert County seat (1859) on Kiowa Creek originated as a stagecoach stop. While Elbert and Elizabeth battled it out for county seat honors, Kiowa officials quietly built a two-room courthouse and began holding trials in what is now the Hitching Post Tavern. It remains a lively country tavern, but its rival, the old Weather Vane Bar, has been converted to a used-car dealership.

Hitching Post Tavern
222 Comanche St. (Colorado 86), (303) 621-2723

To handle the raucous if friendly locals in this jolly joint on Colorado 86, the bartender has been known to grab the backbar Kiowa Indian spear adorned with ruffled feathers. An old-fashioned wooden sidewalk and awning front this two-story clapboard box. Built in 1880 as a general store, it may be the oldest building in town. Large, 30-foot-high ponderosa pines cut from the Black Forest just west of town still prop up the roof. Don Cote converted it to the Hitching Post Tavern in 1991.

Daylight streaming through the plate-glass storefront bathes this old hall with its plank floors, narrow board walls, and ceiling retrofitted with electricity for the ceiling fans and gooseneck chandeliers. Locals linger over cribbage boards at the bar or the two pool tables. Homemade signs read "No Tabs," "Complimentary Non-Alcoholic Drinks for Designated Drivers," and "Please Use the Spittoon" (the brass cuspidor at the bar is for tips). Except for chips and nuts, food service is limited to what you bring in or what will fit into the backbar microwave oven. A side room has been devoted to a serious dart-throwing alley. A corner stage promises live bands every other Saturday night. Meanwhile, a raucous country-and-western jukebox offers off-color tunes such as "Were You Born an Asshole?"

Lafayette
Elevation: 5,237 feet

After rich coal veins were found in this area in the 1880s, pioneer farmer Mary Miller turned her homestead into a town and named it for her deceased husband. She was an ardent Prohibitionist who kept the town saloonless. Most of the mines closed by 1950, but Lafayette is now a booming suburb of Denver and Boulder, and the saloons that Mary dreaded have sprouted up along the main street, Public Road.

Lafayette retains its Boulder Valley Grange Hall (1900) at 3400 North 95th Street and the Sonic Drive-In at 50 Waneka Parkway. Some of the old housing survives, such as the Lafayette Boarding House at 600 East Simpson Street. Here miners found furnished rooms and meals for $6 a week, plus an old washhouse, still out back. Other landmarks within the downtown National Register Historic District are the Rocky Mountain Fuel Company Store (1901) at 400 East Simpson Street and the Miller House (1889) at 409 East Cleveland Street (at Michigan Avenue). Born as a coal town filled with immigrants, this is still a blue-collar town with many Hispanic residents and two notable Mexican cantinas.

Efrain's Mexican Restaurant, Cantina & Takeout
101 E. Cleveland St. & Public Rd. (Main St.), (303) 666-7544

Efrain Gomez, an immigrant from Chihuahua, Mexico, cooked for twenty years in various restaurants before opening his own in a miner's cottage here in 1991. Efrain, a bachelor, enlisted his four brothers and five sisters with their children and grandchildren to run what has become a large, popular cantina. It has spread into the neighboring cottage and become a multiroom maze, complete with an outdoor patio and a library lounge (the old master bedroom) where you can browse and sip superb gold margaritas (Jose Cuervo Gold Tequila and Cointreau). They serve only Mexican food—including both refried and whole beans. The service by Efrain's nieces and nephews is fast and friendly.

This hot spot serves torrid chili verde and costillas (Mexican baby-back ribs). Pay close attention to the thermometer by each menu item—I did not and had to put out the fire with Capirotada, a ceremonial Indian wedding bread with rum.

La Familia Mexican Food Restaurant
201 N. Public Rd. (nw corner of Genesco St.), (303) 665-8592

In a homely stucco-and-Masonite shack with two tiny rear additions, this is a reincarnation of the notorious deejay dive, sometimes called the "Lafayette Knife and Gun Club." It has been retrofitted with glass-brick windows and portholes to reassure you that no one is being murdered inside. On the siding is a large, sunny mural of an Indian pueblo in a saguaro-studded desert-scape. Equally faded on this funky old place are the handpainted chile peppers draped over the front door. Inside, two bars frame a delicious Mexican café.

---

*Notably fond of music, I dote on a sweeter tone
Than ever the harp has uttered, or ever the lute has known.
When I wake at five in the morning, with a feeling in my head
Suggestive of mild excesses before I retired to bed.*

—Eugene Field

Lakewood

Elevation: 5,440 feet

William A. H. Loveland, the ubiquitous pioneer who promoted Golden, built railroads, and in 1878 became the owner of the *Rocky Mountain News,* founded Lakewood in 1889. This agricultural hamlet flourished as a health spa with the 1904 opening of the Jewish Consumptive Relief Society, a tent colony that evolved into a major tuberculosis sanitarium.

Lakewood's sanitarium, turkey farms, and ranches were never the same after the beginning of World War II, which brought construction of the Denver Ordnance Plant. This $35 million federal complex, built on the Hayden Ranch, became the postwar Denver Federal Center, the nation's second-largest concentration of federal workers. It includes major offices for some thirty agencies with about 10,000 employees, of whom 317 can fit into a subterranean bomb shelter to keep the federal government humming in a post–nuclear war world. Such odds could drive even nongovernment workers to drink.

Lakewood did not incorporate as a city until 1969, but then began an aggressive annexation campaign that has made it the fourth most populous city in Colorado with some 140,000 residents. The Jewish Consumptive Relief Society sold off its West Colfax frontage for the JCRS shopping center. Lakewood's grand old mansion, Belmar (at 797 South Wadsworth Boulevard), a replica of the Petit Trianon at Versailles, also succumbed to developers. After demolition in 1970, the 750-acre estate was subdivided for the Villa Italia shopping center, the Lakewood Municipal Center, and Lakewood Heritage Center, a preserve for landmarks in the path of development. For a pristine re-creation of the rural ideal, see the White Fence

Farm (at 6263 West Jewell Avenue), a restaurant and model farm complete with petting zoo, all in patriotic Colonial Revival style beneath an oversize American flag.

Lakewood's old main street, West Colfax Avenue, has been supplanted by Union Boulevard with its concentration of government and private office buildings, but remains the best strip for pub crawling.

Casa Bonita
6715 W. Colfax Ave., (303) 232-5115

To keep this family-oriented place wholesome, the management offers a free taxi ride home for inebriates. In the bathroom they have spelled out the eight surefire proofs of inebriation, starting with "obnoxious behavior" and "glassy, red eyes."

Even the tipsy should be bright-eyed in Colorado's most exotic Mexican cantina. An old department store in the JCRS shopping center was remodeled in 1974 into this south-of-the-border fantasy. The 82-foot, pink stucco bell tower with an observation deck is crowned by a life-size warrior with spear, shield, and plumed helmet. Inside, under a high black ceiling simulating a tropical night, the decor caters to the romantic stereotypes of Mexico cherished by North Americans. A Spanish tile floor winds through a tropical jungle of concrete palm trees, plastic ferns, and strolling, strumming mariachis. Diners can snuggle into a thatched-roof cabaña or a ferny grotto overlooking a waterfall, fountain, and lagoon. Smiling señoritas deliver the margaritas, while acrobatic señors dive into the lagoon.

This 52,000-square-foot complex, with its 30-foot waterfall, pirates' hideout, a mercado, a sixty-game arcade, and other marvels, is the largest link in a chain of Casa Bonitas. Colorado's favorite "dive-in" bar is a great escape from the humdrum.

Edgewater Inn
5302 W. 25th Ave. (sw corner of Ames St.), (303) 237-3524

A long John Elway pass west of Sloan Lake lies the little community of Edgewater and its most famous institution, the Edgewater Inn. Standing proud inside his tiny tavern, Ben DiPietro dressed to match the bright Bronco orange vinyl booths. He opened the place in 1953, but after the Denver Broncos went into business in 1960, he made it a shrine for a team that he, unlike some, never called the "Donkeys" or the "Buncos."

DiPietro specializes in pizza and doesn't worry about chains like Pizza Hut and Domino's. He makes a better pie. His fans are as loyal to him as they are to the Broncos. Ben and his wife, Josephine, have never had to advertise; word of their pizzas, scrumptious meatballs, and cannolis flavored with secret family sauces has spread throughout the metropolis.

Regulars at the U-shaped bar fancy the 18-ounce schooners of beer, ideal for washing down the Howdy Paisano Pizza (Italian sausage, mushrooms, green peppers, black olives, hot chile peppers, and a special seasoning). The Edgewater Inn closes only for the most important holiday of all: the Super Bowl. While Ben and Jo escort a crowd of regulars to the big game, a home team gives their place a thorough annual scrubbing for stray pizza crumbs. The outside decor consists of green, red-orange, and white paint (the colors of the Italian flag) outside and Broncos souvenirs and Coors ads inside. Ben and Jo still run the show, but with considerable help from their son, Dick, and his wife, Caroline.

In one of the few changes since 1953, the DiPietros celebrated the Broncos' 1998 Super Bowl upset win over the Green Bay Packers by finally discarding the orange vinyl seat covers and installing a soft tan replacement. Ben ended customer carping about this shocking change by pointing out that the Broncos, too, had adopted a new uniform.

Ken Caryl Manor House Bar
14432 Ken Caryl Rd., (303) 973-8064

John Charles Shaffer, owner of the *Rocky Mountain News,* named Ken Caryl Ranch for his two sons in 1914, when he bought the 28,000-acre ranch and built the Manor House. In the 1970s the Johns Manville Corporation of New York City bought the ranch and moved their world headquarters here and developed the ranch as luxury ranchettes.

The Manor House, a Georgian Revival–style plantation mansion, opened to the public in 1990 as a bar and restaurant. The library became a piano bar and the sunroom a smoker room, while upstairs rooms were converted to dining. After a few drinks and a stroll around the grounds to admire the view of Denver in the distant haze, guests may soon feel like lords and ladies of the manor.

Lakewood Grill & Bar
8100 W. Colfax Ave.
(se corner of Ammons St.),
(303) 237-8051

In this modern edifice, customers settle into black vinyl booths to bask in the pink neon glow. Built in 1952, this bar replaced

Mike Fuzo's 1940s tavern of the same name. Bruno and Diane Landino took over in 1964 and attracted customers with jumbo drinks and homemade Italian food. Bruno, who worked at Lowry Air Force Base as the commanding general's personal cook, specialized in Paisano Pies (sausage or meatball) and S.O.S. (creamed ground beef on toast) as well as standard Italian fare. The Landinos worked twelve-hour days every day until 1980, when they posted a notice: "To our dear customers. We regret to inform you that for the first time in 15 years we are closing our doors for vacation purposes."

As if he still worked for the general, Bruno kept the place spotlessly clean and promised: "We shoot for seven minutes from order to service. Snappy, fast service—that's what people want. And we don't have pinball machines, drunks, or four-letter words here. We do have a jukebox, but I won't turn it up no matter how much the kids harass me."

Bruno installed thin mirror strips on the backbar so employees could quickly spot anyone in need of another of their jumbo drinks, including happy-hour twofers. "When we started out here, this was practically the edge of Lakewood, which was then a tidy little town," Bruno reminisced with a roll of the eyes. New owners took over in the early 1990s but have kept the legendary Italian dishes, drinks, and ambience.

Lane's Tavern
11400 W. Colfax Ave., CLOSED

An old log shack in an asphalt lot on West Colfax was Lakewood's most storied beer joint. The ceiling was only 8 feet high and the bathrooms were outside behind the building. Benny and Nessie Delacorte served the cheapest beer in town and could pour beer and wash and rinse glasses faster than greased lightning. They opened Lane's in 1936. Benny was wearing a bowtie and a baseball hat the last time I saw him behind the bar. "I found 'em both in the trash," he boasted.

The tavern closed in 1994 but was salvaged by Lakewood's Heritage Center. With the help of volunteers from Colorado Christian University, the fixtures were moved, including the graffiti-smothered wooden tables, benches, and walls, to its grounds at 714 South Wadsworth Boulevard. The saloon building was too delapidated to be moved, but a facsimile will be constructed on the Lakewood Heritage Center grounds, according to director Debbie Ellerman.

Lakewood historians and Christian College students will be challenged to fully resurrect the ambience of this packed, raucous, noisy joint with a loud rock-and-roll jukebox. The dim interior was lit by beer signs, the jukebox, and the cigarette machine. Young singles flocked here and drew encouragement from Benny's wall sign: "Preserve Wildlife. Throw a Party."

Not everyone honored another of Lane's homemade admonitions: "For sanitary reasons please keep feet off the seats." Smooching, dancing, gabbing youngsters kept Lane's rocking until its 2 A.M. closing. There were so many disturbances here that a special emergency yellow light was installed out front in the middle of West Colfax Avenue.

In its early days, perpetual Christmas tinsel draped the bar, which boasted five pinball machines and 10-ounce beers sold at two for a quarter. This rowdy shack saloon where many locals first drank beer and dated seems an unlikely landmark for reconstruction by historians and Christian students. Perhaps this is actually the way respectable folks celebrate the demise of a dive.

Tommy's Corner Bar and Restaurant
5201 W. Mississippi Ave., (303) 937-3760

Leo Hart built a frame restaurant at the corner of West Mississippi and Sheridan Boulevard in 1924. When booze became legal in the mid-1930s, he began serving it along with his famous barbecue. The frame, stucco, and cement place grew with various additions as the Harts started curb service and installed a stage for a live band and

He knew the tavernes wel in every town.
—Geoffrey Chaucer

hula dancers. Leo and Leona Hart and their four children expanded the business to include a hardware store, grocery store, gas pumps, and rental cottages.

Helen Hart, the last of the four children, sold the Corner in 1979 to Phillipe Menelaos and Georgette Moutsos. They fixed the place up, renamed it Tommy's in honor of Tommy Hart, and tried for a National Register designation. The ramshackle, much-altered exterior troubled the majority of the National Register Review Board. They voted no in 1997, with this board member dissenting.

The long, popular, and colorful past of Hart's Corner Barbecue makes it at least a liquid history landmark. Inside, the owners have preserved photographs of this place in its puppy days, showing the extant knotty-pine walls, antique cigarette machine, twenty-five barstools from the 1930s, a vintage jukebox, a ceiling heater, a swamp cooler, and a large, old, walk-in beer cooler.

Lamar

Elevation: 3,622 feet

Lamar is the lowest city in Colorado, but it does have high spots, liquid and otherwise. Before gassing up at local bars, be sure to visit the petrified-wood gas station at Main and Sherman Streets. It's the only one in America.

The history of this city, named for U.S. Secretary of the Interior Lucius Quintius C. Lamar, is well presented at the Big Timbers Museum (1929), 2 miles north of town at the junction of U.S. Highway 50, U.S. Highway 287, and Colorado 196. Founded in 1886, Lamar emerged as the biggest town on Colorado's southeastern plains after the Santa Fe Railroad arrived. The handsome Sante Fe depot has been restored and recycled as the Colorado Welcome Center at South Main and Beech Streets.

The Cow Palace on Main Street has the fanciest bar and is celebrated as the home of Lamar's annual two-shot goose hunt. With Canada geese becoming a ubiquitous nuisance, you might visit here and lobby for a lot more shots at these foul fowl.

The Main Cafe & Rounder Room Bar
114 Main St., (719) 336-5736

This is the oldest saloon in a onetime cow town grown into a regional hub city. Local sandstone was used for the two-story vintage building, which also sports a cast-iron storefront and metal dentiled cornice.

Dora Hernandez, who has owned the bar since the 1980s, produces terrific Mexican food. The café in front has red vinyl, padded booths, wood paneling, plastic plants, and old-fashioned chrome hat and coat racks for each booth. The Rounder Room Bar in the back has black vinyl and brass-studded upholstery. If you have reservations about patronizing an old Main Street saloon, don't worry. Both the Lions and the Rotarians, pillars of respectability and persnickety drinkers and dinners, meet here.

Larkspur

Elevation: 6,680 feet

Some say this town founded in 1860 was named for a local wild-flower. Others say it commemorates cowboys who spurred their horses on larks here, especially after the Denver & Rio Grande arrived to make this a railhead. Long a small country town of fewer than 250 citizens, it began to wake up as suburban sprawl approached in the 1990s, when Douglas County became the fastest-growing county in the country. Newcomers cast wary eyes on the old town tavern, suspecting it is unfit for safe, sanitized suburbia.

Spur of the Moment Bar
8885 S. Spruce Mountain Rd.,
(303) 681-2990

In 1947, a couple converted their small, stucco 1921 house into the Larkspur Inn. It claimed to be "Larkspur's Finest Road House" and had no rivals. Chuck and Sylvia Cockrum took over in 1962 and made the place popular.

Sylvia, who still lives next door to the bar in a trailer, told me in 1996, "After Chuck died, I ran the place until 1982. I'm eighty-three now, but I'm Celtic. I just got back from Ireland. All the kids in the county came here. We were a 3.2 bar and I'd buy 'em a beer on their eighteenth birthday. I helped raise nearly every kid in the county—as many as

two hundred of a weekend night. If they were bad, I'd threaten to spank them. If they were fighting, I'd send 'em outside. If they talked dirty, I'd send 'em home. We had a pool table and a jukebox. We didn't really need chairs for kids that age. They never sit down anyways. And those kids were easier to deal with than their parents!

"When the kids asked me to have a St. Patrick's Day party, I said sure, if they would decorate the place themselves. So they dressed up the whole bar with green crepe and shamrocks. I'd run out of beer on some of those St. Patty's Days.

"Some nights the kids wouldn't go home. I'd threaten to call their families and they'd just laugh. So I'd pull the plug on the jukebox. That did the trick. When they left, I'd warn 'em: 'No stunt driving. People are trying to sleep out there.'" The Douglas County sheriff told me I was doing the county a service by making those kids feel at home here. At least they knew where to find 'em."

Sylvia introduced me to her spunky, white-haired sidekick, Virginia Ashley, who was wearing pink slippers and matching hair curlers. "My husband, Les, and I owned the Spur before Sylvia. We added the dancehall and brought in country-and-western music and had a hell of a time out here. Until the old piano got so filled with beer that it wouldn't play anymore."

"If a couple got real romantic in here, I'd tell 'em to go out back into the bushes. Real troublemakers we'd kick out for three weeks. We had fights—but just fists. No chains. No guns."

Barbara Sheldon, the current owner, bought us all a round and updated the story.

"The owner after Sylvia and before us let the place go downhill. It became a biker bar. They'd ride their motorcycles right into the bar and even change oil in here. The place had been empty seven months when we got it. We had to take out all the grease and a huge beehive over there in the corner. The bar floor was so rotten that my husband fell through when we were fixing it up. We changed the name to Spur of the Moment and began offering 'spurritos,' big smothered burritos. We serve fine meals and have set up a patio out back by the horseshoe pits, where we have the annual Larkspur community pig roast. We also put in a swing back there in the old willow tree." She showed us the huge backyard, which stretches all the way to the railroad tracks.

"Now Larkspur is growing so fast," Sylvia observed. "A lot of those newcomers never come in here. They think this bar isn't good enough for 'em. But Barb's fixing it up real nice. She'll end any talk about this place being a public nuisance."

Leadville

Elevation: 10,152 feet

Leadville was the highest and wildest of America's silver cities. By 1880, the two-year-old town boasted 106 saloons, not counting the billiard parlors, dancehalls, and gambling "hells." Leadville may be 2 miles high, but it was never dry.

The "silver exchanges," places where silver was exchanged for liquid refreshment, lined Harrison Avenue, the main street, and the State (now Second) Street vice district. Charles E. "Pap" Wyman's saloon, on the southeast corner of Harrison and Second, set the pace. Wyman's three-story frame building had a saloon, gambling hall, and dancehall on the ground floor. More serious drinking, gambling, and "dancing" went on in the private rooms upstairs. Pap's place had a legendary Bible on a stand at the door. This was a dirty book, dog-eared and scribbled in, since customers used it to settle bets and theological arguments. Above the Bible, a clock on the wall had "Don't Swear" written on its face, with the added admonition "Damn You!"

The Little Church Saloon & Casino on Harrison Avenue also offered spiritual solace, with its bar tokens for "internal lotions." The corner entrance was Romanesque arched, and the bright, white clapboard siding looked churchy. Inside, most of the worshippers were busy at the casino tables or the bar. Many sinners were shorn of their money, the root of all evil. The bald eagle over the entrance was also shorn, according to a *Leadville Herald Democrat* reporter, who noted that "the feathers dropped out until nothing was left but the stuffed outline."

At the Athenaeum, miners cheered on a trapeze artist trundling a wheelbarrow back and forth along a tightrope. Many of the saloons doubled as theaters where "leg art" thrived. In between stage stints, the actresses sold drinks and other comforts in the private boxes that lined the sides. The Carbonate Concert Garden featured Mollie Newton, "the finest formed woman in America." Her specialty was "a series of beautiful tableaux representing Greek and Roman statuary."

One spectator of these shows reported that the theaters were so cold that the scantily clad actresses turned blue until enough warm bodies showed up to heat the house. Maybe that's why the newspapers in Leadville kept advertising for more girls. Typical was the New Theater's ad in the *Democrat* for

50 WAITER GIRLS
PAY IN GOLD PROMPTLY EVERY WEEK
Must appear in SHORT CLOTHES or no engagement.

The Coliseum offered wrestling matches and dogfights, while the Park Avenue featured boxing bouts. The Leonard and Spencer Billiard Hall in the post office had a cigar stand and bar on one side and a reading room on the other. The five billiard tables had a "full complement of genuine ivory balls ... for fifteen-ball or pin pool." In 1879 this up-to-date place boasted an "elegant Linoleum carpet ... charming in effect and elastic to the tread."

Frozen in time by the silver crash of 1893, America's only 2-mile-high city is still warmed by some old-time saloons.

Manhattan Bar
618 Harrison Ave. (se corner of 6th St.), (719) 486-9939

This bar is so rough that the regulars chew on their beer bottles. In the best surviving example of Leadville's many raunchy blue-collar bars, tattoos and blue jeans are prevalent.

The Manhattan is delightfully shabby, like a real saloon should be. The beer signs are more than the decor; they also provide the lighting and help hold the roof up. The Manhattan also has the other essential ingredient for a saloon: shiftlessness. As noted barfly and *Denver Post* columnist Jack Kisling once put it, shiftlessness can only be supplied by regular customers, by "people who are content to be discontent. People who can sit for hours, inhaling the brutal sanitary chemical odors that disguise the other odors, talking all the while about how sweet the world once smelled."

The Manhattan's waitress, who had a broken heart tattooed on her arm, told us that the front bar dated from 1891 and the mahogany, mirrored backbar from 1905. The knotty-pine wall is smothered with beer-ad beauties, and the pressed-metal ceiling flaunts a fleur-de-lis design. Several decades' worth of messages are carved into the heavy wooden tables. The linoleum floor is worn out in places, exposing the original wooden floor.

Many of the regulars proudly showed us various tattoos in strategic places. A homemade wall sign declared: "No Smoking Area Not Provided." Kamikazes are a

Leadville's Little Church Saloon, at Harrison and Chestnut Streets, gave men something to do on Sundays— and every other day. The "usher" at the door collected tokens that might be good for either a billiard game or a beer. c. 1880 photo of the Little Church by George Wakely, courtesy of the Colorado History Museum; photo of token courtesy of Evelyn and Jim Wright, Tom Noel Collection.

The Pioneer Bar became Leadville's last and best-known residence for "brides of the multitudes." Madam "Ma" Brown and her "belles from hell" sold sex here until the 1950s.

favorite with this hard-drinking crowd, who stay to the bitter end before staggering out into Leadville's freezing night air.

Pioneer Bar and Brothel
118 W. 2nd St., CLOSED

The oldest continually operating brothel in Colorado died in 1970 with its last madam, Hazel Gillette "Ma" Brown, who wore cat's-eye spectacles set with real dia-

monds. Her house, built as the Pioneer Billiard Hall, is a two-story brick structure with rough stone trim. A separate corner entrance leads to the upstairs rooms of this abandoned, decaying bordello. Next door is the Pastime Club, the sole survivor of some twenty-five saloons on once-notorious West 2nd Street. After being closed for several decades, the Pioneer underwent a reincarnation to become residential units in 1998.

Silver Dollar Saloon
315 Harrison Ave., (719) 486-9914

The Board of Trade, an 1879 frame saloon, was replaced by the present two-story brick building. The interior is unusually well preserved, although barn wood now hides the Italianate exterior. An oak partition separates the old-fashioned antechamber from the main barroom. A classical cornice with Tuscan columns frames a diamond-dust backbar mirror. Beyond the main barroom and through swinging batwing doors are a dancehall and back rooms.

The McMahon family, owners since 1943, have filled this 1880s interior with antiques, art, and stuffed animals. The mounted ram's head with a noose around it is a shot at a now-deceased rival at the other end of Harrison Street: The RAM (Raggedy Ass Miner). It is harder to explain the dusty pelican on top of the old-fashioned telephone closet—the world's highest pelican. Proprietor Patty McMahon explained it to me years ago, but the logic and details have since escaped me. The grinning coyote draped over the

Waterford crystal chandelier behind the bar is from Tom Moody. He always paid his bar bill with bounty hides.

The Silver Dollar is a veritable museum. Old photographs, prints, artifacts, and a mounted animal menagerie adorn the flocked, green and gold wallpaper. Old-fashioned oak and glass display cases exhibit everything from mining drill bits to trophies and other memorabilia of the Silver Dollar's fierce girls' softball team in their kelly green uniforms.

The barmaid here in the 1940s, "Bloody Mary" Eitrem, was the toughest barmaid in town, according to regular Donald Mac-Donald. "She called any man she didn't know 'satchel ass.' She was a Bohunk with shoulders like a linebacker and a disposition to match."

Don pointed to the back rooms. "When I was county judge, that was Dago Mike Mongone's gambling den." Don showed me old tables shaped like a spade, a heart, and a club; the diamond-shaped table has disappeared. The Silver Dollar's upstairs rooms were also used for gambling.

On the wall of the bar named for her is a portrait of Silver Dollar Tabor, the beautiful princess born to silver king and U.S. Senator Horace Tabor and Baby Doe. She looks wistful. Her exquisite melancholia suggests the sad end to come—she burned to death in a Chicago flophouse/brothel.

The Silver Dollar always looks like it's St. Patrick's Day. It was here that Judge Neil Reynolds, Don MacDonald, the McMahons, and others dreamed up the St. Patrick's Practice Day Parade. Leadville could not compete with Denver for bagpipers and other marchers in March. Besides, March is snowy, cold, and miserable at this elevation. The best time of year in Leadville is the sunny, warm, and golden aspen time around September 17. So it is that on the Saturday closest to September 17, Leadville holds its St. Patrick's Practice Day Parade.

Patty McMahon is proud of her bar and carries it on as a family tradition. She showed me the trapdoor behind the bar. It leads to the cellar, which became a very busy place during Prohibition when the "M & O Soft Drink Parlor" also offered unadvertised hard drinks. Leadville specialized in "Leadville Moon," the famous Colorado moonshine made in the mines around Leadville. Patty and Donald agree (they often don't) that Leadville never went dry and that gambling was open until the 1950s. It was run by the big boys—the Mafia out of Pueblo. They also agree that the Silver Dollar is Leadville's finest and one of Colorado's finest, oldest, and most storied saloons.

Limon

Elevation: 5,366 feet

John Limon, a railroad foreman, gave his name to this town, founded in 1888 at the junction of the Union Pacific and the Chicago, Rock Island & Pacific Railroads. Limon is also where the Smoky Hill Trail split and I-70 and U.S. Highway 24 now part company, with some traffic heading for Denver, some for Colorado Springs. Although this is the county's sole sizable town, with a population of about 2,000, the only high-rises are the grain elevators, including one painted "Limon."

Before you hit the bars, be sure to visit the Limon Heritage Depot/ Museum, Schoolhouse (c. 1905) & Railroad Park at 899 1st Street. The old Rock Island Depot has been preserved for summer excursion trains and as a museum. The surrounding historical park houses the last of the county's sixty-eight one-room schoolhouses. A 1990 tornado leveled much of Limon, including two fine old saloons, the Stock Exchange Tavern, and the Roman & Peck Billiard Hall.

South Side Food & Drink
680 Main St. (ne corner of C. Ave.), (719) 775-9593

This nondescript, 1991 prefab building of corrugated metal and stucco panels is the area's finest bar and restaurant. It is also the repository of an antique backbar and other relics from the old Roman & Peck Billiard Hall, Limon's legend-ary trackside saloon, which was blown away by the June 6, 1990, tornado.

Owners Pat and Bob Younger had converted the old 1896 pool hall into a bar and café. When the tornado demolished that landmark, the Youngers salvaged the golden oak backbar, some of the antique beer signs, and other items. Bob Younger designed this huge, barnlike bar around the old neoclassical backbar with a mirror framed by Ionic columns. New white Sheetrock walls, many windows, a high ceiling, and bright decor make this a cheery café and family restaurant. It evolves into a bar after the cocktail hour as lights are dimmed and it becomes the town's favorite nightspot. The huge single room has a game area at one end and dining tables at the other.

"We've been in the bar business since 1973, when we started out with the Timberline Tavern in Bergen Park," reported Pat, who operates the South Side with her husband, Bob. "We decided to move to Limon, Bob's hometown, to get away from the mountains, which are filled with turkeys. We have customers who come out to spend the weekend in Limon just to get away from the big city of Denver and the mountain madness. Half of our business is booze, half is food. Local cowboys drink here. So do employees of the new Limon prison, which brought about 250 new jobs to Limon. We stay open late to accommodate the prison shift getting off at 11 P.M."

Locals relish Pat's homemade potato salad and deviled eggs at the salad bar, as well as her green chili, salsa, and Italian sauces. The pizza, calzones, Mexican food, and steak are terrific. All 110 seats are often taken and it's SRO on Friday nights. Even local mule deer, wandering up from Big Sand Creek to graze at Limon's grain elevators, have been known to stop at the South Side, a friendly, local place with fine cheap food and a backbar with nine lives.

Louisville

Elevation: 5,380 feet

Following the discovery of coal in 1877 on Coal Creek, Louis Nawatny platted the town and named it for himself. The last of the many coal mines closed in the 1950s, but Louisville commemorates its earthy origins with a statue of a miner in front of City Hall and well-preserved saloons where miners cooled off after hot, dusty twelve-hour shifts underground.

Unlike nearby towns such as Boulder, which outlawed booze until 1967, this immigrant, blue-collar town was always wet. Thirsty pilgrims from drier areas found twenty-two saloons, thirteen of them in a three-block oasis on Front Street, which fronted the railroad tracks. One saloon, Blent's, disappeared into the earth, swallowed by the coal mines that underlie Louisville.

During Prohibition, the town became a bootlegging center. Saloons revamped as "soft drink parlors" still offered hard stuff whenever the law looked the other way. Taverns are now clustered between Main and Front Streets in a National Register Historic District of seventy buildings. Several ethnic groups settled here, but the town's most frequently encountered culinary fragrances have been marinara sauce and Chianti. Mexican food and drink arrrived more recently with conversion of the old Louisville Theater into Señor T's at 817 Main Street.

The Blue Parrot Restaurant
640 Main St. (se corner of Pine St.), (303) 666-0677

Back in 1919, Mike Colacci left the dark, dirty coal mines to open The Blue Parrot in an old miners' boardinghouse. Originally the Colaccis sold gasoline and oil in front and served their homemade spaghetti in back. Mike's wife, Mary, made her own red sauce, blanching bushels of tomatoes, peeling them, and sun-drying them outside on screens.

Word of this wonderful red sauce and the house wines spread and the place was soon jammed. The Blue Parrot moved into a bigger building, the old Huber Drug Store and Bowling Alley on the corner of Main and Pine, in the 1930s. Even then, the Colaccis often had to turn away customers. Mike and Mary's son, Tony, opened up a second restaurant, Colacci's, two blocks down Main Street. A third family restaurant, the Blue Parrot II, opened in 1967 at 808 Main.

Mike and Mary Colacci's other son, Joe, took over The Blue Parrot, which is now operated by his five children. This tavern is too good to die. After fire destroyed the original Blue Parrot in 1988, the Colaccis quickly reopened in a tent in the parking lot and erected a much larger building.

The Parrot's favorite bartender since 1988, Paul Weissman, was elected the Louisville area's state senator in 1992. The handsome young Weissman has so many fans that he has printed a baseball-style card. "So many people think my being a state senator is a joke," Weissman laughed, "I needed this card to prove it." His best-known legislative coup was his amendment allowing fans to bring their own beer to Colorado Rockies baseball games anytime Coors Field began charging more than $2.50 for a beer. A lightning-fast mixologist seldom at a loss for words, the young Democrat offended more-traditional senators by never wearing a tie. The senate passed a new dress code with which Weissman has complied under the gold-domed capitol, but you'll never

Louisville, a coal town in Boulder County, attracted many Italian miners who later turned to tavern keeping. Colacci's Blue Parrot is one of the oldest and most memorable of these pasta-and-vino havens.

catch him behind the bar at Colacci's putting on ties and senatorial airs.

Colacci's Restaurant
816 Main St., (303) 673-9400

To capture the overflow from The Blue Parrot run by his parents and brother, Anthony Colacci opened this corrugated tavern in 1955 with American flags and beer-art decor. The waitresses wear brown and orange uniforms to match the brown and orange vinyl booths and table. Large, tasty, inexpensive spaghetti and ravioli dinners make this a no-nonsense place for serious eating and drinking. Oodles of noodles with a one-to-one ratio of flour to eggs can be further enriched with pitchers of rich red sauce.

Old Louisville Inn
740 Front St., (303) 666-9982

Behind a clapboard storefront, a 16-foot-high ceiling accommodates the 1880s backbar, Brunswick's top-of-the-line model, "Del Monte." This magnificent rococo altar stands 12 feet high and 25 feet long in shimmering mahogany and cherry. At the base of the front bar is an almost extinct—but once very common—bar fixture: a trough to capture spilt liquor, saliva, and other body fluids. Water no longer runs through this copper trough, which is the only one surviving in Colorado to my knowledge, although I have seen such sanitary devices south of the border in Mexican cantinas.

E. J. "Nick" DiFrancia built the DiFrancia Saloon, later called the Colorado Cafe and the Primrose Cafe. The new ceiling has a stained-glass skylight. The old linoleum floor, red cloth curtains, and corner piano are gone from a now-fashionable restaurant. The bathroom, however, is still the tiny original. The brick foundation is reinforced with railroad track to keep the place from shaking as trains roar by. Along with a pool room, the basement retains its old hand-crank elevator, coal-burning furnace, and the remains of a tunnel, which the owners

say was a Prohibition-era connection to other Louisville saloons.

Pasquale's Restaurant & Bar
809 Main St., CLOSED

Celeste Roman's pool hall still has a classical false front that hides a tiny, hipped-roof house that has evolved into a long, skinny saloon. Pasquale Colabello bought the place in 1960 and renamed it for himself.

Steve Rowe, the proprietor from 1987 to 1997, retained the old name and decor. The original plate-glass front with its fading sign, the tongue-and-groove ceiling, ancient liquor cabinets, and Art Deco backbar with stained glass are still here. Even the old transom window over the front door is still operational. Stout, roomy hardwood booths line the south wall, which is decorated with photographs of old Louisville.

Steve is a smiling, heavyset fellow with a gold earring that matches his gold-rimmed spectacles. Like Celeste and Pasquale before him, Steve lived nearby and walked to the bar, where he spent fourteen to sixteen hours a day.

"I love this place," he confessed, "especially when the old-timers come in and talk about the old days. They showed me the basement tunnel which once connected Pasquale's with other Italian taverns in town. That tunnel used mine shafts, which were also used for stills during Prohibition when booze went underground. You should hear the old guys talk about how they came in here as kids to fetch pails of beer. Celeste would also sell them a nickel double scoop of ice cream, and then the kids would try not to spill the ice cream into the beer buckets they were taking to their fathers in the mines. And they still remember the 10-cent beers and free pretzels."

Pasquale, Rowe recalled, "would go home whenever he damn well pleased. And just tell the customers, 'I'm going a homa. You go homa too. Pizza delivery? You damn lucky I make it,' Pasquale would tell 'em, 'You pick it up!'"

At the bar with its ancient steel foot rail, Julie, the bartender, served us another of Pasquale's fabulous classic pizzas (the pasta, sandwiches, and appetizers are also tasty and inexpensive). She told us that the legal limit is seventy-five customers, but on Friday night's open stage with bands and other performers, "we often shoehorn in 100 customers."

"One really crazy Friday night," she grinned, "this beautiful blonde—she looked a lot like me—started drinking Jose Cuervo Gold shots. One after another. I've never seen anyone hold that much Gold! Then she jumped right up here on the bar and began stripping. She got off her blouse but was too drunk to unfasten her bra. She started to vomit and ran back into the bathroom. Too embarrassed to come out, she stayed in until closing time. Then a real old local, Luther Wilson, who has been sexually inactive for years, went back to the ladies room, picked her up, gave her his coat, and drove her home."

Having got into the heart of the mountain (Leadville), I had supper, the first course being whisky, the second whisky and the third whisky.
—Oscar Wilde

Such gaiety led to the closing of Pasquale's in 1997, but an Englishman, Michael Charnley, plans to reopen it as a British-style pub called the Druid's Arms.

Pine Street Junction
1006 Pine St. (sw corner of Front St.), (303) 666-5232

Joseph Lackner's tavern was renamed by a later owner the Track Inn for its strategic location beside the railroad tracks. After its recent restoration and expansion, it was renamed the Pine Street Junction to celebrate a long-postponed graduation to respectability. This shiplap structure has a corner entry crowned by a large sunburst cornice with hanging ball finials. A south-side beer garden replaces the original and more elaborate one on the west side. The original, ornate backbar, with a sunburst pattern like that of the entry pediment, remains inside, along with boxcar wainscoting and train-lantern chandeliers. The barstools are numbered for the free-drink roulette game conducted by the bartender every time a train roars by.

Manitou Springs
Elevation: 6,412 feet

For Indians, Manitou was a sanctuary where no warfare was allowed. The Ute, Arapaho, Cheyenne, and then the palefaces came to drink from its magic springs. A tourist colony sprang up after the railroad arrived in the 1870s. By 1900 the "Saratoga of the West" boasted some fifty springs whose "magic waters" allegedly could cure everything from heartbreak to wrinkles. During the early 1990s, the Mineral Springs Foundation restored eight public springs, bringing back not only the flowing liquid but the fanciful Carpenter's Gothic–style gazebos that sheltered them.

Of 1,000 buildings in the historic core of the town, 752 are deemed contributing structures in the Manitou Springs Historic District. Hospitable landmarks include Al and Betty's Cafe at 108 Manitou Avenue, a rounded curiosity with a corner glass-brick window that claims to be the "Home of the Fastest Coffee Pot in the West." Coffee and stronger beverages help rinse out the mouth after doses of the local soda, sulfur, and iron waters.

Briarhurst Manor Inn
404 Manitou Ave. (U.S. Hwy. 24), (970) 685-1864

Dr. William A. Bell, a founder of Manitou, built this 1888 English country house guarded by carved stone beasts. A multitude of chimney pots serve eleven fireplaces reminiscent of English castles. The son of a London society doctor, Bell recruited Denver & Rio Grande investors among his father's patients. He attracted so many immigrants that the Colorado Springs and Manitou Springs area was dubbed "Little London." After Bell and his wife had returned to their much larger manor in England in 1920, Briarhurst was converted to a restaurant by chef Sigfried Krauss and his wife. Champagne brunches, elegant dinners, and a lovely beer garden make a visit to this fabulous Tudor castle memorable.

H.M.S. Ancient Mariner
962 Manitou Ave. (U.S. Hwy. 24),
(719) 685-5503

The plastic pirate lurking in the seaweed by this bar's entryway holds a sign: "Welcome to the Ancient Mariner where the Customer is never right." The copper-front bar top is etched with some verse from Samuel Taylor Coleridge's long poem, *The Rime of the Ancient Mariner.* Coleridge, an English Romantic poet driven by fantasy and laudanum, would probably fancy this dark maritime den where his verse is enshrined.

All in a hot and copper sky,
The bloody sun, at noon,
Right up against the mast did stand,
No bigger than the Moon.

Water, water, everywhere,
And all the boards did shrink;
Water, water, everywhere
Nor any drop to drink.

The very deep did rot: O Christ!
That ever this should be!
Yea, slimy things did crawl with legs
Upon the slimy sea.

About, about, in reel and rout
The death-fires danced at night;
The water, like a witch's oils,
Burnt green, and blue and white.

The Ancient Mariner is the only nautical bar on the Front Range besides the Ship Tavern in Denver's Brown Palace Hotel. This offbeat shrine to the poet is not a bright, sunny, airy place like the trendy new bars where people go to see and be seen. This dark, dingy place with its massive, low ceiling beams is more a place to hide and ponder the spirit of such Coleridge lines as "A sadder and a wiser man,/He rose the morrow morn."

Fishnet and glass-ball floats, a sailfish and heavy captain's chairs, and lobster traps and rigging lie about in watery illusions. Old shuttered and leaded-glass windows overlook Fountain Creek, and life preservers line the walls.

The crew in this boozy den is often floundering and in need of preservers. The last night I was there, some tipsy sailors clung to the central log mast and the 3-inch-thick ropes wrapped around it. And a regular pulled the most bizarre bar trick I've seen. He snorted a cocktail swizzle up his nose and spat it out his mouth!

One fellow, who looked like the Ancient Mariner, said he was a real sailor by the

Dr. William A. Bell's Manitou Springs mansion became an elegant public resort, the Briarhurst Inn, after the Bells returned to England. Photo courtesy of the Colorado Springs Pioneers Museum.

name of Melville. He told me about the painting that used to hang

> in the wide, low, straggling entry with old-fashioned wainscots, reminding one of the bulwarks of some condemned old craft. It was a very large oil-painting so thoroughly be-smoked and everyway defaced, that in unequal crosslights by which you viewed it; it was only by diligent study and a series of systematic visits to it, and careful inquiry of the neighbors, that you could any way arrive at an understanding of its purpose. Such unaccountableness of shades and shadows that at first you almost thought some ambitious young artist, in the time of the New England hags, had endeavored to delineate chaos bewitched.
>
> About the bar bustles a little withered old man, selling deliriums and death. Abominable are the tumblers into which he pours his poison. Though true cylinders without— within the villainous green goggling glasses deceitfully tapered downwards to a cheating bottom. Parallel meridians rudely pecked into the glass surround the goblets. Fill to this mark and your charge is but a dollar; to this a dollar more; and soon to a full glass.

The Loop Bar
965 Manitou Ave. (corner of Ruxton Ave.), (719) 685-9344

Hidden behind the Stratton Mineral Springs gurgling in front with free elixir water is a tiny Pueblo Revival–style storefront. Now a family bar with an interior of neon cactus and a Mexican-style fireplace, it was formerly called Los Perditos (Spanish for

"the lost ones"), an apt name for what was a biker-infested public nuisance. The bar slowly cleaned itself up with well-posted warnings: "Motorcycle colors and emblems not allowed. No weapons. I.D. required."

Mission Bell Inn
178 Crystal Park Rd., (719) 685-9983

A large iron bell and thick oak door guard this Mexican restaurant operated by the Masias family since 1962. The exotic building started out as a log cabin built by the Kiwanis Club in the 1920s for use as an Indian museum. The log ceiling, exotic tilework, and turquoise and peach decor make for colorful eating and drinking. Dan Masias, an onion and tomato farmer from Rocky Ford, opened the place. "We bought what looked like a Lincoln Log structure," he reminisced. "We tripled the size, stuccoed it, added vigas, decorated it with tiles from Santa Fe, and the bell from old Mexico." Authoritative margaritas, imported *cervezas,* and tasty Mexican food make this backroad inn worth the visit.

Royal Tavern
942 Manitou Ave., (719) 685-9916

This tiny tavern in the historic Manitou Arcade is hardly royal with its $1 plastic cups of beer, peanut machine, and loud jukebox. Don't miss the huge backbar mural of the Royal with an all-dog clientele putting on the dog. The hardwood floors and glassy walls between stone posts of the arcade suggest that this place may once have been a nobler hangout.

Mesa Verde

Elevation: 7,500 feet

Mesa Verde National Park, the first U.S. World Cultural Heritage Site designated by the United Nations, is still recovering from the greatest fire in its history. From one of the highest spots at Mesa Verde—the bar atop the park's lodge—we surveyed the 5,000-acre black scar, which comes to within 100 yards of the Far View Lodge and Visitor's Center.

Far View Lodge Bar
6262 Far View, (970) 529-4421

The bartender told us that the August 17, 1996, thundershowers left double rainbows over the mesa. But storms continued into the night. A lightning strike smoldering in Soda Canyon, fanned by the next day's hot breezes, burst into flames as high as 100 feet. Racing through dry Utah juniper, gambel oak, and piñon pine, the wildfire damaged 387 archaeological sites but also exposed some previously undiscovered ruins. The inferno closed the entire park and even the Sipapu Bar, where we ordered cold beer and pondered the blaze. Eight centuries ago, the Mesa Verdans abandoned their mesa-top pit-house pueblos for the cliff dwellings. Fires and drought may be the solution to this mystery.

The waitress offered another theory: "It was the women. They got tired of carrying those gallon water pots on their heads and climbing up and down to the seeps in the cliff overhangs. There, water could still be found after mesa-top springs dried up. 'Look, guys,' they said, 'if you want us to keep fetching the water, you need to build us new houses in the cliffs where the water is.'" The men saw the wisdom of these women and also realized that cliff houses would enable them to better defend the waterholes.

The Sipapu Bar tops the brown, rough-stucco Far View Lodge, a handsome Neo–Pueblo Revival–style edifice. You climb to the bar through a circular tower from the dining room and trinket shop below. From the bar's outdoor deck you can see why the place is called Far View. The silvery, snowcapped La Plata Mountains decorate the eastern horizon, while Ship Rock sails through the mesas of New Mexico to the south. To the north lies the Mancos Valley of towns and farms and ranches. Sleeping Ute Mountain dominates the western horizon, threatening to awaken at any moment and chase off palefaces to liberate the Utes from their two Colorado reservations.

The Sipapu Bar is a spirit hole for Indians and cowboys, archaeologists and rangers, service workers and tourists. It is a haven for those who want to linger, to talk, and to ponder the mysteries of Mesa Verde. *Sipapu* is the Hopi word for the tiny symbolic hole in the center of a kiva, the round ceremonial chamber of both the ancient Anasazi and their descendants, the modern Pueblo Indians. In this Indian creation myth, Mother Earth mated with Father Sun and the tribe was born inside Mother Earth. Confined to dark, damp, subterranean regions, the first people prayed to Father Sun and Mother Earth for deliverance. The gods heard and led the good people into a better world. First they climbed to another cave where there was a little more light, the world of twilight. From twilight the people climbed out through the *sipapu* to another cave with still more light, the world of dawn.

So, the *sipapu* opening allowed the human race to move from the dark underworld to a favored place of light and warmth. To celebrate this emergence, Mesa Verdans built *sipapus* into the dirt floors of pit houses and, later, into the kivas of the cliff dwellers. Kivas, like pit houses, were covered over with dirt so that they looked like a womb in Mother Earth. When death comes, the spirit lives by going back through the *sipapu* to Mother Earth.

The bar crew at the Sipapu collect dumb tourist questions such as: Why did they build those ruins so close to the road? What did they practice in the kivas—their own made-up religion? We had no trouble finding the park entrance at Mesa Verde, but where is the park exit? How many undiscovered ruins are there?

Morrison
Elevation: 5,800 feet

George Morrison, a Scottish stonecutter, homesteaded in 1864 along Bear Creek where he found fine red sandstone. He opened one of Colorado's first quarries and built many still-standing stone structures. After the Denver, South Park & Pacific Railroad arrived in 1874, Morrison became a town. It remains a quaint village protected from a sea of suburban development by a National Register Historic District designation, by the Morrison Hogback on the east, by Red Rocks Park on the north, and by steep foothills on the west. Morrison is also defended by The Fort restaurant, which has stockpiled plenty of fine food and booze and aimed its cannons, "Bertha" and "Sweet Lips," at Denver's sprawling suburbs.

The Fort
19192 Colorado 8 (just north of U.S. Hwy. 285), (303) 697-4771

For this 1963 re-creation of Bent's Old Fort on the Santa Fe Trail, Sam Arnold hired craftsmen from Taos, New Mexico. They used local red dirt, straw, and wool to make the 80,000 adobe bricks for the 2-foot-thick walls of this steel-reinforced bastion. The single large entry gate, round corner tower, and accommodations resemble those of Bent's original prairie fortress.

Inside, exquisite southwestern details include Padre Martinez chairs, tile floors sealed with ox blood, and a corner adobe "horno" oven. Owner-operators Sam and Carrie Arnold initially lived here with Sissy, a pet bear. Sam, the premier food historian of the American West, has re-created tasty victuals of the past. Native American and Hispanic delicacies such as buffalo tongue and moose nose are a specialty, along with exotic food and drink you'll find nowhere else. Carrie, a widely known artist, does fine watercolors, such as her portraits of the Bent Brothers in the downstairs bar.

Many small, cozy adobe rooms have hearth-harkening piñon-wood fires. Ask for

Charles and William Bent's 1830s fort on the Arkansas River in southeastern Colorado contained the state's first bar, billiard hall, and tourist dining. Although Bent's Fort is long gone, Sam and Carrie Arnold built a facsimile in Morrison, The Fort, which offers food and drink of the Old West.

the self-guided tour booklet so you can inspect the nine dining rooms, taproom, courtyard, Indian teepee, trapper's cabin, pillory, library, and gift shop. The St. Vrain Bar sports a portrait of the partner of the Bent brothers, Ceran St. Vrain, who introduced fine wines, crystal glasses, and damask tablecloths to the western frontier. In a wall niche is an adobe brick from the original Bent's Fort of 1833. The bar ceiling is classic Hispanic style with *latías* (sticks) laid in herringbone style on the log *vigas* (ceiling poles).

Beware the rattlesnake coiled atop the downstairs backbar. To keep the rattler from doing any harm, you had best order snake medicine right away. Recommended historic antidotes range from Bear's Blood (tequila and pomegranate juice) to Prickly Pear Cactus Margaritas, from Taos Lightning (whiskey, tobacco juice, red pepper, and gunpowder) to Hailstorms (a mint julep served western-style in a mason jar).

If you order champagne, ask Sam to open the bottle with his tomahawk. If you order a mixed drink, ask the bartender to stir your medicine with something they keep hidden behind the bar: a petrified buffalo phallus.

The Morrison Inn
301 Bear Creek Ave. (Colorado 74)
(nw corner of Stone St.),
(303) 697-6650

Over the decades, this red Morrison sandstone building has housed the Pike & Perry Mercantile, Schneider's Drug Store, a barbershop, and the town's first gas station, before Tom Koehler opened the Morrison Inn in 1979. The casual ambience, spicy Mexican food, and "attitude-adjusting" margaritas made the place popular. To discourage bikers, the waitress told me, they stopped serving Budweiser, their beer of preference. Even after expanding into the neighboring storefront, this inn is still jammed.

Red Rocks Grill
415 Bear Creek Ave. (Colorado 74),
(303) 697-9290

Ana DeJesus, who grew up in Spanish Harlem, came to Colorado to rescue this place in 1994. "As the Sportsman Bar," she told me, "it was notorious for drugs, razor blades, and bad bikers." I remember the old Sportsman, where the exasperated bartender finally put a sign on the backbar: "I can only please one person per day and this isn't your day." This surly, shaggy fellow was slow to serve anyone but bikers. The bar and pool tables were the main draws. In the smoky old days, spilled popcorn was stomped into the snot green industrial carpet by a crowd that often exceeded the posted sign: "Occupancy must not exceed 91 & 1/2 persons." Outside, the old signs were bullet-ridden,

including one with a crawling man under the warning "Wino Crossing."

Ana cleaned up the old Sportsman, which had been gathering blood and dust since the 1940s. She upgraded the clientele and the decor with a complex occupying three old storefronts. One is the Creekside Cafe, another a barroom with a U-shaped front bar and captain's chairs, and the third a pizza place in the corner storefront, a former bank with an old walk-in safe.

Tony Rigatoni's Pizza & Pasta
215 Bear Creek Ave.
(ne corner of Stone St.),
(303) 697-5508

Tony's opened in 1991 in the old Tabor Bar, established in 1941 by Sandy and Avery Tabor. They came, as did Baby Doe Tabor, from Wisconsin and commissioned the large Tabor mural that once adorned the west wall. Back in 1982, waitress Jenny Greenwald told me: "That mural takes a beating. This has been a cowboy bar by day and a biker bar at night. Cowboys, at their rowdiest, ride in on their horses, while the bikers try it on their motorcycles."

Tony Rigatoni restored the golden oak, mirrored backbar with its Ionic columns topped by acanthus leaves. He showed up to play the accordion the last time I was there and explained: "I picked the name 'Rigatoni' because it rhymes. And I loved the 1890 building. It started out as a drugstore with a brothel upstairs."

Mosca

Elevation: 7,550 feet

Mosca is the Spanish word for "fly," and flies are very happy here. Mosca offers delicacies few Colorado flies ever feast on, because it houses Colorado's only alligator farm and largest buffalo ranch. Medano Ranch now hosts some two thousand bison. It is one of two antique Hispanic ranches that predate the town, founded in the 1880s on the edge of the Great Sand Dunes National Monument near the foot of Mosca Pass. The other spread, Zapata (1870), has become an exquisite guest ranch with a meticulously restored, hewn-log main lodge and tavern.

The Inn at Zapata Ranch
5303 Hwy. 150, (719) 378-2356

When we checked into The Inn at Zapata Ranch, I worried about all the old-fashioned, galvanized-steel buckets. Not until we were seated at the galvanized-steel bar and reflected on the galvanized-steel signs did it dawn on me: The roofs do not leak. The metal buckets, antiqued with muratic acid, are a design detail—subtle, simple, and practical—with which an ingenious architect has transformed Zapata into Colorado's most remarkable guest ranch.

The buckets are Hisayoshi Ota's idea of a functional yet aesthetic wastebasket. "Hisa,"

as everyone calls him, left Tokyo at age seventeen for the United States. Fifteen years later, he graduated with a master's degree in architecture from Columbia University. In New York he worked on the restoration of Carnegie Hall and in Orlando, Florida, on the corporate headquarters for Walt Disney World.

"I learned a lot of things at Disney," Hisa told me. "Like how to use the smallest details to create a theme, how to transport people back to the Old West. Growing up in Tokyo, I disliked American western movies. I was jealous of all that open space, that freedom. In crowded, noisy Tokyo, and then in New York City, those scenes kept coming back to me. Now I live on a ranch larger than downtown Tokyo!"

In 1988 Hisa bought the Zapata and Medano Ranches, neighboring spreads totaling some 100,000 acres. "Some people were afraid we would build a jet runway to ship in Japanese tourists and ship out bison. But this valley is paradise, and I didn't want it spoiled. I'm here for the long haul."

Hisa and Kris Ota live in the modest foreman's house on the Medano Ranch with some two thousand buffalo and seventy-five Scottish Highland cattle, as well as a herd of three hundred conventional cattle. Hisa took us for a ride in his Grand Cherokee to look for buffalo. "They move around a lot, so they don't overgraze an area or foul their waterholes as cattle do."

"When I first came to this valley, I was a hyper-environmentalist," Hisa reflected. "I was afraid even to step on the land and bruise the plants with my footstep. The first time I took my bison to the slaughterhouse I felt sick. One bison I could never market is my Amelia. Her mother rejected her, so I bottle-fed her with calf formula. Amelia grew up as a pet and she thinks she is human. She watches the herd with interest but doesn't want to join the other bison. She is

> *What is man, when you come to think upon him, but a minutely set, ingenious machine for turning with infinite artfulness, the red wine of Shiraz into urine?*
>
> **—Isak Dinesen**

like my teenage daughter. I can't bear the thought of her with a bull, making babies."

The handsome rancher showed us around his huge spread. He pointed toward bands of buffalo scattered in all directions and drove slowly toward one herd. We got out to sneak up on them. Hisa stopped to show us the big, arcing hoofprints of these animals, which weigh as much as a ton and stand as tall as 6 feet. "These hoofprints capture seeds and the water that lets them grow. And bison provide plenty of fertilizer. They actually improve the land."

The same can be said for this young Japanese cowboy. He has restored two historic ranches, placed the Zapata Ranch headquarters on the National Register of Historic Places, and given the depressed San Luis Valley an economically, environmentally, and historically sound resource by bringing back the bison.

Ouray

Elevation: 7,706 feet

Prospectors from Silverton found silver on the headwaters of the Uncompahgre River and in 1875 set up a town named for the great Ute Indian chief. From Ouray, rich ores rolled to the outside world over the Red Mountain and Uncompahgre Canyon toll road, which later became U.S. 550, the so-called Million Dollar Highway. Although set back by the 1893 silver crash, the town shifted to gold, relying on the Camp Bird, Revenue, Virginius, and other auriferous treasure troves.

The bad old days are recorded in the *Ouray Times,* which reported a July 1881 shoot-out at the Grand Pacific, a saloon on Main Street. "If Todd's pistol had not stopped revolving Monday," the *Times* lamented, "we would have a first-class item this week. As it is we only get a second-class item out of a third-class shooting scrape, causing two fourth-class wounds. Parties who indulge in shooting matches should not disappoint newspapermen." Ouray had twenty-six saloonkeepers and about a hundred prostitutes, according to the *Times,* and could well afford to lose a few. Since the flush times, the town has lost all its brothels and all but a handful of its saloons.

Capitalizing on its spectacular mountain setting, Ouray puffs itself as "The Switzerland of America." It is a tourist nirvana for hiking, jeeping, and skiing, and its famous outdoor hot-springs pool is open all year. In recent years Ouray has emerged as the U.S. center for the emerging sport of ice climbing.

Bon Ton
426 Main St., (970) 325-4951

Catherine "Kittie" O'Brien Porter Heit built this neat brick inn for $10,000. Opened in 1898 as a $1-per-night hotel for miners, the St. Elmo has been rehabilitated as a bed-and-breakfast, offering elegant Victorian accommodations and continental cuisine in the Bon Ton, as Kittie first called the dining room a century ago.

"Aunt Kittie," according to a 1915 obituary in the *Ouray Herald*, "was the miner's friend. They were always welcome whether flush with money or down and out. Her hotel [became] a real home for the lonesome and homeless. Everything was done for the comfort and pleasure of 'her boys.' She was a regular 'mother' to hundreds and no one could possibly be missed more than she."

Kittie's ghost lingers in the downstairs bar, a tiny, L-shaped piece of highly polished mahogany with a church pew for a bench. The subterranean mini-bar and restaurant spill out into a beer garden on the north side of the hotel, where Kittie's original Bon Ton stood. Dan and Sandy Lingenfelter bought the hotel and restaurant in 1984 and transformed them into a superb bed-and-breakfast inn.

The Outlaw
610 Main St., (970) 325-4458

This bar, museum, and restaurant is a treat in many ways, although the dim, wagon-wheel chandeliers make it hard to

"Kittie" O'Brien Porter Heit, founding proprietor of Ouray's Bon Ton Restaurant, poses with her canary, her dog, a potted plant, and prized customers. The Bon Ton still offers some of the best food and drink to be found in Colorado's San Juan Mountains. Photo courtesy of the Denver Public Library, Western History Collection.

inspect all the antiques, stuffed animals, outlaw portraits, and hats (including a Stetson that John Wayne wore while here filming *True Grit*). The storefront had to be redone after a Trailways bus crashed into the bar in 1946, but it retains the old metal cornice and rough stone foundation. Under the high, pressed-metal ceiling, local cattle brands are burned into the wood-paneled walls. Steaks are a specialty, and in summer The Outlaw hosts mountain cookouts that are the pinnacle of local social life.

Since 1938 the Bonatti family has owned what current proprietor Christina Bonatti claims is the oldest continuously operating saloon in town. It opened in 1911 as Feletti & Cresto's Free Coinage Saloon and became The Outlaw in 1969. Taverns of various names have been here since 1876, most notably The Miners Pick, a notorious hangout for miners.

Ouray's Western Hotel Bar remains relatively unaltered with a grand old potbellied stove that warms customers and the scantily clad women in the bar art. 1942 photo courtesy of the Denver Public Library, Western History Collection.

They came in after payday, slapped down a hundred dollars on the bar, and swore they weren't going to leave until it was all drunk up.

Silver Nugget Cafe
740 Main St. (sw corner of 8th Ave.), (970) 325-4100

This corner commercial block retains its cast-iron columns and plate-glass storefront beneath a fancy cornice. According to an 1898 newspaper account, the $8,000 structure opened as "a saloon with a female rooming attachment on the second floor"

where "nymphs exposed their anatomy to passers-by." During Prohibition, the first-floor Columbus Pool Hall became a bootleg joint. In 1992 the upstairs bordello reopened as the Columbus House Bed and Breakfast with seven small bedrooms, a bath, and a parlor. The downstairs saloon is now a sedate café.

Western Hotel Bar
210 7th Ave., (970) 325-4645

This 1891 three-story, frame hotel has a full-length front porch and plate-glass storefront with colored-glass transoms. Stable management and electricity came in 1897 when the Western was taken over by Denver hoteliers William Holt and H. P. Foster, whose names still decorate the pediment. The hotel became a home for many miners, while tourists gravitated to the more elegant Beaumont Hotel. Maria "Ma" Flor, who ran the place from 1916 to 1961, welcomed even the poorest and sickest miners, never letting anyone leave hungry. A single large bathtub on the second floor was used by both guests and the Flor family. After Ma died, the hotel closed, then became a museum, and later a jeep rental. The Western reopened in 1982 as a hotel and saloon.

A 140-pound female mountain lion perched atop the magnificent backbar keeps her glassy eyes fixed on a pheasant, ignoring other stuffed animals around the room. A huge potbellied stove adorned with chrome heats both the room and a naked lady shivering in a nearby wall painting.

Palisade
Elevation: 4,727 feet

amed first for peach orchards and now for its vineyards, Palisade flourishes along the Colorado River as it emerges from its Rocky Mountain canyon. Between 1940 and 1960, it produced a million bushels of peaches a year, but orchards have given way to suburban growth and almost half of some eighteen Colorado wineries. Although a few brave souls experimented with wineries in Colorado before Prohibition, the so-called "noble experiment" killed that business. In 1968, Dr. Gerald Ivancie resurrected the idea with the winery he opened in Denver using grapes grown in and around Palisade.

Grand River Vineyards
787 Elberta Ave. (via I-70, Exit 42), (970) 464-5867

The Grand River boasts a nifty tasting room and gift shop open year-round in a handsome Mission-style building. Since its 1990 opening, this has become Colorado's largest vineyard, producing almost half of the state's wine grapes. Besides merlots and chardonnays, Grand River specializes in its signature Viognier and Meritage. This is a good place to start a wine tour, which should include the nearby Plum Creek Cellars and the Rocky Mountain Meadery.

Palisade Livery Saloon
215 Main St., CLOSED

A relic of the 1890s, this two-story brick livery has the original, high-ceilinged first floor and is still 150 feet deep, although the livery doors have been replaced by a storefront. Inside, a 42-foot-long oak front bar stretches beyond a majestic mahogany backbar with tapered Ionic columns. Its oversailing cornice with egg-and-dart trim echoes the front façade's stacked cornice. In back are a dance floor and pool tables—but no horses.

Palmer Lake
Elevation: 7,225 feet

William J. Palmer, founder and president of the Denver & Rio Grande Railroad, is commemorated by this rail town of some 1,500 souls. Palmer Lake sits on the high divide between the South Platte and Arkansas River drainages. Despite the large, boatable body of water called Palmer Lake and the spectacular Estemere Estate, it never became the great tourist haven its founder envisioned.

The quaint railroad depot and water tower are gone, the lake is a half-drained mess, and the town sold its pride and joy, D&RG Steam Locomotive No. 71, to Colorado Central Station Casino in Black Hawk. At least Palmer Lake has not lost its long-lived tavern, which has had as many lives as a cat.

Joseph O'Malley's Steak Pub
104 Colorado Hwy. 105 (nw corner of Pie Corner), no phone available

This rickety country tavern occupies a two-story 1912 house that served as a hotel until its 1950s conversion to a saloon and steak house, the Palmer Lake Lounge. In the 1970s the building wore a tattered tarpaper overcoat and knotty-pine interior walls. It was rowdy with country music, yee-hawing, and Indian war whoops greeting incoming sidekicks. The special steak dinner was $3.95 and a homemade sign on the wall read, "Sorry, folks, we've tried to hold down our beer prices. But our beers will go up to 60 cents on March 1, 1977." Beers were served without glasses and old beer bottles doubled as salt and pepper shakers. The pool table was busy and other regulars gambled with cards and dice.

Two decades later, not much has changed except the name and the prices. It is still a hodgepodge of eating and drinking rooms with a hodgepodge of furniture and decor. Sue McCoy, a friendly and competent bartender, told us, "This bar is a survivor. We survived the Sons of Silence and other motorcycle gangs, the 1965 cyclone, and even Wilbur driving through here one night in his Chevy pickup. Wilbur Spade was a big Cherokee Indian—and strong. One night he and a friend picked up this front bar and threw it out that window. He tore the place all to hell with his truck, too. He's in a wheelchair now and back on the reservation in Oklahoma. He was the wildest of a lot of wild people we've seen in here. And I've been coming since I was eighteen and the cops treated me to my first beer here!

"We're not an uppity bar like the places up at Larkspur have gotten to be. Now they want you to wipe your feet before you come in. They keep kicking out good drinkers, and we just take 'em in."

Let schoolmasters puzzle their brain,
With grammar, and nonsense, and learning;
Good liquor, I stoutly maintain,
Gives genius a better discerning.
　　　　　—Oliver Goldsmith

Pueblo

Elevation: 4,695 feet

E l Pueblo started out as an adobe trading post that sold liquor to Indians. Later it became a workingman's city of smelters and steel mills, filled with immigrants who also liked their liquor. Colorado's finest blue-collar saloons are to be found in the city that long called itself "The Pittsburgh of the West."

As Colorado's industrial giant, Pueblo developed many ethnic, working-class neighborhoods. Italians initially clustered around the steel mill in Bessemer; many Slavs worked at the Philadelphia Smelting and Refining Company and lived nearby amid the cottonwoods lining the Arkansas River in the area known as "the Grove." More recently, Hispanics settled in Pepper Sauce Bottoms and along Salt Creek. Germans, Greeks, Irish, Japanese, and others also staked out turf in the Steel City. Hispanics and Italians flavor the city's extensive menu of saloons.

Pueblo was Colorado's second largest city from the 1880s to the 1950s. It initially consisted of four separate towns: Pueblo, South Pueblo, Central Pueblo, and Fountain City. Union Avenue was constructed across the Arkansas River in the 1880s to help unite the city and provide access to Union Station. After the Pueblo flood of 1921 and the Great Depression of the 1930s, once-spiffy Union Avenue became Skid Road. The avenue had never lacked saloons. Coors, Schlitz, Tivoli, and Pueblo's hometown brewery, Walter's, all constructed groggeries there. The Schlitz Building at 223 South Union has Colorado's most ornate saloon façade. The Coors Building, just across B Street from Union Depot, sits next to a huge wall sign for Walter's, which urges beer drinkers to buy it because it was "not controlled by foreign capital." "Foreign" in this case meant Milwaukee (Schlitz), St. Louis (Budweiser), Golden (Coors), and Denver (Tivoli).

The Palace Bar at 307 South Union Avenue courted Pueblo's many immigrant and indigenous groups with its slogan "All Nations Welcome But One (Carry)." Gambling halls, billiard rooms, sporting clubs, and bordellos also sprang up on and around this avenue. Union Avenue rivaled Denver's vice districts on Larimer and Market Streets, proclaiming itself "the naughtiest street in Colorado." Damon Runyon, the famed Pueblo writer, celebrated Union Avenue types—hookers, gangsters, and gamblers—in his famous 1932 book, *Guys and Dolls*.

After a long, slow decline, Pueblo is making a comeback. Union Avenue is now a historic district that sparkles with rejuvenated taverns. The Union Avenue Historic District helped stabilize the core city, which also boasts El Pueblo Museum. Pueblo's Historic Arkansas River Walk project is transforming the entire river valley into a wonderful amenity for boaters, walkers, joggers, skaters, shoppers, and barhoppers.

Before the Walter Brewery Company closed in 1975, its floats often stole the show in the Labor Day Parade. Pueblo's steel mills and breweries helped make it Colorado's second-largest city. Both once-mighty industries are gone today, but Pueblo still glories in its many small working-class saloons. Photo courtesy of the Pueblo Regional Library.

Cafe Del Rio
5200 Nature Center Rd.
(corner of Arkansas River & 11th St.),
(719) 549-2009

On the banks of the Arkansas in a cottonwood grove, this spacious Pueblo Revival–style café opened in 1995. Its extensive outdoor space overlooks the river, which lures anglers, waders, swimmers, kayakers, and rafters. Nearby is a nature center, the Pueblo Raptor Center, and paved riverfront paths to Pueblo and Pueblo Reservoir. You can either mosey along these urban trails, raft the river, or ponder possibilities while enjoying Del Rio's full bar service and tasty, reasonably priced meals.

Do Drop Inn
1201 S. Santa Fe Ave.
(sw corner of Mesa Ave.), (719) 542-0818

In 1993 the Do Drop moved from 117 Main Street, opposite the bus depot, to this old, two-story, corner brick building. Freshly restored, it now has a mirrored backbar and sparkles in a grungy neighborhood near the steel mills. According to the *Pueblo Chieftain,* the Do Drop has "the best pizza in the universe with its thick and sweet crust, light but tasty sauce, gooey cheese and great toppings." *Pizza Today: The Monthly Professional Guide to Pizza Profits* (January 1996) called the Do Drop "the pizza pacesetter" with its "new oversized kitchen." "Unlike the chain pizza places," Donna told me, "we have developed gourmet pizza with ingredients such as jalapeño peppers, artichoke hearts, spinach, broccoli, and eggplant."

Proprietors Donna and Mike Redinger, who bought the old Do Drop Inn (formerly Frankie & Johnnie's Tip Top Tavern) in 1977, have decorated their new pizza palace with photos of old Pueblo. They have made this a hot spot, but with good fire protection—Mike is a Pueblo fireman (twenty-four hours on, forty-eight hours off to work at the Do Drop).

El Valle Mexican Restaurant & Lounge
208 W. Northern Ave. (se corner of I-25),
(719) 564-9983

Inside this nondescript stucco building is Pueblo's most celebrated Mexican food and a museumlike bar. "My folks opened this place in 1937 as La Valencia," owner-operator Tom Sebastian Valle told me in 1998. Located just off I-25, today it is filled with family memorabilia, Franklin Mint plates, hundreds of toy cars, a fabulous Jim Beam bottle collection, and a smirking Mona Lisa framed by Chianti bottles.

"This used to be the biggest and best nightclub in Pueblo," Tom reminisced. "During Prohibition my folks made their own whiskey. We fed the mash to our chickens. The cops could smell it, but they'd check all our Italian neighbors, not us Mexicans. We've had various nightclubs—the Tico Room, the Sebastian Club, the Tom Cat, Tonto's Tamale House, the Pink Lady, the Arcadia. We'd hire lots of cops to help out and stay open all night. We had Booker T & the MGs, Fats Domino, Nancy Wilson, Chubby Checker, Chuck Berry, and a lot of famous Mexican singers play here.

"I introduced the margarita to Pueblo and a lot of other special cocktails, including our banana drinks. I also experimented a lot with the menu, coming up with specialties such as our Valencia hotdogs [with green chili inside the wiener and a sopaipilla bun], avocado and pork burritos, and cheespas [little Mexican pizzas with *chicharrones,* chorizo, sour cream, cheese, and jalapeños]. We have $3.95 luncheon specials—the best deal in town—and fruit flautas for dessert."

Tom Valle has been working in restaurants since 1940, when he turned fourteen. His swank, storied place sports red floral rugs, a beamed ceiling, brown "leather" vinyl booths, memorable food, exotic bar drinks, and Tom's wonderful stories.

Favorite Tavern
119 W. B St. (corner of Victoria & B Sts.), (719) 545-1311

Opposite Pueblo's fabulous Union Station, this local tavern wakes up after dark. A Spanish and country-and-western jukebox is fed by raucous pool players thanks to the rule "25 cents for jukebox if any ball falls on floor." Pink plastic lights flicker on the Art Deco backbar. The foot rail is steel and the barstools have been repaired with duct tape. An acrylic-on-flannel señorita smiles from the walls, surrounded by beer ads. Proprietor John Gallegos owns the street-level bar and dancehall and upstairs apartments in this 1903 edifice called the L'Union Block for the newspaper once published here.

Grand Prix Restaurant
515 E. Mesa Ave., (719) 542-9825

Sadie and Nick Montoya, two Pueblo natives who had worked at other restaurants together, opened the Grand Prix on January 1, 1970, in what used to be Anzick's Bojunk Restaurant and Bar. The surrounding blue-collar, residential neighborhood, like the tavern, has evolved from mostly Slavic to mostly Hispanic. Behind an unpretentious exterior, this Mexican cantina has a thick floral carpet, low acoustic-tile ceiling, and wood-paneled walls decorated with family photographs. The Art Deco–style backbar has fluted, pink end lights, a linoleum top on the curvy oak front bar, and heavily padded, red vinyl bar chairs. A huge walk-in cooler is reassuringly full of Mexican, Colorado, German, Chinese, Philippine, and Canadian beers.

Snappy, cheerful service and terrific food are due to family loyalty and humane working conditions; the large front living room complete with easy chairs, sofa, and a television is for waitresses (and their children) to rest in whenever their feet get tired.

"We make everything from scratch," explained Gloria Montoya Hoffert. "This really is authentic Mexican food. We buy our pinto beans out in the country and cook 'em all day long in 15-gallon vats. Then we add the Snowcap lard—it's not healthy but it tastes good. Nick and Sadie—or their children—do all the cooking. Family members start working here at age fourteen. We don't need to hire any outsiders off the street."

Most locals agree that the Grand Prix has Pueblo's best margaritas, chiles rellenos, and refried beans. Its sizable business led to the purchase of the adjacent Trophy Room Pawn Shop for conversion to a banquet room. The Montoyas live next door in a well-kept bungalow behind a huge, red rosebush.

Gray's Coors Tavern
515 W. 4th St. (ne corner of Elizabeth St.), (719) 544-0455

This dim, narrow saloon occupies a high-ceilinged commercial building on the industrial western edge of downtown Pueblo. Busy 4th Street to the south rushes within a few feet of the plate-glass frontage, so grand entrances and tipsy exits are better negotiated through a side door in the gray stuccoed wall facing the west parking lot.

Inside, another era reigns. Rustic wooden booths with hat racks line the west wall. Tables sit on aged and scuffed linoleum flooring. The Streamline Moderne–style backbar and beveled mirror along most of the east wall are highlighted in red neon. Frosty mugs of beer dot the bar in front of customers whose dress ranges from business suits to sleeveless undershirts. Loud conversations and laughter echo off the wood-paneled walls hung with photos of athletes, past and present. An old-fashioned sports betting board under two televisions offers the point spreads for upcoming games. Michelob is the fanciest beer here.

John Carleno and Joe Greco opened the tavern in about 1934 to celebrate the repeal of Prohibition. They used the first floor of what was then Schaefler's Railroad Boarding House, next to the now-gone Santa Fe Roundhouse. Look for the photo of John and Joe posing out front before the second-story boarding rooms were removed. Dolph Otterstein, the Coors distributor for Pueblo, later owned this bar and gave it the Coors name before Don and Gary Gray bought it in 1977.

John Carleno and Joe Greco remained regular customers into the early 1990s. According to Ginger, the friendly and professional barkeep, "Joe is real sick, but John still comes in like clockwork at 11:20 every day. You can set your watch by him." For John and other Pueblo old-timers, this bar is far more than a business. It is home base.

Gray's is the "Home of the Original Slopper," a Pueblo phenomenon from the 1930s now served at several bars around town. A "Slopper" is an open-faced hamburger with one or two patties in a bowl smothered with chili. The menu's most expensive item is a Double Green Slopper at $4.95. The S.O.B. is an Italian sandwich on a bun. If you're not that hungry, the beer comes with complimentary oyster crackers. But the sloppiest hamburger in Colorado, doused with chili, cheese, and onions, should not be dismissed lightly.

Gus' Place
1201 Elm St. (sw corner Mesa Ave.), (719) 542-0756

Colorado's best-known blue-collar saloon is a small, one-story brick corner tavern that blends into a working-class neighborhood. Augusto "Gus" Masciotra, an Italian immigrant, went to work at the nearby CF & I steel mills at age fourteen and saved enough to buy the house at 1201 Elm. In 1926 he added a grocery. When happy days returned with the end of Prohibition in 1933, Gus opened a tavern in the front of the grocery. He also sold beer in buckets-to-go from a take-out window on the north wall that has been filled with glass blocks. In 1937, 1939, and 1941, *Ripley's Believe It or Not* pronounced Gus' the national leader for beer sales per square foot.

Inside, booted steelworkers have worn out two steel foot rails at the front bar. A section of the second rail is mounted in a wall trophy case. Clean design prevails in this little-altered saloon, which displays the green, white, and red colors of the Italian flag on its front awning, in the ceiling tiles, on the linoleum floor, and even in the neon stripes of the mahogany backbar. The walls are smothered with clippings, photos, memorabilia, and other liquid history.

Although Gus died in 1965, his son and grandsons keep polkas on the jukebox, and still serve 18-ounce beer schooners and the famous Dutch lunches with heaping stacks of bread, ham, salami, provolone, lettuce, tomatoes, and cherry peppers. After basking in the glory of Gus' Place, check out two other little neighborhood saloons nearby,

Gus' Place, the most legendary of Pueblo's taverns, is in a converted cottage in a working-class neighborhood near the steel mills. Joanne Dodds, the Pueblo author-historian-librarian, and her husband, Edwin, are among Gus' many content customers.

the Mill Stop Cafe, 317 Bay State St., and Eiler's Place, 326 E. Mesa Ave.

Irish Brewpub and Grille
108 W. 3rd St., (719) 542-9974

Theo Calantino opened this restaurant in 1944 and captured a liquor license in 1948. His son, Ted, who has managed the place since 1963, added the brewpub in 1996. Colorado wild game and pasta are the specialties, along with Blarney Stone Irish Red Ale and Lucky Leprechaun Gold Ale.

The Mozart
1120 N. Main St. (se corner of 12th St.), (719) 542-9662

In a two-story Spanish Colonial Revival–style palace built as a Ford Motor Company showroom, the Mozart is a stylish Italian restaurant and bar with rich floral carpets, heavily textured stucco walls, a stained-glass map of Italy, and a gilt bust of Mozart. Originally located at 6th and Main, The Mozart moved here in 1979. Savio Concaldi, an immigrant who started out as a Pueblo shoemaker, became a prominent restaurateur. This is his last and most elegant place. His son, Savio, keeps it genteel with soft candlelight and tapes of oldies but goodies, especially Frank Sinatra, one of his dad's favorites.

Star Bar
300 Spring & C Sts., (719) 542-9718

This drab, two-story corner building with no name on it in the derelict Grove neighborhood can be found thanks to a few lighted beer signs. Once it was the pride of what used to be a Slavic neighborhood, with its grand garlanded mahogany backbar and red and gold, hexagonal tile floor. The high ceiling and high-back booths with old-fashioned coat and hat racks survive. Old-timers come in for shots and schooners, which they nurse for hours, while the young and hungry try the famous Star Burgers, triple-deckers loaded with calories and flavor. Ben Palumbo, the proprietor since 1973, told me the Star is Pueblo's oldest operating bar.

Union Station Bar
Victoria & B Sts., no phone available

In one corner of the grand passenger waiting room, the old lunch counter was converted to a bar in 1997. The original Mission Deco–style backbar now graces the Phantom Canyon Brewing Company in Colorado Springs and has been replaced by a less illustrious replica. But the original ornate tile, including a wagon train in bas relief on the front bar, are still here.

Beautifully restored in the 1990s, this is Colorado's most picturesque train depot, crowned by a six-story mansard clock tower. The bar and waiting room are lit by tall windows in the red Manitou sandstone edifice. Stained-glass Art Nouveau–style transoms, rich golden oak wainscoting, a 20-foot-high parquet ceiling, and hexagonal ceramic tile floors enhance this period piece. At the bar inside, the bartender warned us about the female ghost who hangs out here. She suggested that we buy her a glass of Chablis and leave it by her chair next to the fireplace.

Rollinsville

Elevation: 8,420 feet

his hamlet was named for John Quincy Adams Rollins, who erected the Rollins Steam Quartz Mill nearby on South Boulder Creek. Today this dilapidated crossroads retains the ruins of the mill, an icehouse, an assay office, some modest homes, and a memorable tavern.

Stagecoach Tavern
**Colorado 119 & County Rd. 16,
(303) 258-3270**

Dominating the landscape and social life of Rollinsville, this two-story, board-and-batten former inn was built as the Toll Gate Barn of the Butterfield Stage. It has accommodated a hotel, grocery, general store, boardinghouse, and several taverns over the years. The tongue-and-groove, hardwood-floored hayloft is now a dance-hall. The backbar is an 1860s mahogany classic supposedly brought from Missouri by covered wagon. The barroom chandeliers were constructed from pulley wheels of the now-demolished Rollins Steam Quartz Mill.

When I asked the saloonkeeper about the house slogan, "Good Food & Drink Since 1868," he brought out a property deed to prove it. If you want take-out booze, just order it from this same resourceful bartender. He'll send you outside to a side door. Then he will walk through a door behind the bar into another little room. He closes the door so that he's legally out of the bar and in the liquor store when he sells customers liquor to go.

Salida

Elevation: 7,036 feet

Founded in 1878 as a railroad town, Salida takes its name from the Spanish word for "exit" or "gateway" because of its location at the west end of the Arkansas River Canyon. The D&RG built a splendid depot, roundhouse, hotel, hospital, and shops in Salida, a strategic division point for trains headed south over Poncha Pass to the San Luis Valley, west over Marshall Pass to Gunnison, or north up the Arkansas to Leadville. The seat of Chaffee County has an unusually well-preserved downtown with terrific old bars such as the Main Bar and Steakhouse, with its antique horseshoe bar counter, stainless-steel beer cooler, and shuffleboard court. Club Rio, the oldest saloon in town, is now The Silverado, where they used to stable horses and still have barn-wood decor.

First Street Cafe
137 E. 1st St., (719) 539-4759

This Mexican cantina occupies a swell 1880s Italianate-style commercial building. The back room housed Salida's first Ford garage, which opened in 1937, but it is now a dining room separated from the front room by a mini-bar. The furnishings and decor are mostly salvage, much of it from Denver.

Il Vicino Wood Oven Pizza and Brewery
126 E. 2nd St., (719) 539-5219

Owner-operator Tom Hennessy opened this gem in an 1888 building that had been the town mortuary. Tom's Wet Mountain Pale Ale, which won a silver medal at the 1997 World Beer Championship, has more color (amber) and flavor (sweet and hoppy) than most India Pale Ales. The restaurant specializes in pizza and beer, of course, but also has calzones, pastas, coffees, and desserts.

Victoria Hotel Bar
**143 N. F St. (sw corner of Sackett Ave.),
(719) 539-4891**

The two-story, 1886 brick-and-stone hotel boasts a splendidly preserved corner saloon. A large adjacent room has a dance floor and a stage. After a 1979 restoration, the hardwood floor, pressed-metal ceiling, mahogany backbar with festoons and garlands, and antique Walter's Beer clock mirror the scene in a large old photograph of the interior kept on the wall to settle arguments about how things used to be. The Vic boasts "live music since 1903" as well as shuffleboard, two pool tables, Ping-Pong, and a dance floor—if the peanut shells don't get in the way.

In this den I met the sage of Salida, the Homer of the hills, Ed Quillen. He is a columnist for the *Denver Post*, editor/publisher of *Colorado Central* magazine, and a bright, eccentric, and witty spokesperson for keeping rural Colorado rural. A latter-day Horace Greeley with his long scraggly beard, thick spectacles, and irrepressible opinions, Ed started his career in Greeley at the University of Northern Colorado, where he ultimately became editor of the student newspaper.

The bar is usually crowded and noisy, something Ed hates. "If Salida keeps growing," he promised, "I'm going to move to Saguache, where it's safe to jaywalk. And where they still put out the *Saguache Crescent* on one of the last hand presses in the U.S. Salida is in danger of becoming another Boulder or Aspen."

Salida's Victoria Hotel Bar has changed little, outside or inside, where old-timers have posted old-time photos of the saloon to document how things used to be.

"I'm appalled at all these slick, glossy publications that commodify Colorado with lascivious real-estate ads and glowing montane photography. These sleek landscapes are like the women in *Playboy* magazine. Real women have unwanted hair, stretch-marks, moles, and body fat. This month's Playmate does not. Real mountains have power lines, road cuts, and traffic jams. The glamorous mountains of Colorado—our state's Playmates of the Month—are virginal bosoms, with curvaceous streams and untouched alpine meadows." Such pornography, Ed fears, is luring city slickers into the mountains, where too many newcomers are settling in havens such as Salida.

San Luis
Elevation: 7,965 feet

The 230-mile pilgrimage from Denver to the "Oldest Town in Colorado" takes about five hours. Only a few slow, winding roads cross the 14,000-foot-high Sangre de Cristo and San Juan mountain ranges that separate the San Luis Valley from the rest of Colorado. Like other shrinking towns in "El Valle," San Luis survives by falling back on an antique system of bartering and communal life. It is the only town in Colorado to retain a communal *vega* (common grazing area) and the communally built People's Ditch, for irrigating fields and operating flour mills. San Luis emerged as the mill town not only for the San Luis Valley but also for early gold-rush towns in northern Colorado. The San Luis Ditch sustained the farmers from northern New Mexico who first settled in this high, dry desert valley. It averages only about 7 inches of moisture a year, much of which falls as snow.

San Luis usually looks sleepy and cold. During most of the year, piñon smoke sweetens the nippy night air and leaves shiver on the willows and cottonwoods. On my last visit, the full moon cast a spooky glow on the snowy Sangre de Cristos to the east by the time we spotted the neon cocktail glass on Emma's old sign, "El Patio Inn Dine & Dance."

El Patio Inn
Main St. & Gaspar Ave., (719) 672-3321

Emma's red chili enchiladas and sopaipillas with honey are mouthwatering, especially with the blue margaritas from Joe's Saloon. Fortunately, Emma's restaurant and Joe's bar are two sides of the same inn on Main Street. Emma is usually in, but her husband, Joe, a longtime mayor of San Luis, is often out.

Emma Espinosa, a well-dressed, dignified woman, welcomed us to her hacienda, which she opened in 1949 as El Patio Inn. In an adjacent room, Joe opened what another sign calls "Joe's Saloon." Joe M. Espinosa was mayor from 1968 until 1982, when he lost to Sam Medina Jr. of the Covered Wagon Bar & Cafe. Joe regained the mayorship in 1986, 1990, 1994, and 1996. A wiry man with a wispy white mustache, horn-rim glasses, and a cowboy hat with curled sides, he boasts, "I'm the oldest mayor in the oldest town in Colorado."

The Espinosas' inn has irregular hours, but it is usually open around mealtimes. Nor does it have a specific address—exact street numbers and even home mail delivery have never caught on in San Luis. If you want someone or something, just ask. No one has ever been lost for long in San Luis, which has a population of around 900—if you count the outlying villages of Chama, San Acacio, San Francisco, San Isidro, and San Pablo.

Tavern talk turned to the question of the oldest bar in the oldest town in Colorado. Eulogies were offered for the now-closed Garcia's Town Tavern, the Liberty Grill, Gordo's Bar, and other deceased groggeries. The first saloon listing for San Luis in the *Colorado State Business Directory* is the Gallegos Saloon, which was in business from the 1870s until the early 1900s. It was located in the old Salazar Store, the oldest store in Colorado. Joe and Emma's saloon is in a

No poems can please for long or live that are written by water-drinkers.

—Horace

century-old adobe building, but it was not a bar until they took over in 1949.

The oldest operating tavern is not Emma and Joe's, according to Josie Lobato, a long-time resident and curator of the Fort Garland Museum for the Colorado Historical Society. "My uncle, Sam Medina Sr., bought the old Riverside Dance Hall and two other buildings and reopened them in the early 1940s as the Covered Wagon Bar and Cafe. He loved to parade around town in his old covered wagon to promote the restaurant and bar. In 1982, Sam was riding high with his wagon and his restaurant, and even defeated Joe Espinosa for a term as mayor. His son, Sam Jr., still runs the place, but now they serve beer and mixed drinks instead of the whiskey punches of the old days."

I once investigated the Covered Wagon, a pink adobe building with a pink neon sign that boasted the fastest cook in town, with meals in less than five minutes. Emma's was slower and safer—she keeps a crucifix over the kitchen and a holy picture of San Martín sharing his cloak with a beggar. Inspired by San Martín, the Espinosas happily share their food, drink, and stories.

Severance

Elevation: 4,890 feet

David E. Severance, who owned much of the town site and applied for a post office, founded this community in 1894. A hamlet of about 100 residents, it is far famed for its oyster bar, which gives a new meaning to the word "severance."

Bruce's Bar

1st St. & 4th Ave., (970) 686-2320

"I was a broke farm boy when I opened this in 1957," Bruce Ruth told me. He bought the Severance Recreation Hall, whose principal asset was a pool table, and added a bar and a kitchen. Initially, his place became a big hit with his duck- and goose-hunting buddies. He supplies them with food, drink, shells, and hunting blinds to this day.

But it is the "oysters" that made Bruce's nationally famous. Taking advantage of Weld County's many cattle feedlots and slaughterhouses, he began serving Rocky Mountain oysters. Bruce's soon became the largest and best-known purveyor of bull fries. Publications far and wide, from *The New York Times* to *Penthouse* magazine to *People* magazine, have featured Bruce's, as have many television stations and the *Today* show.

Bruce's is in a long, low, stuccoed ramshackle building. With its many additions, it almost fills a block. It is now the biggest as well as the busiest place in Severance. Cartoon murals of protesting bulls decorate the walls. Customers sit at long picnic tables covered with plastic, red-checked tablecloths. Steaks, seafood, and sandwiches are served. Country music, live and recorded, is a mainstay. On weekends the dance floor helps attract as many as three hundred people, who come from all over to check out the purported aphrodisiac served here. Some of the cowgirls in tight jeans cause beer bottles to foam over.

Bruce is often on hand, packing a Colt pistol and boasting, "We don't have scuffles or shootouts in here much anymore … unless I do it!" This tiny town now has a sign at the main intersection: "Severance, where the geese fly and the bulls cry."

214

Silver Cliff

Elevation: 7,982 feet

Named in 1878 for rich silver discoveries in the nearby cliffs, Silver Cliff boomed into the third largest town in Colorado by 1880, when it boasted a population of 5,040, twenty-five saloons, twenty groceries, three hotels, and four newspapers. Silver Cliff rivaled Leadville, then the state's second- largest city, with it numerous saloons and a red light district along Cliff Street. But flush times soon faded. The silver panic of 1893 devastated the town, as did several serious fires. Worst of all, the Denver & Rio Grande bypassed Silver Cliff for Westcliffe, a mile to the west. Ultimately, the county seat, the Episcopal church, and many other buildings were moved to Westcliffe. Today this is a hamlet of around 300 residents—and America's only geodesic-dome saloon.

The Silver Dome
Saloon and Music Hall
110 Ohio St., (719) 783-9458

Charles Behrendt Jr., a boilermaker and mechanic, was drinking at the Raccoon Saloon the night an arsonist burned it down. He left the blaze muttering, "We're going to build this town another bar, a dome bar." Behrendt began to erect a geodesic dome around a huge Engelmann spruce in a field at his parents' place. The tree served as a central pole and its branches supported the balcony over the bar. For the only geodesic-dome bar in America, Behrendt engaged local architect Henry Gottgetreu to help with the design. His younger brother, Terry, who also helped, reported: "We spent five years researching it and over $50,000 building it. We opened July 4, 1984, although there were a great many parties in here to celebrate every stage of construction. We cut the timber up on Locke Mountain and used beetle-kill ponderosa for the trim."

The dome is 58 feet, 8 inches, in diameter. The plywood exterior skin is painted a shiny silver. Inside, the bar is well lit by pen-

The Silver Dome in Silver Cliff claims to be the world's only geodesic-dome saloon.

tagonal windows in the dome. In a unique fashion that might be called "Paul Bunyan Stick" style, huge stumps serve as barstools, log chairs as thrones, and thick polished planks as the front bar. There are two pool tables, a dance floor, and a stage for the many live bands who perform here.

Terry Behrendt said: "The older the dome gets, the tighter it gets. The walls fall into themselves. This is the biggest building in town but also the warmest. We can heat all 4,400 square feet with a little Kero-Sun heater. The structure is perfect. This is the liveliest, most unusual spot in Custer County, attracting bands and fans from all over." In 1996, Charles Behrendt put the bar on the market for $275,000, complete with a shaggy, devoted, hard-core collection of customers.

Silver Plume
Elevation: 9,118 feet

 eathery pieces of silver gave a name to this community founded in 1870. "Commodore" Stephen Decatur, editor of the *Colorado Miner*, celebrated the puppy town with a poem in his paper:

> The knights today are miners bold,
> Who toil in deep mines' gloom!
> To honor men who dig for gold,
> For ladies whom their arms enfold,
> We'll name the camp Silver Plume!

Clear Creek County lawyers and politicians, merchants, and mine owners gravitated to Georgetown, the county seat 3 miles down Clear Creek. Silver Plume housed most of the mines and miners in a narrow, steep-sided valley that harbored 1,000 people by the early 1890s.

At one time, Silver Plume had nine saloons, but in the 1960s, when the population sank to fewer than 100, it became saloonless after the old Round House Tavern burned down. The insurance company refused to pay off the owners after it was discovered that all the expensive liquor had been carefully removed before the fire; arson investigators found only Budweiser bottles.

Bypassed by I-70 and Colorado's late 1900s boom, Silver Plume seems to be in a time warp. One of the best-preserved mining towns, it retains a miniature dirt Main Street lined with false-fronted, frame buildings.

The Plume Saloon
776 Main St., (303) 569-2277

Since 1975, Silver Plume has rejoiced in The Plume Saloon, located at the west end of Main Street. The Plume is a quirky building, with parts of the old Mill Site Motel snuggled up against an old house for warmth. Motel units are still available, at some of the cheapest rates along the entire I-70 mountain corridor. Plume saloon-keeper Joan Anderman also spruced up a nifty old Queen Anne–style house next door as the Brewery Inn Bed & Breakfast.

The bed-and-breakfast commemorates the Silver Plume suds plant of Otto Bosche, who operated a brewery, beer garden, and bowling alley here in the 1870s. The brewery's old Carpenter's Gothic–style spring house still sits across the street, and the spring flows between The Plume Saloon and the Brewery Inn to a backyard pond, gazebo, lawn, and bocci ball and volleyball courts overlooking Clear Creek.

A century after Bosche's brewery closed in 1876, the Plume Saloon opened on its old site. Without a sign, advertising, or printed menus, The Plume has attracted locals and a few stray tourists with its good, inexpensive food and drink. Beverages flow from a splendid miniature backbar over a copper-topped front bar. A piano and tiny dance floor are in a back room, while a potbellied stove warms the tiny pool room, as do French Art Nouveau posters of bare-breasted femmes. Above the big stone fireplace is a framed portrait of Frances Willard, founder and president of the Woman's Christian Temperance Union. This great champion of prohibition is condemned to stand there helpless, watching people drink night after night, day after day.

Silverthorne

Elevation: 8,790 feet

F ounded in 1962 as a construction camp for Dillon Dam workers, this town traces its origins to Judge Marshal Silverthorne's 1881 placer claim on the Blue River. Some of the homes and businesses destined to be drowned by the Denver Water Department's Lake Dillon relocated to Silverthorne. Riding the ski and summer resort boom, Silverthorne has become Summit County's largest town and has two outstanding liquid landmarks.

The Mint Saloon
321 Blue River Pkwy. (Colorado 9), (970) 468-5247

Dating from the 1880s, the clapboard hall behind a classic false front was transplanted from the dammed and drowned town of Dillon. This barnlike edifice, which once housed Jim Ryan's Saloon, still draws thirsty locals and tourists to a splendid old backbar. This longtime dive has gone upscale in recent years, replacing burgers with pick-your-own-cut steaks, and what used to be the cheapest beer in Summit County with fancy brews and costly wines.

Old Dillon Inn
311 Blue River Pkwy. (Colorado 9), (970) 468-2791

Like The Mint next door, this false-fronted frame tavern escaped the watery grave created by Dillon Dam. Mexican beers, margaritas, and good Mexican food bring large crowds into this old-timer with plank floors, wagon-wheel chandeliers, and barn wood–and–burlap walls.

The Old Dillon Inn of yesteryear lives in *It's Easy, Edna, It's Downhill All the Way* (Carbondale, Colo.: Sirpos Press, 1981) the autobiography of Edna Dercum, who with her husband, Max, first brought skiing to Summit County with the Arapahoe Basin Ski Area and Ski Tip Ranch. When the Dercums arrived in 1942, Dillon consisted of "four bars and two liquor stores on the one-and-a-half block of Dillon's main

Like the best wine ... that goeth down sweetly, causing the lips of those who are asleep to speak.

—Song of Solomon

Silverthorne's Mint Saloon opened in Dillon in 1862 and moved when Lake Dillon drowned the town. Now an up-scale steak and seafood saloon, The Mint is finally paying off.

street." Inside the inn, the Dercums ordered breakfast and looked around: "It was dim and cool inside with a juke box playing cowboy songs. The jangling of several slot machines lined up near the front of the long room competed with the juke box. ... The bartender set the bottle in front of the customer who poured his own. I heard the bartender say to one fellow down the bar who looked like a miner, 'You plannin' on taking a bath?' I was puzzled but later learned that when a customer poured himself too generous a drink, that was the usual sarcastic remark.

"On all sides of the barroom walls I saw excellent western paintings by Gerard Delano, whose works now sell for thousands of dollars." That morning, the Dercums witnessed a barroom brawl. The sheriff finally arrived and pushed his way through the crowd to announce: "It's a fair fight, folks, so let 'em finish it. Just stand back, folks."

Silverton
Elevation: 9,318 feet

San Juan County's oldest town and county seat has been preserved by its economic poverty and geographic isolation. The quaint mining town has been used as a set for many films, including *Naked Spur*, *Ticket to Tomahawk*, and *Maverick Queen*. By shifting to gold and other metals, Silverton survived the 1893 silver crash. Mining fed the town and the county until 1991, when the Sunnyside Mine closed. Silverton is the only live town in San Juan County, which has the lowest population of any Colorado county—fewer than 500 souls reside here year-round.

Tourism is the mother lode today, and the Durango–Silverton Narrow Gauge Railroad disgorges some 2,000 summer tourists daily between May 1 and October 31. Motorists also reach Silverton from Ouray and Durango by U.S. 550, the "Million Dollar Highway." From the notorious red light district on Blair Street, some of the former bordello buildings survive, most notably the Welcome Saloon at 1161 Blair and the Shady Lady Bar at 1154 Blair.

Bent Elbow Saloon
1134 Empire St. (ne corner of 11th St.), (970) 387-5775

Louis Pedroni and Ernest Zanoni, the builders and original owners of this 1907 saloon, named it The Florence for the city in their native Tuscany. Now a Hollywood-ish invitation to tourists, the saloon once staged mock shoot-outs and hangings. The Brunswick-Balke-Collender backbar, "Union Made by Amalgamated Woodworkers of America," is a nifty backdrop for the good, reasonably priced food and drinks. The owner-operator is now Mike Zanoni, Ernest Zanoni's nephew, who grew up across the street. He has livened this place up with honky-tonk piano, personal hospitality, and the best fast food in town, although

Silverton's main street has changed little since its early 1900s heyday. The stone town hall (left) and Wyman Block (right) still crown the town. c. 1909 photo by George L. Beam, courtesy of Jackson Thode.

the Elbow no longer offers, as it did during the fast-drawing 1950s, a "Free, Exciting Gunfight during Lunch!"

Grand Imperial Hotel Saloon
1219 Greene St. (nw corner of 12th St.), (970) 387-5527

Boosters of out-of-the-way communities like Silverton built grand hotels to bring the world, or at least some investors, into town. Englishman Charles S. Thomson built this splendid hotel in 1883 with a mansard third story clad in silvery metal.

The county courthouse occupied the second floor before the present courthouse was completed in 1907. This grand hotel also housed mining companies and the offices of the *Silverton Standard,* the oldest newspaper on the Western Slope, before it moved to its own office a few doors down the street. The Grand Imperial also boasted, according to the June 12, 1886, *Standard,* "a reading room furnished with carpet, chairs, writing desks, writing paper and envelopes, cards, chess and checker boards and over 400 books."

The Grand Imperial was the hub of Silverton, inspiring the original name of the saloon. Louis Wyman described the old Hub Saloon in his memoirs, *Snowflakes and Quartz*

(Silverton, Colo.: San Juan County Book Company, 1977): "There's one thing you can do in a saloon when you're broke: Find a chair, sit down and watch the world go whirling by. ... The chairs in the Hub Saloon were fairly comfortable. I tilted mine back against the wall and hooked my heels on the bottom rung for easy setting ... . From early evening to early morning, [the saloon was] filled with men, cigar and tobacco smoke, and the sour reek of malt liquor. It pervaded the establishment, pushing the foul stench of the 'john' into its corner at the back alley wall. The odor spilled out the front and back doors like an over-full bucket." Yet, Wyman added, the Hub "had one redeeming feature—the bar and back bar—beautiful islands of sparkling crystal and plate glass mirrors." Another benefit was its "whiskey-soaked preacher" who blessed anyone who bought him a drink.

The Grand Imperial Saloon is still elegant, with its magnificent, mirrored, cherry backbar with diamond-dust mirrors framed in three ornate arches springing from Corinthian capitals. The matching front bar, however, now rests in the Miners Union Hall, and the Grand Imperial has a less grand replacement. In the 1950s, someone hungry for the tourist trade drilled into the fleur-de-lis medallion of the backbar arch a hole now attributed to "a bullet intended for Rosie Stewart." Further titillation comes from two life-size Rubenesque nudes, one posed as a classical bather, the other as Leda shying away from an unseen swan.

The bar has a brass rail and red-and-gold floral wallpaper. Saloon hall commotion is quieted somewhat by new pressed-metal ceilings from the venerable W. T. Norman Sheet Metal Manufacturing Company of Missouri. These shiny ceilings brighten the common rooms with reflected light and reflect sound down and away from upstairs sleeping rooms. Quiet nights have been a problem, apparently: A sign at the foot of the stairway, next to the full-length painting of Lillian "Diamond Lil" Russell, cautions, "Registered guests only." Another notice reads, "Firearms must be left with the bartender."

It is better to hide ignorance, but it is hard to do this when we relax over wine.

—Heraclitus

Miners Union Hall
1069 Greene St. (sw corner of 11th St.), (970) 387-5560

A small, square tower and flagpole atop the corner entry make this two-story brick hall easy to find. Members of the socialistic Western Federation of Miners (WFM) donated labor to build this hall in 1902, only to be evicted during the 1903–1904 strikes.

The Union Hall subsequently housed a store, a funeral home, and various saloons. Somehow this place acquired the fancy Brunswick front bar that matches the fancy backbar at the Grand Imperial Saloon. Only

past came back to life in 1989, when the upstairs hall reopened as the Miners Union Theater. The hall was filled with old seats from the Star/Lode Theater for performances starring townsfolk and local high school students.

Since the 1970s, I've found this bar has the cheapest beer and the best stories in Silverton. The bartender here shared some of his collection of dumb tourist questions:

Q. When do the deer turn to elk?
A. There is a school for deer in Ouray. When they graduate they become elk.

Q. When do you paint the mountains white?
A. When we get tired of tourists.

Q. Is that real snow on the mountains?
A. No, it's cocaine.

Q. How do I get back to the train?
A. Follow the tracks.

after the National Labor Relations Board stepped in during a bitter 1939 strike to stop the kidnapping and deportation of union organizers did union men get a fair shake in Silverton. The Colorado Supreme Court ordered in 1941 that the hall be returned to the Silverton Miners Union, Local No. 26. In 1948, the financially strapped union sold the hall to the American Legion. Its union

And one dumb local questions, "If this is tourist season, why can't I shoot them?"

Sphinx Park
Elevation: 7,040 feet

Without even a post office, Sphinx Park is little more than a tavern surrounded by a few homes, a squiggle in the road named for a massive nearby granite formation. Hidden in the hills of southwestern Jefferson County, this rustic retreat is only 25 miles from Denver.

The Buck Snort Saloon
15921 S. Elk Creek Rd.,
(303) 838-0284

Decades ago, the Sphinx Park Mercantile became The Buck Snort Saloon, a trashy biker bar. Tom Paton bought the dive for $50,000 in 1981 and, with years of hard work, turned it into a legendary, and usually packed, mountain escape. It became popular for its fast, friendly service, delicious Buck Burgers, barbecue sandwiches, burritos, steaks, a wide selection of cold beers, and spectacular setting in a log cabin perched above Elk Creek. The scenic Elk Creek Canyon into which it is squeezed is famous as a rock-climbing haven boasting Elephant Rock and the Sphinx itself.

The narrow serpentine road to Sphinx Park often leaves first-timers wondering if they are lost. But the long, slow trip is worthwhile—this bar is unique. Inside this log-cabin inn, the walls are rough sawn lumber, the seats are log stumps, and the tables are wooden spools. Condiments and napkins are served in cardboard six-pack cartons. A rustic, back-porch bar counter overlooks the jubilant rush of Elk Creek, which flows downhill to meet the South Platte River.

The Buck Snort is famed for its live country-and-western, blues, folk, and rock music. Joe Bye, a blues guitarist and vocalist who has been a longtime favorite here, bought the bar in 1996. You may find him busing tables, taking out the trash, singing,

When I demanded of my friend
what viands he preferred,
He quoth: "A large cold bottle,
and a small hot bird."

—*Eugene Field*

Customers usually fall in love with this place and stay until dark, so be sure to look south if you enter by daylight to see the stony face of the Sphinx. Inside this bar, which you have to see to believe, the faces are friendlier among a crowd ecstatic about finding such a swell saloon in the middle of nowhere.

or doing whatever it takes to keep The Buck Snort a fine place to eat, drink, and be merry. Joe, a Norwegian, gives the credit to his wife, Galina, a Ukrainian-born poet, songwriter, and chef. Their son and daughter also work here. They have made The Buck Snort more popular than ever. "We have as many as four thousand people come through on a weekend," Joe claimed. "Even more if it rains."

Steamboat Springs
Elevation: 6,695 feet

he Routt County seat at the junction of Soda Creek and the Yampa River was established in 1875 and named for the most exuberant of some 150 local springs. The chugging of the spring's blowhole could be heard for miles away, reminding the pioneers of steamboats. Another spring fills the municipal hot-springs pool, which is a starting point for a walking tour of some showcase springs under restored gazebos.

After the Moffat Railroad arrived in 1909, Steamboat became one of the largest cattle- and sheep-shipping points in the United States. Haying and ranching were the main businesses until after World War II, when Steamboat boomed as a ski town celebrated for deep powder snow. Skiing had been the favorite local sport since the 1914 founding of the Steamboat Springs Winter Sports Club. Norwegian Carl Howelsen ("The Flying Norseman") laid out the Howelsen Hill Ski Jump and launched one of America's first winter carnivals, with cowboys skiing behind horses and the high school band marching on skis.

Despite such quaint local festivities, travelers on U.S. Highway 40 scurried past this ranching town located in a snow bowl averaging 164 inches a year. The town was so desperate for tourists that the Women's Club offered them free baby-sitting. The population remained under 2,000 until the 1960s, when the ski business began to draw visitors. Since then it has soared to more than 7,000.

The stretch of U.S. 40 known as Lincoln Avenue is a 100-foot-wide main street once used for cattle drives. This main street sports notable saloons both new and old. Après-Ski Way and Ski Time Square in Steamboat Village up at the Mount Werner Ski Area do not lack watering holes, either.

Old Town Pub
600 Lincoln Ave. (nw corner of 6th St.), (970) 879-2101

Since its 1904 construction as the Albany Hotel, this edifice has housed a hospital, general store, Odd Fellows Hall, post office, library, and movie house before it was converted to the Old Town Pub in 1969. Gaudily restored, it now boasts a popular restaurant and a raucous nightclub. In the old days, cowboys rode their horses in to order beer by the hatful. Today the cowboys are mostly wannabes and one sees almost as many llamas as horses around town. But boisterous young crowds still flood the pub late into the night, inspiring the management to switch to plastic beer pitchers.

Pine Grove Barn, Bar & Restaurant
1465 Pine Grove Rd., no phone available

Rancher Jerry McWilliams built this barn of local pine in 1910. Sixty years later, David Lindlow converted it into a restaurant, adding another barnlike wing and a round, silolike, two-story entry and stairway. The open-raftered second story contains a dance floor and dining areas and, like the rest of the building, is decorated with antiques, old photos, and other souvenirs of ranching days displayed on barn-wood walls. The surrounding pine grove was sacrificed for commercial development, but this old barn is still a great place for a drink and a dance.

Steamboat Springs Brewery & Tavern
434 Lincoln Ave. (se corner of 5th St.), (970) 879-2233

This brewpub is the hub of a 1993 commercial complex. It is a modern, split-level, low-ceilinged place adorned by bear and buffalo heads. Try a sampler or plunge into a 22-ounce bomber of Hahn's Peak Gold Ale, Alpenglow Strong Ale, or Whitewater Wheat from brewmeister Dave Brereton, a veteran suds-maker who formerly worked at Vail's Hub Cap and Denver's Wynkoop breweries.

Steamboat Springs Yacht Club
811 Yampa Ave., (970) 879-4774

The original, 1922 river-rock structure was a state fish hatchery, later converted to an indoor rifle range. It was incorporated into a larger building erected in 1985 for a restaurant, bar, and nightclub with a nautical decor of dark mahogany, brass fixtures, life preservers, and even a lifeboat. High water on the Yampa in springtime may yet put these lifesavers to work. From the deck overhanging the rapid river, you can savor a drink and stay dry while watching rafters, tubers, and kayakers glide by in the summer or ski jumpers fly off Howelson Hill in the winter.

Sterling
Elevation: 3,935 feet

Founded as an agricultural colony in 1873, this town was laid out by a railroad official who named it for his hometown in Illinois. Sterling moved 3 miles south to its present location in 1887, when the Union Pacific Railroad agreed to make this its division point on the line to Denver. When the Chicago, Burlington & Quincy Railroad reached Sterling, the town's role as a major trading center for northeastern Colorado was confirmed. Industry, business, and saloons sprang up along the shiny, silver railroad tracks. The Office Bar and the Silver Dollar down on Front Street by the tracks are still going, although the old Farmers Lounge is closed. Other old-time saloons still line the tracks near the UP depot amid grain elevators and the gigantic Great Western sugar beet plant. But the most notable tavern in town is in a Baptist church.

Delgado's
116 Beech St. (ne corner of S. 2nd St.), (790) 522-0175

Azure margaritas and scrumptious Mexican food have replaced Bible classes in the basement of this former First Baptist Church. The upstairs sanctuary is a bar, dancehall, and banquet room favored for Christmas parties, high school proms, and weddings. Lou Delgado, a Sterling building inspector, acquired the church after the congregation moved out, and converted it to a cantina in 1978. From the beginning, the place has been so popular that Delgado never bothered to put a sign on the building. Just look for a homely, asbestos-sided church with Gothic windows on the corner tower—and a crowd waiting to get in the door.

It may take awhile to choose among the blue, banana, melon, peach, strawberry, raspberry, and regular margaritas. The decor (plastic plants and Masonite paneling) is inexpensive, but so are the meals. The most popular Mexican restaurant in northeastern Colorado recently opened Delgado's II in Fort Morgan to relieve the waiting lines here.

Stratton

Elevation: 4,414 feet

Born in 1888 as Claremont, this High Plains hamlet renamed itself in 1906 for Winfield Scott Stratton, the Croesus of Cripple Creek. With the exception of a grandiose new mansion, the Claremont Inn Bed & Breakfast, little of Stratton's golden magic rubbed off on this now-typical, stagnant rural town.

The Brand Inn Iron
230 Colorado Ave., (719) 348-5209

The Brand Inn Iron's stuccoed, boxy additions seem to be stuck together to protect the plank inside walls, which are charred with local brands. The large back room is held up by huge elm-tree stumps and boasts a back wall completely covered by a Budweiser beer-wagon mural.

When my girlfriend asked for a Corona, the shaggy, white-bearded bartender snarled, "We don't have no fur-in beers." He grudgingly provided a glass for her Budweiser. A greasy-looking, stringy-haired cook-dishwasher appeared like some Halloween nightmare, but we ordered food anyway. She told us that The Brand Inn Iron had been here "forever" and sighed.

This bar has dim lights and dark crannies, the lonely spaces of wasting lives drowning in beer. The neglected country-music jukebox played all by itself every thirty minutes to remind customers that it was there and needed feeding. We left quietly so as not to disturb the snoozing, grumpy, old bartender.

Telluride
Elevation: 8,750 feet

The San Miguel County seat sprouted up in 1878 after a gold strike. Although mines operated until the 1970s, twentieth-century production never matched that of the nineteenth-century boom. Between the 1920s and the 1970s, Telluride stagnated. Poverty preserved the town, as did its remote location at the dead end of a paved road. Much of old Telluride is a National Historic Landmark District with some notable saloons and four landmarked whorehouses that helped this town earn the nickname "To-Hell-U-Ride."

Isolation came to an end in the early 1970s, when Joseph T. Zoline, a plastics manufacturer from Beverly Hills, California, began building the Telluride Ski Area. A new airport helped bring in many newcomers, including monied transplants from California, Illinois, and New York. Festivals devoted to bluegrass, jazz, film, wine, ideas, the future, and mushrooms helped turn Telluride into a year-round tourist destination.

New Sheridan Hotel Bar
231 W. Colorado Ave., (800) 200-1891

This hotel's patrons included Lillian Gish, Sarah Bernhardt, and Colorado's three-time choice for U.S. president, William Jennings Bryan. The latter delivered a silvery speech in front of the hotel for Telluride's July 4, 1903, celebration (a photo of this grand event hangs in the hotel saloon). During the labor wars of 1903–1904, the New Sheridan Hotel was commandeered by the Colorado National Guard as its headquarters for suppressing striking miners. Since then it has been rehabilitated for modern-day travelers.

This three-story, red brick, 1890s hotel originally had a saloon with calfskin-covered walls and velvet-curtained booths equipped with telephones to order meals, drinks, and female companionship. Many

The Roma Hotel & Saloon in Telluride passed out 12½-cent tokens useful for buying only one thing—a beer. Photo courtesy of the Robert & Evelyn L. Brown Collection.

of the original Victorian furnishings were sold to Knott's Berry Farm for their Southern California amusement park, although a 30-foot-long mirror framed in Corinthian columns still reflects the surviving Austrian cherrywood bar.

Audrey, the famed standing nude, has survived. According to the most-often-told tales, she worked Pacific Avenue cribs, where she befriended an itinerant artist. Audrey's shoulders and arms are poorly proportioned, but her hips and bosom have never been found wanting. Audrey hung around various Telluride saloons over the years. She delighted customers at the National Saloon, the Cosmopolitan, and The Diamond before moving on to the Roma, where she was quickly expelled by the owner's wife. I last saw Audrey on the New Sheridan Hotel landing. She seemed to be heading for one of the upstairs rooms.

Roma Bar
133 E. Colorado Ave. (nw corner of Spruce St.), (970) 728-3669

One wild night, the jam-packed Roma Bar fell into the basement—or that's how the story goes. Actually, it was carefully moved downstairs piece by piece, allowing a much higher roof and atrium to capture some of the barroom racket. Before its lowering, the Roma had three trapdoors and a big, stone-walled basement. Its tunnels supposedly led to nearby St. Patrick's Church to supply the Roma with sacramental wine during Prohibition. On a subterranean tour of the joint in 1972, I saw a lot of spooky things, but no catacombs to St. Patrick's.

The Roma has operated under that name since around 1900. It catered to the town's many Italians and also attracted many other miners, as it was the closest bar to the mines. An 1860 Brunswick-Balke-Collender carved-walnut backbar frames 12-foot-long French mirrors that visually enlarge the tiny, crowded space. This false-fronted saloon has housed some wild times. When snow is in short supply, regulars conduct a strange ritual known as the "ski sacrifice," piling up skis and setting them afire to send incense to the snow god.

San Juan Brew Pub
300 S. Townsend Ave., (970) 728-0100

In 1991, a century after the Rio Grande Southern narrow-gauge railroad built this classic little depot, it reopened as Telluride's first brewpub. San Miguel County had gutted this Queen Anne–style depot for heavy equipment storage. Charles Cunliffe, an Aspen architect, put it back together again and doubled the space to accommodate a basement microbrewery. The old depot now has a fine restaurant and saloon with a double-sided fireplace. A mural depicting Telluride's history wraps the barroom and flows into the etched canopy for the bar, which resembles a railroad observation car. A deck outside steps down to the San Miguel Riverwalk, which connects with the free ski-area gondola. In this lovely beer garden, you can nibble on eggplant and goat-cheese baguettes as you sample the house elixirs. Try the hoppy Galloping Goose Golden Ale and a local favorite, the dark, bitter Black Bear Porter.

Senate Saloon
125 S. Spruce St., no phone available

Mrs. McDougal's Boarding House opened here in the 1890s as a respectable place, but soon became the Senate, whose boarders became brides of the multitudes. In the 1960s it was restored as a bar and restaurant, but lost the second-story boarding rooms. Nude paintings and statues, instead of the real thing, linger in what is now a restaurant. Just around the corner on Pacific Avenue, the three small Victorian cottages are, like the Senate, rare landmark examples of a threatened building type: the whorehouse.

Swede/Finn Hall
472 W. Pacific Ave.
(se corner of Townsend Ave.),
(970) 728-2085

Finns who spoke Swedish as a result of Sweden's 700-year occupation of their country built this clapboard hall with a diagonally laid hardwood floor in 1899. During Prohibition it became the Swede-Finn Temperance Hall. A 1992 restoration left it a large, primitive hall whose beauty lies in the fine woodwork, complemented by a grand, new cherrywood bar. Pacific Avenue, between Townsend and Oak Streets, the heart of the neighborhood once occupied by Finnish miners, still contains the Finn Town Flats and Finn Hall (1896), at 440 West Pacific.

Muriel Sibell Wolle, the artist and author who wrote the first classic book on Colorado's ghost towns, *Stampede to Timberline* (Denver: Sage Books, 1949), visited the Swede/Finn Hall in 1942 and found "a long narrow frame building with seats around the walls, long thin windows, and a huge potbelly stove near the door and a stage at the far end of the room. On the stage stood an upright piano, some bits of scenery, a table and festoons of crepe paper from the last 'Name Day' [birthday] party. At Finn Hall's 'toe socials,' girls exchanged shoes and stuck their feet out from under curtains, the only clue men had when picking their partner for the evening."

Trinidad

Elevation: 6,025 feet

According to legend, sheepherder Gabriel Gutierrez named this town for a sweetheart he left behind in New Mexico, Trinidad Baca. To console himself, he opened a tavern that brought other settlers. His inn helped make Trinidad the gateway to southern Colorado. So did the town's location at the foot of Raton Pass on the Santa Fe Trail and the Goodnight-Loving Cattle Drive Trail.

Trinidad boomed between the 1880s and 1920s, when the thriving coal industry made it Colorado's fourth largest city. As natural gas and electricity began to replace coal in the 1930s, Trinidad began to shrink. Many antique saloons linger, although the coal miners who once filled them are gone. And the huge Schneider Brewery has been dry for decades, a dusty relic of Trinidad's flusher times.

Thanks to economic stagnation, the town is unusually rich in historic buildings that embellish the Corazón de Trinidad ("Heart of Trinidad") National Historic District, which includes virtually all of the downtown. The Colorado Historical Society's Baca House and Bloom Mansion Museum, as well as the Colorado Visitor's Center, are good places to get oriented before you hit the red brick streets in search of bars.

Many saloons are only shadows of their former selves. Del Monico's Bar at 313–315 West Main Street lost its magnificent backbar to the Hotel Jerome in Aspen. The Green Light Bar & Cafe at 306 West Main has closed, but the Alamo Lounge next door at 303 Main is still fighting to stay alive behind an eagle painted on the front door and the slogan "Where Friends Meet." The foundering Atlantic Bar at 225 West Main tried most recently to revive itself as Black Jack's Saloon & Steakhouse. The last time I went into the Golden Nugget Restaurant & Lounge at 110 Santa Fe Trail (719-846-9053), they offered to sell it for $35,000. That would be a steal, for this fine two-story edifice had been a classy bar and restaurant, although fire badly scarred the antique backbar. A bar and restaurant, Roberto's, once occupied the basement of the former First Christian Church at 400 East Main. It later became a Presbyterian church and then a warehouse. In the 1970s it arose again as a restaurant, Arturo's. Renamed Roberto's in 1996, it subsequently reverted to storage use and awaits yet another spiritual awakening.

The Big House Restaurant & Bar
Main & Animas Sts., no phone available

This establishment occupies the storefront of the West Block, an imposing, three-story 1889 edifice with a façade of native sandstone. Edward West, who also built the West Theater at 432 West Main, erected this office and retail block. The large corner storefront evolved from a mortuary to a J.C. Penney store, then became The Big House in 1993. A grand ballroom, now unused, occupies the second floor, and a walk-in safe survives on the first.

Columbian Hotel Bar
111–119 N. Commercial St.
(nw corner of Main St.), (719) 846-3133

Trinidad's grand old hotel opened in 1879 as the Grand Union Hotel. The three-story brick landmark trimmed in stone and pressed metal was renamed in honor of the 1893 World's Columbian Exposition. A terrazzo-floored lobby leads to a rococo-style ballroom, a billiard hall, a smoking parlor, and the saloon.

President Herbert Hoover, actress Mary Pickford, cowboy movie star Tom Mix, and Will Rogers were among the celebrities to stay here, while Doc Holliday and Bat Masterson might be found in the basement gambling parlor. An unwilling guest was Mary "Mother Jones" Harris. For rallying striking miners, she was locked up in the Columbian during the "law and order" reign of terror culminating in the slaughter of miners' wives and children at Ludlow by the National Guard. The Columbian had been seized by law enforcement officials as their headquarters for suppressing the United Mine Workers, who had dared to strike John D. Rockefeller Jr.'s Colorado Fuel and Iron Company coal mines.

Licker talks mighty loud w'en it gets loose from de jug.

—Joel Chandler Harris

Trinidad's Columbian Hotel opened in 1878 as the grandest accommodation in southern Colorado. The hotel saloon glistened with electric lights, a leaded-glass and mahogany backbar, and carved cupids. Interior courtesy of the Denver Public Library, Western History Collection; exterior c. 1950 photo by Glenn Aultman, Tom Noel Collection.

The Columbian's grandiose saloon, resplendent in shining mahogany and walnut, featured a great high altar for King Alcohol: a massive, carved backbar with leaded-glass panels. Angels filled this place in the guise of naked cupids cavorting in the ceiling frieze and enormous nude paintings of Love and Psyche. Real ladies were not allowed in the saloon but were confined to an adjacent "retiring room." Since the 1970s, this hundred-room hotel has been vacant, awaiting an angel to restore "the grandest hotel in southern Colorado."

Lone Star Cafe
200 W. Main St.
(sw corner of Convent St.),
(719) 846-6101

One of Trinidad's less genteel bars occupies the Franch Block, an elegant two-story sandstone structure erected in 1887. What opened as the American Savings Bank was converted to a saloon by Max Franch. Once splendid, it became the most dangerous place in town. Barstools and lounge seats, as well as customers, wear knife slashes and scars. Red wallpaper and a dusty old piano linger from better times. The ceiling has been lowered, but some of the new panels are knocked out or broken to reveal the original, high, pressed-tin ceiling. Drunken commotion prevailed during our visit, but we caught some typical scenarios.

"Gimme a cigarette."

"Hell, no!"

"I'll blow up your car!"

"I ain't got no car!"

Another customer was begging the bartender to either give him another drink or "take me to detox."

"I've worked all my life," pleaded a voice from the depths. "Can you buy me just one beer?"

Monte Cristo Bar
124 Santa Fe Trail (se corner of Main St.),
(719) 846-6314

This 1910 brick building with its fancy, second-story bay window is angled to fit its corner lot. Max Maloff built this place with a fine terrazzo floor and classic cherrywood backbar. One of Trinidad's more respectable groggeries, it has a good restaurant, but, like most places in Trinidad, it also has its peculiarities. Owner-operator Ethel Ritzus cautions: "We don't have regular hours. I open when I like and when people need me to open."

Montelli's Bar
137 W. Main St.
(nw corner of Convent St.),
no phone available

This is one of the few bars in Colorado to have been built as a saloon. Saloons generally occupy generic storefronts designed to accommodate a wide variety of businesses. This one's marble terrazzo floor and grand backbar remain, but the original plate-glass storefront and the bay window fronting the upstairs gambling parlor are gone. Long known as "The Palace," it is now somewhat less palatial and operating as Montelli's Bar.

Vail

Elevation: 8,150 feet

Vail boasts North America's largest ski area and some notable liquid landmarks. The first tourist of note, Sir St. George Gore, eighth baronet of Manor Gore, County Donegal, Ireland, arrived in the 1850s. Mountain man Jim Bridger guided Lord Gore's forty-one-man retinue composed of a chef, gun bearers, and a trout-fly artist, as well as 112 horses, several milk cows, twelve yoke of oxen, six wagons, twenty-one carts, and hunting hounds. Lord Gore's exploits are commemorated by a mountain range and a creek that flows through what is now the town of Vail. There, modern-day tourists emulate Gore's penchant for conspicuous consumption.

Peter D. Seibert, a veteran of the famed Tenth Mountain Division of World War II ski troopers, and his associates founded Vail in 1962. They replaced John Hanson's Sheep Ranch with a ski resort named for Colorado Highway Department chief engineer Charles D. Vail, a balding, bespectacled bureaucrat.

Gasthof Gramshammer
231 Gore Creek Dr. (at Bridge St.),
(970) 476-5626

Austrian ski star Pepi Gramshammer and his wife, Sheika, the daughter of an Austrian innkeeper, founded what is now Vail's oldest inn in 1964. It includes the Antlers Dining Room, which specializes in wild game and a Sunday Austrian dinner buffet with live German music, in a bar filled with memorabilia. Guests can bask in front of an inviting fireplace or on a sunny deck overlooking Vail's main pedestrian intersection. In 1997, Sheika's nightclub in the basement, the mainstay of Vail nightlife for two decades, became a health club where aging patrons do aerobic dancing.

Waitresses in clogs and dirndls serve bratwurst, salmon "Norge," German schnitzel, Austrian *knödels,* Hungarian goulash, hot apple strudel, and beers and wines from all over the globe. Beautiful and tan, Sheika Gramshammer still looks like the model she became in 1954 when she dropped out of a Swiss convent school. She entertained us on the sunny outdoor patio with the story of her legendary inn:

"Pepi and I came here to ski at the beginning in 1962, when he was rated the world's third-best downhill skier. We bought this land in 1963 for $1.50 a square foot. Then there were thousands of sheeps here. We built a *gasthof* [guest house]. Pepi wanted to call it Gasthof Tyrol or Gasthof Austria, but I told him he had a great name that we should use. We built the bar first, then opened the hotel in 1964. Then Vail was beautiful and wide open People built what they thought was beautiful, not what they thought would sell. We've had many celebrities here at the Gasthof. Leonard Bernstein. Rock Hudson. Gregory Peck. Gerald Ford. Barbra Streisand. Princess Diana. We try to make everyone feel like a celebrity, darlink."

Hub Cap Brewery & Kitchen
143 E. Meadow Dr.
(in Crossroads Shopping Mall),
(970) 476-5757

Hundreds of hubcaps decorate this large, high-tech brewpub in what was originally a Burger King in the basement of a shopping mall. Camp Hale Golden Ale, Powder Pig Porter, and Beaver Tail Brown Ale are favorites, augmented by some of Vail's most reasonably priced meals, a combination that has kept the Hub Cap hopping ever since its 1990 opening.

Kaltenberg Castle Royal Bavarian Brewhouse
486 E. Lionshead Cir., (970) 479-1050

His Royal Highness, Prince Luitpold of Bavaria, led this 700-year-old brewery to open its U.S. branch in 1998 in the old Lionshead Gondola. Besides a brewery producing some 7,500 barrels a year, this place offers traditional Bavarian food in a restaurant modeled after Musician's Hall in the famed Neuschwanstein Castle in southern Germany. Hidden in a functional concrete structure, this fantastic hall has high ceilings with exquisite chandeliers and rich European scenes painted on the wood-paneled interior. The brewhouse seats 300, and another 120 patrons can be accommodated in the outdoor beer garden overlooking the ski slopes while they sip Kaltenberg's prize-winning pilsner, dark malt, and traditional wheat beer.

Prince Luitpold, the great-grandson of the last king of Bavaria, Ludwig III, told the *Vail Times* on October 8, 1997: "After a day of skiing on Vail Mountain, I feel that the fun atmosphere, delicious Bavarian food, and traditional beers of Kaltenberg Castle Royal Bavarian Brewhouse will be popular with skiers and non-skiers alike. Just think of it as a year-round Octoberfest!"

Victor

Elevation: 9,693 feet

After the Cripple Creek gold rush began, Victor was platted in 1893 and named for homesteader Victor C. Adams. While mine owners and businessmen gravitated to Cripple Creek, Victor housed miners and other working-class residents in cottages built amid head frames and mine dumps. By 1900, Victor's 4,986 residents made it Colorado's eighth most populous city. Like Cripple Creek, however, the town has shriveled since World War I, with barely 300 year-round residents today.

Victor's downtown is a six-block National Historic District with sixty-six business buildings and modest, brick-and-frame cottages, including several bed-and-breakfast inns. These are great places to sleep it off after your saloon tour.

Adeline's Cafe
Victor Ave. and 3rd St., (800) 748-0870

Built in 1900 as a bank, this edifice sat atop its own gold mine. While excavating for this four-story structure, the Woods brothers discovered a 20-inch-wide vein of gold ore. Mining continued far underground during and after construction. The bank and the mine lasted until the Great Depression. Later reincarnated as the Victor Hotel, this beige brick structure retains a pressed-metal ceiling, 12-foot-high plate-glass windows, original Otis birdcage elevator, and a huge safe. In 1993 a $1 million restoration revived the building as a thirty-room hotel with this cozy café in the mezzanine.

Elks Lodge No. 367 Bar
3rd St. & Diamond Ave., (719) 687-6978

In a fortress built in 1892 as an armory, Elks and Elkettes maintain an elegant saloon reflecting Victor's golden years. A 12-foot-high ceiling and huge windows make this an unusually bright bar, with light gleaming on the grand, oak, mirrored backbar with its beveled- and leaded-glass cabinets. A full-size pool table, monthly bingo games, and socials keep this place alive. "During the flush times," bartender Mike Nolthaus sighed, "the door never closed here and the fire never went out in the fireplace."

It's Someplace Else
306 Victor Ave., no phone available

A big glass storefront topped by a garland frieze fronts this funky, popular saloon. Opened in 1993, this was once the Amber Inn before that joint closed in 1986. It is the place for locals—and their dogs. In this dim and dingy bar, you'll find the best (and often the only) food in town. Informality is an art form here, with a chalkboard menu. Rolls of paper towels sit on each Formica table in case customers ever need a napkin, placemat, or mop for spills.

The 16-foot-high ceiling drips with memorabilia and artifacts, most notably panties and bras swinging from an old pipe over the bar. Two pool tables, loud rock music, and intense conversation prevail. Among the most remarkable antiques here are real live gold miners reworking the still-rich ores in Victor's cyanide heap-leaching operations.

Zeke's Place Bar
108 S. 3rd St., (719) 689-2109

Zeke Bennett opened what is now Victor's oldest and best-known bar. He was followed by George Yeager and then by George's son, Ohrt, who ran this dive with splendid dignity, serving even the scruffiest customers in his starched white shirt, red suspenders, and bow tie. With his beautifully trimmed, bushy, handlebar mustache, he was a master saloonkeeper and also a great coach for Donkey Derby Days and Victor's outhouse racing team. The bar is festooned with prize ribbons, including awards for the Black Forest Outhouse Race, in which teams pushed an outhouse on wheels with someone inside. "The secret," Ohrt confided shortly before his death, "was to get the prettiest and lightest girl in town to ride inside."

Some bars are too good to die. Zeke's had four different locations before settling into what used to be the Stope Cafe. Since 1990, Les Mattson has run this ramshackle joint, which is given some sense of security by a huge, steel I-beam supporting the wobbly north wall. Les serves three meals a day, operates a patio out back, and has added to the wealth of photos, memorabilia, and artifacts smothering the log walls. "Victor doesn't have a town drunk," boasts one backbar sign. "We all take turns." Despite the "No shoes, no shirt, no service" sign at the door, neither are worn by the bar nudes decorating the walls. Pool tables, a dartboard, a jukebox, two ancient iceboxes, a can crusher for recycling, and a nude photo of Marilyn Monroe help the old stove heat this place up.

Walsenburg
Elevation: 6,185 feet

O riginally named La Plaza de Los Leones for founder Miguel Antonio Leon, the Huerfano (Spanish for "orphan") County seat was renamed for Frederick Walsen in the 1870s by German settlers. Walsen was a pioneer storekeeper and coal mine operator who became the first mayor. Following the Denver & Rio Grande Railroad's arrival in 1876, Walsen's burg grew into a rail and coal-mining hub. By 1900 the U.S. census taker found twenty-six different nationalities among the 1,033 residents, most of whom worked in mines with ambitious names such as Ideal and Sunshine.

Once a crowded coal town overflowing with saloons, Walsenburg is much quieter today, having shrunk from a peak population of almost 6,000 in 1940 to half that. The old Colorado & Southern Depot at 112 East 4th Street is a visitor center and also contains the Colorado Barbed Wire Collectors Museum.

Inside the post office at the corner of South Russell and East 6th Street is a moody 1937 mural, *The Spanish Peaks*, by Ernest L. Blumenschein, one of the founders of the Taos, New Mexico, art colony. The mural depicts the saddle-shaped peaks in silvery snow, with a foreground of Ute teepees and a Hispanic sheepherder.

The Huerfano County Courthouse and Jail dominate Walsenburg's downtown, reflecting in its rich detail, noble sandstone walls, and shiny silvery roof, the county's more opulent days. The steel cells and steel beds are still in the jail, which in 1994 became the Walsenburg Mining Museum.

In 1973, when I stayed here at the Kirkpatrick Hotel, the town had about twenty-five bars, which seemed to occupy every third building. Most

242

were closed even then. During the flush times, Walsenburg sported thirty-three saloons. Only seven survive. The 1880s Pioneer Bar at 512 Main Street had evaporated, as had its Main Street neighbors, The Monte Carlo Saloon and a dozen more. Gone, too, was the Silver Dollar, which opened at 112 West 7th around 1900. The Silver Moon had sunk from Main Street, too. In the 1970s, we found it a classic with a high-pressed tin ceiling, high wooden bar booths painted red, and a magnificent mirrored backbar with matching merchandise cabinets. It had vomit yellow stucco walls and dim beer-ad lighting, Spanish jukebox tunes, and a wall notice that impressed us:

WARNING

Walsenburg Police Must be Immediately Notified of all
Disturbances in this Establishment—Walsenburg Ordinance 661

The Central Tavern at 524 Main, The Wonder Bar (now Los Hermanos) at 620 Main (719-738-1833), and Aly's Fireside Bar & Cafe at 606 Main linger on, as do Lucky's Bar at 52 Main, the Moon Glow Inn at 716 Walsen Avenue (719-738-9980), and Sarti's at 823 Main (719-738-2522), where Gino Sarti and other old-timers are still sipping on memories of Walsenburg's better days.

Aly's Fireside Cafe
606 Main St., (719) 738-3993

A rusty, old neon cocktail glass still adorns the outside of this faded glory, as does an Art Deco–style curved-glass façade with jet black glass tile. I remember it as Shosky's Cafe, which had 25-cent beers and a $1.75 breakfast of steak, eggs, hash browns, toast, and coffee. The linoleum, high-backed  booths were topped with rock specimens, cactus, and sagebrush decorated with Christmas tree ornaments.

The Central Tavern
524 Main St., no phone available

In this bar dating back to 1900, we found 25-cent frosted schooners of Walter's Beer in 1973. There was a grand Philippine mahogany backbar adorned with a backward wall clock, a jackalope, and a sign: "T-bone 25 cents. With meat $2.75." I was studying all the paper money from different countries pasted on the wall when a dozing, long-haired hippie crashed to the floor from his stool. The bartender threw up his arms: "You can't win 'em all." He and I hauled the fellow off the floor and into a booth, where he slept like an angel.

An eagle came to rest permanently on the elegant backbar of the Starlite Inn in the southern Colorado town of Walsenburg, a history-rich coal mining hub.

I am going to a tavern alone to eat a steak, after which I shall return to the office.

—Richard Steele

Starlite Inn
110 W. 6th St., (719) 738-9968

Three generations of Archuletas had owned this bar since it opened around 1910, according to owner Ben Eolida "Paco" Archuleta. Under a fine, pressed-metal ceiling, locals in overalls congregated at the marble-topped front bar, drinking red beer and listening to country-and-western music. Atop the backbar is a screaming golden eagle with its wings spread. In 1997 we were treated here by super-friendly locals. Several contractors were buying—and hiring. Sad-looking men came in to ask them for construction jobs, which was about all the work left in this long-depressed coal town.

Ward

Elevation: 9,258 feet

In the spring of 1860, Calvin Ward found gold on a mountainous western fringe of Boulder County. The town named after him sprouted out of a deep ravine in Left Hand Creek. By the 1880s, half a dozen stamp mills thumping day and night kept Ward humming. According to the federal census, the population peaked at 424 in 1890, then sank to 10 in 1950. During the 1960s, Ward began growing again as a haven for dropouts and pursuers of alternative lifestyles.

Remnants of the Big Five Mines still pockmark the surrounding hills, although pine, spruce, fir, and aspen have erased most of the scars. This disheveled town spills down Left Hand Canyon along a rutted road lined with an exquisite collection of old cars and trucks, even a battered old Citroen with Paris plates.

Other than the Old Mill Site Saloon, the Ward Store is the only consistent vital sign in this spooky community, which nearly became a ghost. More typical is the Ward Dance Hall, a crumbling stone ruins across Main Street from the store. Behind the store, a large frame ghost, the two-story Columbia Hotel, looks like it may blow away any day. The pale white, wooden Congregational church, a landmark dating from 1894, has been rechristened the Ward Community Church, but it is attended mostly by varmits trying to get in out of the cold.

Old Mill Site Inn
44365 Colorado 72
(Peak to Peak Highway)
(0.4 mile n. of Ward),
(303) 459-3308

One place that never freezes over is Ward's Old Mill Site Inn. The inn is a rustic log cabin with its name spelled out in the log balustrade of the large front porch. I snooped all around the place, but found no trace of the gold mill that once stood here.

Opened in 1935 as the Aspen Grove Inn, this inn has a cozy interior with bentwood furniture, venerable sofas, and a stone fireplace made with sparkly ore specimens from surrounding mines. The log posts inside are a maze of graffiti, including a beautifully carved snowplow, the signature of plow operator Ed Martinek. The small, copper-topped front bar has microbrews and good, cheap meals. The blue-jeaned clientele are ecologically minded, honoring the bathroom admonition "Flush Only When Necessary. If it's yellow, let it mellow. If it's brown, flush it down."

A sign on the bar promised, "In times of great stress it's good to remember that there's someone just around the corner waiting to help you—your bartender." The bartender turned introspective one night and told me, "Ward is weird. We have the highest per capita education in Colorado, and probably the lowest income. Ex-mayor Farley was typical. He lived on food stamps, slept above the Ward Store, and could be found here at the Mill Site. He didn't do much for a living and died drunk. We figured a dead mayor could do less damage than a live one. So we elected him. He was the kind of do-nothing politician we like in Ward. And he got along with everybody, even Conan the Vegetarian. Conan dresses in a loincloth, lives in a mine up by Brainard Lake with his woman, and never comes down here to the Mill Site. We don't serve vegetables here. Ward's other crazies include a woman who grazes around town stark naked on all fours.

"Patty Hearst did live here," the bartender swore. "She hung out up at Duck Lake by the Modoc Stamp Mill. Ward is a psychiatric ward! We're competing with Nederland as the most drug-crazed town in Colorado. But we don't have an ATM, which in Nederland they call 'the coke machine.' Our biggest dealer worked at the post office, so you could buy dope and stamps at the same time."

Ward is definitely weird. But kind. They have big wakes for anybody who dies up there, with free Bushmills whiskey at the Mill Site. The dead, as the Mill Site bartender said, should be honored, no matter how weird their lives.

They [The British] claim to be the first inventors of those recondite beverages, cocktail, stonefence, and sherry cobbler.

—Washington Irving

Yampa

Elevation: 7,892 feet

ounded in 1894 and named with the Ute word for "bear," this tiny town began as a cluster of homesteads that emerged as a hub for the local cattle, coal, lettuce, and lumber industries. Years after Yampa's most famous saloon closed, patrons are still talking about the bearlike curmudgeon who ran it with snarling service.

Antlers Cafe & Bar
Main St. & Moffat Ave., (970) 638-4555

This false-fronted classic opened in 1896 as a saloon and survived as a pool hall and soft-drink store during Prohibition. In 1933, Michael and Emily Benedict began operating the one-story tavern as an unreformed, nineteenth-century, western saloon. The stark white lap-siding and plate-glass façade opens to a bare plank floor and paneled walls that make the neoclassical backbar look magnificent. Mangy stuffed deer, wildcats, elk, and eagles eye the two life-size nudes. One ornate Victorian bar is for drinking and the other is a lunch counter in this long and lean watering hole.

"Everything about this bar is beautiful," quipped grumpy, old "Smiling" Mike Benedict, "except the customers." His gruff humor is immortalized in handmade signs such as "This is not Burger King. You get the son-of-a-bitch my way, or you don't get it at all!" Mike Benedict went into a nursing home and Emily closed the place a century after it opened.

The Antlers Cafe & Bar housed a fantastic collection of stuffed critters.

Further Reading

Caughey, Bruce, & Dean Winstanley. *The Colorado Guide, Fourth Edition.* Golden, Colo.: Fulcrum Publishing, 1997.

Dallas, Sandra. *No More Than Five in a Bed: Colorado Hotels in the Old Days.* Norman, Okla.: University of Oklahoma Press, 1967.

Earley, Karen O'Neill. *Noteworthy Pubs, Taverns & Saloons of Colorado.* Florissant, Colo.: Colorado Adventure Publications, 1995.

Noel, Thomas J. *Buildings of Colorado.* New York: Oxford University Press, 1997

———. *The City and the Saloon: Denver, 1858–1916.* Lincoln, Nebr.: University of Nebraska Press, 1984.

Noel, Thomas J., Paul F. Mahoney, & Richard E. Stevens. *Historical Atlas of Colorado.* Norman, Okla.: University of Oklahoma Press, 1994.

Powers, Madelon. *Faces Along the Bar: Lore and Order in the Workingman's Saloon, 1870–1920.* Chicago: University of Chicago Press, 1998.

St. John, Bill. *Rocky Mountain Restaurants.* Boulder, Colo.: 3D Press, 1997.

Todd, Tony, & Craig Jones. *Discovering Colorado's Brewpubs.* Silverthorne, Colo.: Peak Publishing, 1997.

West, Elliott. *The Saloon on the Rocky Mountain Mining Frontier.* Lincoln, Nebr.: University of Nebraska Press, 1979.

Index

Boldface page numbers indicate a photograph.